Forever Prisoners

FOREVER PRISONERS

How the United States Made the World's
Largest Immigrant Detention System

Elliott Young

OXFORD
UNIVERSITY PRESS

Oxford University Press is a department of the University of Oxford. It furthers
the University's objective of excellence in research, scholarship, and education
by publishing worldwide. Oxford is a registered trade mark of Oxford University
Press in the UK and certain other countries.

Published in the United States of America by Oxford University Press
198 Madison Avenue, New York, NY 10016, United States of America.

© Oxford University Press 2021

Library of Congress Cataloging-in-Publication Data
Names: Young, Elliott, 1967– author.
Title: Forever prisoners : how the United States made the world's
largest immigrant detention system / Elliott Young.
Description: New York : Oxford University Press, 2021. |
Includes bibliographical references and index
Identifiers: LCCN 2020018277 (print) | LCCN 2020018278 (ebook) |
ISBN 9780190085957 (hardback) | ISBN 9780190085971 (epub) | ISBN 9780190085988
Subjects: LCSH: United States—Emigration and immigration—Government policy. |
Immigrants—Governemnt policy—United States. |
Alien detention centers—United States—History. | Detention of persons—United States. |
Human rights—United States.
Classification: LCC JV6483 .Y68 2021 (print) |
LCC JV6483 (ebook) | DDC 365/.4—dc23
LC record available at https://lccn.loc.gov/2020018277
LC ebook record available at https://lccn.loc.gov/2020018278

9 8 7 6 5 4 3 2 1

Printed by Sheridan Books, Inc., United States of America

For
Reiko, Zulema, and Ryo
And all the migrants who strive to be free

CONTENTS

ACKNOWLEDGMENTS

This book emerged in a moment of political crisis when detention and deportations have reached unprecedented levels in the United States. I had been studying transnational migration for years, but I became more aware of the problem of mass incarceration and policing through conversations with my partner, Reiko Hillyer, and a friend, David Menschel. I began to see how policing and immigrant detention were inextricably linked. What began as a book about immigrant detention became a project about mass incarceration.

Following the election of President Trump, a group of immigration historians consulted with each other over email about how to confront what was likely to be an all-out assault on immigrants. Sanctuary campuses was one idea that we advocated given our location in universities. In the coming months, US Immigration and Customs Enforcement (ICE) began an intense effort to round up undocumented immigrants inside courthouses, and outside of hospitals and schools. Immigrant advocates responded by passing ordinances to disentangle local law enforcement with immigration enforcement in what became a widespread sanctuary movement across cities and universities. We knew what was happening around us, but the genealogy of the immigrant detention system remained shrouded in mystery. Furthermore, the activist calls to abolish ICE ignored this much longer history of detention and deportation. Hopefully, this book can serve advocates as a reminder of the many ways immigrant incarceration has happened in the past so we do not simply replace one form of prison for another.

Since 2014 when I began researching and writing this book, I have written more than 250 expert witness declarations for asylum cases in Mexico, Honduras, Guatemala, El Salvador, and Venezuela. It is that work that put me in touch with Mayra Machado. My testimony has also helped many of these families to gain asylum and reminded me that my academic knowledge can be useful in the real world. I thank Stephen Manning of the

Innovation Law Lab for getting me involved in such work. My hat goes off to the many immigration attorneys across the country and in the United Kingdom with whom I have collaborated on asylum cases. They are doing amazing work under the most difficult conditions.

Intellectually, I have been sustained by the Tepoztlán Institute for Transnational History of the Americas, an institute I co-founded with Pamela Voekel in 2004, which brings together scholars from across the Americas in a small town outside of Mexico City each summer. I have learned and drawn inspiration from the amazing array of scholars, artists, and activists who have participated. The collective that runs the institute has become my alt-family. I want to particularly thank collectivistas Josie Saldaña, David Kazanjian, Alejandra Puerto, Marisa Belausteguigoitia, Micol Seigel, David Sartorius, Jorge Giovannetti, Anna Moore, and Shane Dillingham for their comradeship and ideas. I want to also thank my colleagues in the History department at Lewis & Clark College who have read various chapters of this book in our colloquium, and especially Mo Healy and Andy Bernstein for their comments in an intensive summer workshop. Law scholars and professors Stephen Manning, Juliet Stumpf, and Aliza Kaplan were my legal dream team who helped me get the legal details right for the final chapter. Over the years I have also been lucky to have amazing Lewis & Clark College student research assistants who helped me do archival research in Washington, DC; Mexico City; Seattle; San Francisco; and New York City: Kate Wackett, Megan Scott-Busenbark, Alexander Castanes, Lauren Krumholz, Maya Litauer Chan, Will Sarvis, Maggie Costello, and Sofia Knutson.

This kind of project could not have happened without the scholarship and mentorship from many scholars of migration (too many to name), including the following: Ana Raquel Minian, Madeline Hsu, Mae Ngai, Erika Lee, Maria Cristina Garcia, Maddalena Marrinari, Hidetaka Hirota, Torrie Hester, Naomi Paik, Adam Goodman, and Alexander Stephens. Mad props to Kelly Lytle-Hernández who invited me to participate in a special issue on the Carceral West, resulting in the article, "Caging Immigrants at McNeil Island Federal Prison, 1880–1940," *Pacific Historical Review* (2019) 88 (1): 48–85, which eventually formed the basis for the first chapter in the book. Through her activism in Los Angeles, her rigorous scholarship, and her keen editorial eye, Kelly is a model for scholar-activists.

History does not get written without the archivists, so thank you to those at the National Archives in Washington, DC, and Seattle, the Washington State archives, the Atlanta History Center, and the Canadian Archives who made this book possible. Thanks to the two anonymous reviewers who gave me detailed and intense feedback that pushed me to hone my argument.

And to Susan Ferber at Oxford University Press, who understood what I was trying to do with this book and helped me to make it the best version that it could be.

I especially want to recognize the people shared their personal and traumatic stories with me. Elsa Kudo, Seeichi and Angelica Higashide's daughter, who was herself locked up in a detention camp in Texas as a child, told me about her and her family's experiences. Tami Kudo Harnish, Elsa's daughter, also generously commented on the chapter about her family. Gary Leshaw, who provided legal defense for Mariel Cubans at Atlanta Penitentiary, and Sally Sandige, who coordinated the Coalition to Support Cuban Detainees, both granted me interviews and allowed me access to dozens of boxes of documents that provided me with a unique understanding of the detainees' own views on their incarceration. Finally, Mayra Machado has been a constant source of inspiration for me. Seeing how she organized her own legal defense, coordinated solidarity from around the country, and supported her children, all from inside an ICE detention center in rural Louisiana, was a lesson in persistence. She has lost all of her legal battles thus far, but she refuses to give up. Big shout out to Isabel Medina and Benjamin Osorio, attorneys, who both took on Mayra's case pro bono and who continue to pursue justice for her.

What often gets forgotten is that research is an embodied enterprise, and one needs food and lodging while digging through dusty boxes in the archive. In Atlanta, Johnny Hillyer provided shelter, food, and a makeshift photography studio, and J. T. Way stayed up with me until the wee hours one Saturday night in a clandestine scanning operation at Georgia State. In Washington, DC, David Sartorius runs the best secret residency program out of his apartment (take note Mellon Foundation) and gave my students and me a place to crash.

Finally, Reiko Hillyer continues to be my best interlocutor and editor for this book, and so many other life projects. Ryo Havana, our daughter, has watched me for the first four years of her life pound away at the keyboard working on this book. She recently asked me if my story would have lots of pictures. When I said it would have only a few, she predicted it would be a boring book. Let's hope other readers are more generous.

ABBREVIATIONS

AEDEPA	Antiterrorism and Effective Death Penalty Act of 1996
BOP	Bureau of Prisons
DACA	Deferred Action for Childhood Arrivals
DHS	Department of Homeland Security
HIAS	Hebrew Immigrant Aid Society
ICE	Immigration and Customs Enforcement
IIRIRA	Illegal Immigration Reform and Immigrant Responsibility Act (1996)
INS	Immigration and Naturalization Service
NDLON	National Day Laborer Organizing Network

Forever Prisoners

Introduction

I'm not a bad person. I shouldn't be here. . . . I'm not a threat to society and I'm not going to hurt anybody. I should be taking care of my children.
—Mayra Machado, from a Louisiana immigrant detention center, 2016

Migration stories are inherently about mobility, people plowing across oceans and rivers, boarding trains and buses on dangerous journeys, and trekking across deserts in the dark of night. But those hopeful stories of flight to freedom, escaping from poverty, violence, and political persecution at home, have ended for millions with imprisonment behind bars in the United States. The caged butterfly is an apt metaphor for migrants caught in the steel jaws of a detention system that now locks up half a million people each year. This book is about these butterflies and the cages we have built for more than a century to keep their wings clipped.

In December 2015, Mayra Machado took her three kids to shop for Christmas decorations in a mall in Springdale, a suburb of Fayetteville, Arkansas. Ever since her miscarriage a few months earlier, her family was depressed, so she hoped Christmas decorations would bring some cheer to their lives. Dominic (10), Dayanara (8), and Dorian (6) were excited about the upcoming holidays. On the car ride home, Dominic realized he had left his eyeglasses at the Hobby Lobby they had visited, and so Mayra turned her car around and returned to the store. Raising three kids was difficult after the father of her children had abandoned the family. But she had a good job as an ophthalmologist's assistant and had a new fiancé. Her hopeful future came crashing down when a police officer pulled Machado over for failing to yield, an offense she claims never happened. He discovered that

Machado had an unpaid traffic fine for another failure to yield charge. Although she offered to pay the ticket immediately with a credit card, the officer arrested her and had her car towed away. In 2019, Machado told me her story from an Immigration and Customs Enforcement (ICE) detention facility in Louisiana.[1]

On the side of the road, Machado's three children witnessed their mother being handcuffed and arrested, an image that still haunts them to this day. This was not the first time they had heard of family members being snatched by police. At the station, Machado knew many of the police officers because they had visited the ophthalmologist where she worked. She figured she would pay the fine and be home by evening. However, an old, bald officer said, "Bring her over here," and he demanded to know where she was born and her immigration status. The officer flashed a 287(g) badge that authorized him as an ICE agent. After checking the immigration status of her mother, sister, and grandmother, the officer said he was issuing an immigration hold based on her undocumented status and felony convictions for a writing a hot check a decade earlier. Machado was born in El Salvador and brought by her mother to this country when she was five years old. Her three children were born in the United States. At that point Machado was told she was being taken to Fort Smith detention center in Arkansas where she would be issued a bond and released. Instead, Machado was shackled and sent to an ICE detention center in rural Louisiana where she was ordered deported to a country she left as a child and where she knew nobody.[2] For the relatively minor crime of writing a bad check when she was a teenager, Machado was punished with banishment and separation from her children. Even for a criminal justice system rife with extreme sentences, this was an absurdly disproportionate outcome. And yet, for immigrants such extremities are the norm.

This book begins with Machado's story because it illustrates how tough-on-crime laws intersected with harsh immigration policies in the last three decades to make millions of immigrants vulnerable to deportation based on criminal acts, even minor ones, that had been committed years or decades earlier. Machado's history also shows how much had changed between 2004, when she was first arrested on felony charges for writing the fraudulent checks, and 2015, when her immigration status became the central issue in what was a routine traffic stop. The integration of local police with immigration enforcement in the 2010s cast a much wider net, entrapping millions of long-term immigrant residents in the jaws of an enhanced deportation machine. By the end of Obama's second term, he had earned the dubious distinction of deporting over three million people, more immigrants than any other president in history. In doing so, the twenty-first century became an era of mass immigrant detention and deportation. There are millions of other immigrants like Mayra Machado who have their own stories of living in the United States, some with US citizen children, some having committed crimes, but all sharing the experience of being locked up and deported. Machado's story should be familiar to us from recent media accounts, but the long history of how we got from there to here is less understood. Building on the exciting new scholarship in recent years, this book provides an explanation of how, where, and why noncitizens were put behind bars in the United States from the late nineteenth century to the present. Through select granular experiences of detention over the course of more than 140 years, I explain how America built the world's largest system for imprisoning immigrants.

HISTORY OF IMMIGRANT DETENTION

From the late nineteenth century, when the US government held hundreds of Chinese in federal prisons pending deportation, to the early twentieth century, when it caged hundreds of thousands of immigrants in insane asylums, to World War I and World War II, when the Federal Bureau of Investigation (FBI) declared tens of thousands of foreigners "enemy aliens" and locked them up in Immigration and Naturalization Service (INS) camps in Texas and New Mexico, and through the 1980s detention of over 125,000 Cuban and almost 23,000 Haitian refugees, the incarceration of foreigners nationally has ebbed and flowed.[3] Although far more immigrants are being held in prison today than at any other time in US history, earlier moments of immigrant incarceration echo present-day patterns. In fact, the legal debates about incarcerating immigrants indefinitely pending deportation stretches all the way back to the late 1880s, and the rates of institutionalization (all forms of incarceration) in the early to mid-twentieth century rival those of the twenty-first century.

Until very recently, the study of incarcerated immigrants has fallen in the crack between prison and migration studies. Migration scholars focus on movement of people across borders and the communities they establish in their adopted countries. Prison scholarship has mostly ignored the question of migrant incarceration, focusing instead on the mass imprisonment of largely Black and Brown citizens.[4] Although the issue of migrant incarceration is touched upon in both fields, there is little sustained effort to describe, measure, or account for their imprisonment, especially before the 1980s. Recent books focusing on the rise of immigrant and refugee detention since the 1970s help to flesh out the latest period of mass immigrant incarceration and particularly the link between immigration and criminal law. These scholars show how legislation and specific policies from the 1980s to the present have resulted in the massive growth of migrant detention.[5] The historical studies of Ellis Island in New York and Angel Island in San Francisco help us to understand where and how immigrants were detained in the first half of the twentieth century. The government incarcerated 300,000 migrants on Angel Island from 1910 to 1940, more than half of whom were Chinese (100,000) and Japanese (85,000), making it by far the largest detention center at the time. Ellis Island processed many more than Angel Island (around 12 million) but fewer people were held there and they were detained for shorter periods.[6] Legal historical studies of deportation also offer a framework for understanding the laws that provided for detention pursuant to deportation, but oftentimes these works pay short shrift to the experience of detention itself.[7]

Various scholars have argued that when writing about immigration and citizenship, we must not only focus on those coming from outside the country hoping to become part of the national community but must also consider the ways in which insiders have been rendered non-citizens and foreigners.[8] Native Americans and enslaved Africans are the most obvious examples of people who were very much inside the nation and yet were rendered "aliens" legally, politically, and socially. Free Blacks had citizenship rights in certain states, but their legal subordination made them into non-citizens in slave states and rendered them vulnerable to efforts to "repatriate" them to Africa. And even though Black people gained formal citizenship in 1868 and Native Americans in 1924, obstacles to voting, Jim Crow, and other discriminatory practices continued to limit their citizenship rights. Native Americans were subject to congressional plenary power in the late nineteenth century even after the 1887 Dawes Act conferred citizenship on individual land-owning Indians, and certain states barred Native Americans from voting up to 1962, suggesting the extent to which citizenship rights were limited for non-white people. Although formally citizens, white US women were also considered to have less than full citizenship rights well into the twentieth century. In 1907, Congress passed a law that stripped US women of their formal citizenship if they married a non-citizen, and women lacked voting rights until 1920. The poor of all races also had limited voting rights and were subject to vagrancy laws and incarceration at extremely high rates. Thus, insiders of many stripes were rendered non-citizens or second-class citizens. Throughout the nineteenth and twentieth centuries, women, non-whites, and the poor have gained formal citizenship rights, although even today these rights are constrained through legal and extralegal means, but the line between non-citizens and citizens cuts more deeply than ever.

Although this book does not focus on the "insiders" whose citizenship rights have been stripped or limited, its aim is to draw connections between the incarceration of non-citizens and second-class citizens. Many of the same prisons and detention centers for immigrants also held citizens who were poor, Black, and disenfranchised. Japanese Americans were locked up in spite of their being citizens, and many Latinx Americans have been swept up in deportation raids notwithstanding being born in the United States or having become naturalized citizens. Historian Laura Briggs has shown how the same practices of stripping children from their parents that happened on the US-Mexico border have precedents from the colonial era through the present for Native Americans and African Americans; oftentimes the very same carceral sites and facilities have been used for non-citizens and citizens.[9] The bright line between citizen and non-citizen is much clearer in the law books than on the street. The eroding of rights of non-citizens and their increasing criminalization since the late nineteenth century has gone hand in hand with the denial of rights to subordinated citizens. It is not a coincidence that the dramatic expansion of immigrant detention and deportation happened at the very same time that mass incarceration of citizens exploded.

The book's title, *Forever Prisoners*, takes its name from the term used by journalists and others to refer to the terrorist suspects being held at the US prison at the military base at Guantanamo Bay, Cuba. Some of those picked up in 2001 in the midst of the War on Terror in Afghanistan and elsewhere are still being held in Guantanamo, never having been charged with a crime and with no foreseeable end in sight to their incarceration. After almost twenty years behind bars, they are forever prisoners. From the late nineteenth century, many immigrants also found themselves facing indefinite detention, either having never been charged with a crime or having years earlier completed their criminal sentences. The forever prisoners are a small subset of the millions of all non-citizens locked up domestically or held in US-controlled prisons outside the country, but their stories demonstrate the extent to which foreigners in the United States and in US-controlled territories have found themselves beyond the protection of the Constitution or any semblance of human rights. What makes immigrants forever prisoners is not just the indeterminate time they spend locked up, but that they often remain vulnerable to detention and other forms of restrictions after release; they are never truly free. Non-citizens live in perpetual fear of incarceration and deportation for minor offenses that may have occurred decades earlier. And even naturalized citizens are under threat of having their citizenship stripped. Like twenty-first-century slave catchers, ICE agents roam highways, fields, and factories, snatching people from their homes and workplaces, and separating parents from their crying children. If immigrants are deported, they often live circumscribed lives far from their families and hemmed in by violent gangs and corrupt police. Mayra Machado spent almost three years in prison pending deportation proceedings and although she was deported for a second time in January 2020, she still feels like a prisoner in El Salvador, hiding out in a room, cut off from her family, friends, and home. As Machado put it while fighting back tears a few days after being deported, "Nothing has changed."[10]

In this book, immigrant, migrant, foreigner, non-citizen, and refugee are used to refer to the people who have been imprisoned. Not all migrants intend to become immigrants who establish long-term residence, and some of the people discussed did not even choose to come to this country but were brought here at gunpoint by the US government. However, all of the people in this book shared a legal status as "aliens." Although the term "alien" or "illegal alien" will not be used unless referring to the government's designation, tracking the criminalization of non-citizens and the making of the idea of "illegal aliens" is the point.[11] While each of the abovementioned labels carries a precise legal meaning, these labels tend to obscure the common experience shared by all of those who do not enjoy the benefits of full citizenship. That commonality is what I want to highlight.

A concept known as plenary power is the reason immigrants have found themselves so exposed to state power with little protection from the Constitution or the courts. The plenary power doctrine vests the right to devise and enforce immigration laws with the legislative and executive branches, and the Supreme Court has been reticent to review such statutes even based on constitutional constraints.[12] There is a long and complicated legal history of indefinite detention of non-citizens, with courts alternating between granting the government unlimited powers to incarcerate non-citizens and imposing time limitations on their detention pending a hearing or deportation. Recently the Supreme Court decided two important cases that upheld the right of the government to hold certain classes of immigrants in detention indefinitely without a bail hearing.[13] Although legal scholars argue that the Court left open the possibility of a constitutional challenge to indefinite detention, the current practice allows the government unfettered and unlimited detention authority. To most lay people, the ability of the government to imprison people without end and without a criminal conviction seems unfair and a blatant disregard of the most basic of civil rights, the right to freedom.

This study of immigrant deportation and detention builds on the important work of scholars who have investigated particular periods and forms of detention by examining all the ways foreigners have been imprisoned in the United States from the late nineteenth century through the present. This wider and more comprehensive perspective highlights the waxing and waning of particular forms of incarceration over time as it appreciates the magnitude and scope of carceral institutions that have locked up millions of non-citizens for more than a century. Many recent studies argue that the recent wave of mass immigrant detention is a dramatic departure from the past, pointing to the supposed hiatus of immigrant detention from 1954 through the 1970s.[14] A wider and deeper examination of the pre-1980s period, however, challenges that conclusion. Although the last thirty years have been a time of mass incarceration for both citizens and non-citizens, the rates of institutionalization in the early to mid-twentieth century, which include people locked in hospitals for the mentally ill and other charitable institutions, were equal to the rates in the twenty-first century. Broadly speaking, more people were locked up in insane asylums than prisons in the early twentieth century, and by the 1960s, psychiatric institutions began emptying out and prisons began filling up. People suffering from mental illness were likely to be found in insane asylums in the early twentieth century, but in the late twentieth century those people were being incarcerated in jails and prisons. Given this reality, one needs to look beyond jails, prisons, and immigrant detention centers to the hospitals for the mentally ill and other institutions where foreigners were denied liberty. Similarly, during World War II, tens of thousands of foreigners ended up behind bars after being accused of being "enemy aliens," not to mention the 120,000 Japanese and Japanese Americans interned in forced relocation camps. Examining all of these different forms of non-citizen incarceration in one volume reveals for the first time that mass immigrant incarceration was as prevalent in the early twentieth century as it is in the twenty-first century. The justifications have changed and the names emblazoned on the prisons have altered, but roughly the same proportion of immigrants were deprived of their liberty then as now. As we imagine a different future, we must be cognizant of the variety of ways that immigrants have been locked up in the past. The solution to the immigrant incarceration crisis is therefore not to return to a rosy past when foreigners were welcomed, but to create a radically new vision of rights beyond citizenship.

Incarcerating poor and mentally ill immigrants has a long history in America. Before the federal government took over the enforcement of immigration restrictions in the 1880s, states like New York and Massachusetts practiced their own immigrant processing, detention, and deportation.

New York established a station at Castle Garden in lower Manhattan in 1855 where immigrants deemed excludable due to their poverty or criminal past were detained and deported.[15] When Ellis Island was created in 1892, the federal government took over enforcement of immigration restrictions, but almost all foreigners transferred through the center in a few hours, and those detained longer were usually held for just a few days. In contrast, at Angel Island, the immigrant processing center established in San Francisco Bay in 1910, Asians, particularly Chinese, were held for much longer periods of time, often for weeks at a time, while their eligibility to enter was determined by immigration officials.[16] Although immigrants detained at either Ellis Island or Angel Island were not legally considered prisoners, they experienced their detention as imprisonment. Bennie Woon Yep, who was detained for one month at Angel Island, described sleeping on metal beds and being separated from family members as "just like a jail."[17] One author estimated that 3,500 immigrants died at Ellis Island, including 1,400 children. Although accurate data are unavailable, multiple reports of immigrants in detention committing suicide at both Ellis Island and Angel Island illustrate their desperation when faced with the prospect of deportation or indefinite detention.[18] Even as detentions of prospective immigrants on Ellis Island waned, it became a convenient place for the federal government to imprison foreign radicals pending deportation. The anarchist Emma Goldman, longshoreman union leader Harry Bridges, and a host of other radicals were locked up on Ellis Island before it was finally shuttered in 1954.[19]

Since the late nineteenth century, the infrastructure to incarcerate immigrants has grown in periodic bouts of prison-building frenzies. From the early 1950s to the late 1970s, however, there was a pause in a long-standing policy of detaining immigrants and refugees while their claims for asylum were being adjudicated. Immigration was at a historic low in the early 1950s, and the proportion of the foreign-born American population had been in decline from the early twentieth century, so there was little public pressure to keep immigrants locked up.[20] Another reason for the policy of generally paroling refugees and immigrants rather than detaining them was that the United States was projecting itself as a beacon of freedom and hope in the midst of the Cold War with the Soviet Union.[21] A supposedly "liberal" attitude toward immigrants was part of US foreign policy propaganda, even as the Cold War–inspired 1952 McCarren-Walter Act stepped up deportations and placed severe restrictions on Asian migration. In 1954, Attorney General Herbert Brownell Jr. announced the new policy at a naturalization ceremony on Veterans Day at Ebbets Field in Brooklyn: "In all but a few cases, those aliens whose admissibility or deportation is under study will no longer be detained. Only those deemed likely to abscond or those whose freedom of movement could be adverse to the national security or the public safety will be detained." All others, Brownell asserted, would be released on parole. Brownell predicted that the number of those detained in exclusion proceedings outside of the Mexican border would drop from 38,000 in 1953 to fewer than 1,000 under the new policy. The new initiative was so "far reaching in scope and effect," Brownell declared, that the Justice Department was closing six detention centers at seaports in Boston, Seattle, San Francisco, San Pedro, Honolulu, and the paradigmatic one in New York at Ellis Island.[22] In 1958, four years after Brownell's announcement, Supreme Court Justice Tom C. Clark said, "The physical detention of aliens is now the exception."[23]

Like magicians using sleight of hand, Attorney General Brownell and Justice Clark pointed to the closed detention centers at seaports to distract attention from the Border Patrol's temporary camps for Mexicans in the Southwest. At the very moment Brownell was announcing the end of immigrant detention, "Operation Wetback" had reached a record number of over one million Mexicans returned to Mexico. These operations involved short-term detentions and were not formal removals involving a legal process, but they required a massive detention structure nonetheless. The intense focus on apprehending and deporting Mexicans began well before 1954, with Mexicans accounting for over 90 percent of the hundreds of thousands of national apprehensions (1943–54) each year. Migrants were processed quickly in temporary detention centers, some in converted tomato warehouses, and then either transported to the border by bus or train, or flown to the interior on airplanes.[24] Thus, even in this period when immigrant detention was supposedly the exception rather than the rule, there were still hundreds of thousands of immigrants being rounded up, detained, and deported. The duration of detention was shortened, the locale had shifted from seaports to the southern border, and the detainees were Mexicans rather than Europeans, but the detention regime did not end.

The closing of Ellis Island in 1954 led to other problems when detained immigrants were transferred into New York City jails. A few days after Brownell's announcement of the new policy, author Pearl Buck complained in a letter to the *New York Times* that due to the closing of Ellis Island, immigrants were being transferred to jails alongside common criminals. "They are locked up with murderers, drug addicts and other degenerate types," Buck wrote. "Their food is inadequate, their bed mattresses dirty. They have little opportunity to get fresh air, and they must perform labor such as criminal persons perform."[25] Publicly shamed, the Justice Department rescinded its order to hold immigrants in jails and instead ordered them moved to the Empire Hotel in Manhattan until the agency could establish its own detention facilities.[26] The 1952 Immigration Act allowed the government to provide various parole alternatives to detention, even after a final order of deportation was handed down, and time limits were established so that no immigrant would be held for longer than six months after a final deportation order.[27]

Scholars have pointed to Brownell's and Justice Clark's words to argue that immigrant detention was "effectively abolish[ed]" in the 1950s.[28] However, these scholars gloss over hundreds of thousands of Mexicans who were rounded up, detained, and deported, perhaps because the INS simply left Southwest border detentions out of the count in the 1950s, as historian Judith Irangika Dingatantrige Perera has shown.[29] In 1960, the INS reported that fewer than 7,000 aliens were "taken into custody under warrants of arrest," but in that same year close to 60,000 were deported, almost all of them Mexicans who were detained in three staging areas on the border. These Mexicans were apparently not part of the official count and were simply referred to as "other aliens." The INS was proud that it had managed to process them quickly, with an average detention of only seven days, but shorter detentions also allowed more people to be processed and removed.[30] In 1962, the INS began reporting all detentions, including those of Mexicans, and also listing which of those were in INS facilities versus other jails and prisons. Throughout the 1960s, the number of detentions grew from under 35,000 to over 215,000 in 1970. By 1978, detentions had reached a record of more than 340,000. Over time, the INS expanded its detention facilities, and by 1979, it held 204,000 immigrants in its own prisons and outsourced another 112,000.[31] However, even these large numbers omit the vast majority of Mexicans who were arrested by Border Patrol and dumped across the border without ever setting foot in an official detention center. The fact that the INS made over one million apprehensions in 1979 suggests the extent to which mass detentions were occurring well before the era of mass deportations supposedly began.[32]

The policy of limiting detention for asylum seekers, at least in terms of duration if not numbers of people, began to erode with the arrival of Haitians fleeing violence, political instability, and economic crisis in the 1970s. Out of 50,000 Haitian asylum petitions from 1972 to 1980, fewer than 100 were granted. Instead of paroling asylum seekers into the United States while their petitions moved through the hearing process, the INS began to detain all Haitians in hastily erected detention centers. In March 1980, the INS entered into an agreement with the Bureau of Prisons to use their facilities to "screen, process and detain aliens who are in the United States illegally," and a Haitian processing center was created at the Federal

Correction Institute in South Florida. In the very same month, the 1980 Refugee Act established a universal procedure to determine eligibility for all people claiming refugee status. The long-standing automatic parole for Cubans was summarily ended; for the first time, Cubans would have to undergo a review to determine if they were refugees.[33] It is no coincidence that mass immigrant detention was revived with the arrival of tens of thousands of poor, Black Haitians. Racism has always been central to immigration restrictions and enforcement.[34]

In April 1980, Castro's announcement that he would open up the port of Mariel and allow people to leave the island triggered a massive exodus of people. In what became known as the Mariel Boatlift, 125,000 Cubans boarded rickety boats and fishing trawlers to make the short journey across the straits of Florida that spring and summer. The INS quickly established detention and processing centers in the Orange Bowl and Krome, a former missile base in Miami, as well as military bases in Fort Chafee, Arkansas; Fort Indiantown Gap, Pennsylvania; and Fort McCoy, Wisconsin. Over 300 Cuban refugees even ended up in a federal prison on McNeil Island off the Pacific Coast near Tacoma, Washington. Within a few months, almost all of the Cubans were released on parole to US-based family members, but the Haitians and many Black Cubans, most of whom had no family in the country, found themselves in detention for longer periods of time. By May 1981, the INS had a blanket policy of mandatory detention of Haitians with no possibility of release on bond. In the first ten years, only eight of 25,000 Haitians were allowed to pursue asylum claims. Although immigrants in the United States theoretically had some constitutional due process protections, the government attempted to circumvent these by interdicting refugees before they reached US shores and by creating a new status of "Cuban/Haitian entrants" that defined them as being still outside the United States even though they were inside. In August 1981, nearly 800 Haitian asylum seekers were detained in the US military camp, Fort Allen, in Puerto Rico.[35] These measures were designed to deny Haitians and Cubans the right to petition for asylum and to limit their constitutional protections. In September 1991, following a new wave of exiles fleeing a coup, Haitians were interdicted at sea and locked up at the US naval station at Guantanamo Bay, Cuba, where they would have an even harder time to claim asylum due to lack of access to lawyers. What began as a policy for Haitians and Cubans was soon expanded to include Central Americans.[36] A Justice Department spokesperson defended the new policy in 1982 by arguing they were just doing their jobs: "The rules say that if illegal aliens come to this country without proper documentation they will be detained. All we're doing is enforcing the law."[37] In that same year, a young Justice

Department lawyer, Rudolph Giuliani, went to Congress to make an urgent plea for $35 million to build two new prisons to "enforce our immigration laws."[38] As mayor of New York City in the mid-1990s, Giuliani ordered police to use a heavy hand to enforce low-level offenses. Giuliani was therefore one of the principal architects of mass incarceration for both citizens and immigrants.

CRIMMIGRATION

The harsh detention and asylum policies applied to Haitians and Cubans in the early 1980s morphed into a much more expansive criminalization of immigrants by the 1990s. What law scholar Juliet Stumpf aptly calls "crimmigration," the merging of criminal and immigration law, has been mostly seen as a late twentieth-century phenomenon. Stumpf acknowledges that criminal and immigration law emerge from a common state interest in exclusion, but she argues that detention of non-citizens with criminal backgrounds was "less common than now."[39] However, the overlapping of criminal and immigration law began in the late nineteenth century with Chinese being imprisoned for unlawful entry, and there is ample evidence that non-citizens with criminal records were being imprisoned at high rates in the early twentieth century. In the 1990s, harsher immigration restrictions expanded the crimes for which immigrants could be deported at the same time that police across the country began to step up their enforcement of low-level offenses. Expanded policing of low-level offenses and mandatory sentencing laws for drug and other charges led to the explosion in incarceration rates for citizens, and for immigrants it resulted in increasing numbers of mandatory detentions due to the Illegal Immigration Reform and Immigrant Responsibility Act (IIRIRA) of 1996. Within five years of the act, the number of non-citizens detained by the INS more than doubled, from around 72,000 in 1994 to over 188,000 in 2001.[40] While increased detentions were already apparent by 2000, the number of detentions continued to grow as local police were more fully integrated with immigration authorities during the Obama administration. Criminal immigration prosecutions remained at less than 20,000 per year from the 1970s through the early 2000s, and then shot up to over 80,000 a year from 2008 through 2014. Criminal immigration prosecutions have remained high ever since.[41] The number and length of detentions increased along with the growing number of criminal prosecutions and deportations from an average of four days in 1981 to 30 days in 2001, where it has remained.[42] Since the average length of stay of immigrant detainees is about a month, the total admissions on an annual basis is much higher than the daily count. The number of immigrant detentions has been dramatically growing as the Trump administration has sought mandatory detention of almost all immigrants, adults, children, and even infants, who come into the country without proper papers. In 2019, a record of more than half a million immigrants were detained. For the first time ever, the US government held more than 50,000 immigrants in their detention centers each day, and Trump's 2021 budget asked for increased funding to detain 60,000. Equally significant, an additional 3.3 million other immigrants were under ICE supervision, either on parole or bond, or were being sought by the government as fugitives.[43] Given that an estimated one-in-ten immigrant families, both citizens and documented immigrants, live in mixed-status families with someone who is undocumented, the impact of immigrant detention and deportation ripples out to millions more.[44] Asylum seekers who present themselves to immigration officers at the border are also being held in detention, or sent to dangerous border cities in Mexico, while the lengthy legal process for claiming asylum unfolds. The immigrant detention archipelago echoes infinitely inside and outside the borders of the nation.

To apprehend and hold all of these migrants has required a massive build-up in the prison infrastructure, including the construction of government detention facilities and private prisons, as well as the use of hundreds of local jails and state and federal prisons. In 1980, the INS spent just over $21 million on detention. By 2010, ICE spent almost $1.8 billion annually detaining immigrants, and by 2018, its yearly spending topped $3 billion.[45] While the government does not publicize the extent of its detention footprint, a Freedom of Information request revealed that from 2003 to 2017, millions of immigrants in the United States were imprisoned at 1,685 facilities solely on civil charges. In fiscal year 2018, immigrants had spent nearly 18 million "mandays" locked up; that's 18 million days immigrants spent behind bars in just one year.[46] In 2016 alone, more than 350,000 new immigrants were booked into 637 civil detention facilities around the country, in addition to about 115,000 immigrants locked up in state prisons and local jails for other offenses.[47] The number of immigrants being detained in non-criminal proceedings has increased since 1994 from less than 7,000 to well over 50,000 per day in 2019.[48] Although the point-in-time snapshot incarceration rates of foreign-born individuals is significantly lower than that of native-born citizens, from 2011 to 2016 an average of more than 380,000 immigrants have been expelled from the country every year.[49] Viewed as elimination, deportation together with incarceration serves to disappear about half a million immigrants from civil society annually. Therefore, almost 5 percent of the undocumented immigrant population (whose total is estimated to be around 10.5 million) is removed from society and put in detention centers or deported each year.[50] The devastation of losing one in twenty people each year cannot be overestimated. The cumulative effect of this massive deportation machine over the past two decades has touched nearly every immigrant family in the country, particularly from Mexico, Guatemala, El Salvador, and Honduras. The loss of human potential by caging people for 18 million days a year is incalculable.

DETENTIONS AND DEPORTATIONS
IN HISTORICAL PERSPECTIVE

It is difficult to grasp the magnitude of immigrant detentions because such data have been sporadically and inconsistently reported. Since 1892, when the government started tracking removals, the US has deported more than 57 million people.[51] Many immigration scholars focus on formal removals as a proxy for tough restrictionist policies because of the existence of consistent deportation data since 1892. Looked at from this perspective, deportations remained low through most of the twentieth century and then dramatically shot up in the 1990s. However, that truth is only part of the story. Since 1927, the government has distinguished between removals and returns, the former being a formal deportation while the latter is a "voluntary return" after being apprehended near the border. Although formal deportations remain low up to the 1990s, returns read like the electrocardiogram chart of a cardiac patient, with sudden spikes almost every decade since the 1950s. Since the late 1990s, voluntary returns have fallen to levels not seen since the 1960s, but removals have spiked. What this means is that more people are spending longer in detention while their deportation cases wind their way through the courts.

Unlike detentions, which have only been sporadically and inconsistently recorded by immigration bureaucrats, apprehensions have been steadily tracked since 1925. These data do not measure the number of individuals apprehended, since one person can be apprehended multiple times. Nonetheless, tracking apprehensions measures the total number of temporary detentions, a subset of whom will be held for much longer periods of time. The chart shows various spikes in apprehensions, reaching highs of 1.8 million in 1986 and again in 2000.[52] Since 2000, the total number of apprehensions has steadily dropped to fewer than half a million per year. Looked at in terms of arrests, immigration detention has fallen

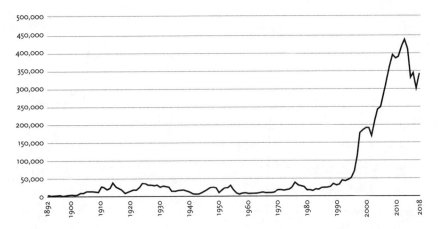

Figure I.1 Alien removals, 1892–2018.
Source: Department of Homeland Security, Table 39, FY 2018.

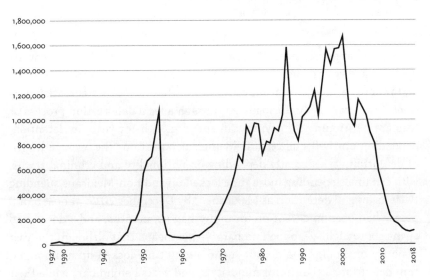

Figure I.2 Alien returns, 1927–2018.
Source: Department of Homeland Security, Table 39, FY 2018.

dramatically since 2000 signaling a shift in immigration enforcement. The vast majority of immigrants formerly were detained for brief periods by the Border Patrol before being released across the Mexican border, but increasingly more immigrants are being detained by ICE and held for weeks, if not months or years.[53]

For the purposes of understanding the ebb and flow of detention, removals, involving a formal legal procedure, are more significant than

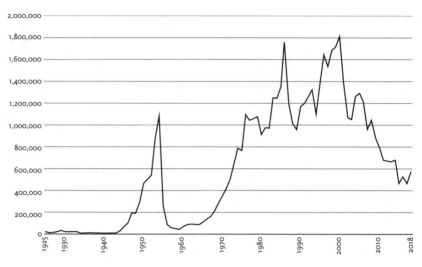

Figure I.3 Alien apprehensions, 1925–2018.
Source: Department of Homeland Security, Table 33.

returns or apprehensions. Migrants captured near the border may be held for a few days before they agree to voluntarily return to Mexico, and therefore their detention experience, while perhaps traumatizing, is brief. Immigrants who formally go through a legal deportation process or who are petitioning for asylum can spend months or years in detention, depending on their ability to fight their deportation. The average length of detention varies greatly depending on nationality and criminal status, with criminals spending more time locked up and non-Mexicans spending twice as long in detention as Mexicans.[54] By December 2012, almost 5,000 people had been in detention for more than six months, and a dozen had spent six to eight years behind bars.[55] This means that although the vast majority of immigrants do not spend a long time locked up in immigration detention, a significant minority spend years behind bars while their cases drag on in the courts. It is important to remember that in addition to ICE, the Border Patrol is also detaining hundreds of thousands for shorter periods of time. Furthermore, by 2019, ICE was monitoring an additional 120,000 immigrants on a daily basis through home and office visits, court tracking, and ankle bracelets.[56] In short, the forty-year trend has been toward lengthier and greater numbers of immigrant detentions, reaching a record-breaking half a million in 2019.[57]

Even though US immigration data show an increasing number of long-term detentions, especially in the last decade, they significantly underestimate detentions and deportations because they do not account for the

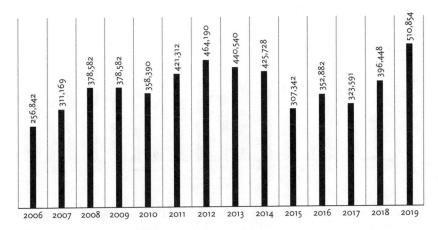

Figure I.4 Book-ins to ICE detention, FY 2006–2019.
Source: Department of Homeland Security, Immigration Enforcement Action Reports.

increasingly large number of Central Americans who are being captured in Mexico and deported without ever reaching US soil. Mexico's vigilance over its southern border with Guatemala increased with the second phase of the Mérida Initiative, when the United States pumped $200 million into Mexico's efforts to police its border (2014–18) and made border security one of four pillars of the Initiative. As a result of this funding and US diplomatic pressure, Mexico began to apprehend, detain, and deport hundreds of thousands of Central Americans each year. Mexico deported 600,000 people between 2014 and 2018, almost all of them coming from Central America's northern triangle (El Salvador, Guatemala, and Honduras) heading farther north. While the Mérida Initiative pumped money into these efforts, Mexico has been cooperating on enforcing US immigration policy for quite some time. From 2002 to 2017, Mexico deported 1.9 million from these three Central American countries, compared to US deportations of 1.1 million.[58] Thus, in addition to the millions of immigrant detentions taking place on US soil, the US has been funding and directing millions of additional immigrant detentions in Mexico. Since these are really US deportations through remote control, they should be included in attempts to account for the number of detentions and deportations done by or at the behest of the United States.[59]

There is no doubt that the United States locks up far more immigrants than any other country. Just as with incarceration of citizens, the nation has the dubious distinction of being a global leader in imprisoning foreigners. Mexico detains the second highest number of migrants, reaching close to 100,000 in recent years, but almost all of those detentions

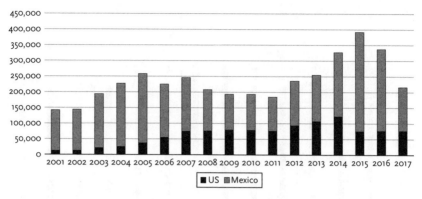

Figure I.5 Total removals and returns of people from Northern Triangle Countries (El Salvador, Guatemala, and Honduras), 2001–2017, by US and Mexico.
Source: Based on DHS data, https://www.dhs.gov/immigration-statistics/yearbook. DHS data include only removals from 2001–2008. Mexico data from Secretaria de Gobernación, "Extranjeros presentados y devueltos," tables 3.2.1 and 3.2.7, http://www.politicamigratoria.gob.mx/es_mx/SEGOB/Boletines_Estadisticos.

are at the behest of the United States. Although accurate data and lack of standardized reporting makes global comparisons difficult, the well over 500,000 annual US immigrant detentions far surpass those of other countries with high detention rates (Malaysia, 87,000; France 46,000; Russia 38,000; and the United Kingdom 33,000).[60] The very absence of globally accepted definitions of what constitutes migrant detention or accessible data helps explain why these prisons have remained understudied and in the shadows.[61]

STORIES, NOT NUMBERS

The figures in this introduction excepted, *Forever Prisoners* avoids reducing the story of immigrant detention to a dizzying pile of statistics on apprehensions, detentions, and deportations, and instead narrates this history through intimate portrayals of six illustrative stories. One of the stories focuses on an incident involving a group of Chinese detainees whose names are barely mentioned in government documents, while others focus on a single individual or family whose stories have been the subject of numerous newspaper articles. All of the stories capture the feelings of helplessness and uncertainty experienced by people who faced indefinite detention based on their status as "illegal aliens." Some of the stories end in deportation or death in detention; others end with the immigrants winning their legal battles and gaining US citizenship. In early January 2020,

Mayra Machado was deported to El Salvador while her appeal was still pending in the 5th Circuit Court of Appeals. Whether she remains in El Salvador hiding from violent gangs or returns clandestinely to the United States, evading ICE and traffic cops, she will live in fear.

The five stories that comprise this book are told in chronological order and also address different themes: immigration violations, mental illness, national security, criminality, and terrorism. The criminalization of migration, indefinite detention, and racism are the threads that have stitched this carceral landscape together for more than a century. Criminalization of migration began with Chinese labor exclusion in the mid to late nineteenth century. Not only were Chinese in the Pacific Northwest locked up in the McNeil Island federal prison and sentenced to hard labor for immigration violations, but a large number of immigrants served time in the prison for drug and alcohol violations. The suggestion that criminalization of migration was not a fundamental part of the immigration system until the latter part of the twentieth century obscures these early carceral experiments.[62] The first chapter explores the western birthplace of these criminalization efforts by focusing on the thousands of Chinese and other immigrants locked up on a remote prison island near Seattle, many of whom were deported after serving their sentences.

Just as criminalization of immigration has an earlier genesis than is typically acknowledged, so does mass incarceration. If one considers "insane asylums" and other so-called charitable carceral institutions, the rate of incarceration at the beginning of the twentieth century is equivalent to that experienced in the last few decades. Hospitals for the mentally ill locked up far more immigrants (and citizens) than did jails and prisons in the early twentieth century. Between 1960 and 1980, mental hospitals began emptying out and jails and prisons began to fill up. After the mid-1970s, immigrants and citizens alike were more likely to be incarcerated in jails and prisons than in mental institutions, a trend that has continued to the present. Chapter 2 explores this world of foreigners trapped by psychiatrists and immigration agents through the story of a Russian-Jewish-Brazilian immigrant who was declared insane in 1914 and deported.

Foreign policy is always part of the calculus of immigration control, but during moments of heightened fears about national security provoked by wars or imagined threats to the nation, immigrants and marginalized citizens face greater threats of incarceration and fewer legal protections. The primary example of this is the detention of more than 120,000 Japanese and Japanese Americans during World War II, but World War I and the War on Terror in the twenty-first century also have led to spikes in detention of immigrants and even citizens perceived as "aliens." The third chapter explores the intersection of national security and immigration policy through the story of a little-know program run by the FBI during World War II to kidnap Japanese, Germans, and Italians living in Latin America and incarcerate them in camps run by the Immigration and Naturalization Service (INS) in Texas and New Mexico.

The most recent wave of legislation criminalizing immigrants in the 1980s and 1990s led to a massive growth in the immigration detention footprint and the steady growth of the number of immigrants put behind bars. "Tough on crime" policies and a carceral turn in the country prompted a prison-building frenzy for citizens and non-citizens alike. In both cases, Black and Brown men were the ones occupying the new cells. In the 1970s and 1980s, tens of thousands of Haitian refugees arrived in the United States, along with 125,000 Cuban refugees in 1980. Instead of releasing them on parole, as had been the general policy since the 1950s, the United States set up mass detention camps to process the asylum seekers. It was not simply a coincidence that the liberal parole policy ended when a group of largely Black migrants arrived on our shores. Although more Cubans than Haitians were eventually paroled into the United States, the Cubans who ended up remaining in prison due to prior criminal convictions or mental illness were almost entirely Black. And when Cuban parolees com-mitted minor criminal offenses in this country, they also ended up back in prison after serving their sentences, waiting to be deported to a country that refused to accept them. The indefinite detention of the Cubans be-cause of their criminal histories augured what would become an increas-ingly overlapping system of criminal and immigration law. Chapter 4 focuses on a two-week prison uprising in 1987 by Mariel Cuban refugees in Oakdale, Louisiana, and Atlanta, Georgia, when they discovered they would be deported back to Cuba. Following this prison takeover, legisla-tion demanded mandatory detention of immigrants who had committed an ever-expanding list of crimes. By the 1990s, the INS had developed a robust network of detention facilities capable of caging asylum seekers, those fighting deportation orders, and those labeled "criminal aliens." It was the era of mass incarceration of citizens and also the era when millions of immigrants were put behind bars and barbed wire.

The Haitian and Cuban detentions were the opening salvo in the re-cent trend of criminalizing immigrants that saw its fruition in the first two decades of the twenty-first century. In this period, the number of immigrants facing criminal prosecutions skyrocketed as did the number of immigrants detained and formally deported. Since federal immigration en-forcement began in the 1880s, the vast majority of immigrants were allowed to return voluntarily without going through formal deportation procedures.

Although people were being forcibly removed from the country, very few were subject to lengthy detention in immigration detention facilities. The historic shift from voluntary removal to formal deportations in the second decade of the twenty-first century resulted in millions of immigrants accruing criminal records based on their illegal entry and reentry. It was also in this decade when technological advances allowed local law enforcement to identify those who were in the country without authorization during routine police stops. The penultimate chapter explores our present moment of criminalization of immigrants through the story of Mayra Machado, the woman from El Salvador whose story opened the book.

The incarceration of foreigners and those turned into non-citizens by white settlers has been a feature of the United States since its origins as a British colony. Native Americans and Africans were enslaved and forced to work on plantations and farms, which were themselves essentially prison work camps.[63] The United States restricted the mobility of Native Americans, forcing them onto reservations and attempting to wipe out indigenous cultures by forcing Native children into assimilationist boarding schools. Slave catchers kept enslaved Africans on the plantation under the whips of their overseers, and in the post-emancipation period vagrancy laws and Jim Crow limited the mobility of African Americans. In the antebellum period, state governments deported poor Irish immigrants to other states or back to Ireland. However, it was not until the late nineteenth century that the US government developed an immigration enforcement bureaucracy that allowed it to detain thousands of immigrants for violation of immigration laws. Since that time, unauthorized immigration has been criminalized, and immigrants have been disproportionately incarcerated for other low-level criminal offenses and for mental illness. While all evidence suggests that immigrants commit crimes at levels lower than native-born citizens, in the early twentieth century they were locked up at rates higher than those of the general population for low-level crimes where police discretion is more of a factor.[64] Police targeting these immigrant communities rather than criminal behavior explains the high rates of immigrant incarceration in the early twentieth century. Numerous studies have found that in the twenty-first century, immigrants, both legal and undocumented, either have no effect on crime rates or help to lower them in the United States.[65]

Even though there have been peaks and valleys in roundups of immigrants over the course of the last 140 years, beginning in the 1980s, we entered a new era in the mass imprisonment of immigrants, coinciding with the mass incarceration of citizens. In both cases, Black and Brown men are the ones most likely to be locked up. Although there have been serious efforts to reduce mass incarceration of citizens, especially in California, bipartisan immigration policies have led to more immigrants being put behind bars for longer periods of time.[66] Today, the same country that declares itself a "nation of immigrants" locks up far more immigrants than any other country on earth.[67]

CHAPTER 1

Dawn of Immigrant Incarceration

Chinese and Other Aliens at McNeil Island Prison

The penitentiary will soon be full to overflowing with contraband Chinamen. As the subject now stands, they are subject to indefinite imprisonment.
　　—William H. White, US Attorney, Washington Territory, 16 January 1888

In the mid-1880s, a strange thing was happening at McNeil Island prison, off the coast of Washington Territory. A growing number of Chinese were being held there after completing criminal sentences for immigration violations, but the government was unable to deport them to Canada, the country from which they had entered the United States, because they lacked the money to pay the steep $50 head tax required by Canada. The indefinite detention of the Chinese was the first time the government was faced with the contradiction between the still emerging immigration law and the demands of justice. This episode also reveals that the standard narrative claiming that immigration was not criminalized until 1929 is wrong. Further investigation into this prison's population from 1880 to 1940 uncovered a world of immigrant incarceration, largely based on drug and alcohol offenses. The early history of McNeil Island prison is evidence that the criminalization of immigrants and migration began long before our present era of mass immigrant detention.

McNeil Island is just two and a half miles off the coast, near Tacoma, Washington, but it might as well have been in the middle of the Pacific Ocean when a territorial jail opened there with just three prisoners in 1875. This remote island is located in what was then a sparsely populated part of

Washington Territory; in 1870 there were fewer than 1,500 people in the county in which the island was situated.[1] McNeil Island was the western birthplace of immigrant incarceration, and it was the only federal prison on the West Coast until the 1930s. In 1891, the Three Prisons Act incorporated McNeil Island into the Federal Prison System, along with penitentiaries in Atlanta, Georgia, and Leavenworth, Kansas.[2] McNeil was not set up as an immigrant detention center, but it quickly filled up with foreigners. The prison represented exclusion from the nation by its very geographical location at the edge of the frontier. It was here that many non-citizens found themselves most exposed to state power and without rights at the dawn of the deportation era.

Before federal immigration law, before the United States was even created, and even 2,000 years before Puget Sound was formed, McNeil Island was inhabited by the Puyallup, Nisqually, Steilacoom, Squaxin, and Fox Island nations.[3] That a 15,000 year-old indigenous territory was turned into a prison for immigrants by recently arrived white settler colonists suggests the deeply ironic history of this small coastal island. The fact that a good number of the people imprisoned at McNeil Island were Native Americans suggests the ways in which this prison was part of the settler colonial project in which white newcomers incarcerated both native inhabitants and non-white immigrants. The Chinese were the first to be locked up on McNeil Island on immigration-related charges, but this chapter also explores the large number of foreigners who ended up in the prison for a variety of different reasons, mostly immigration, and drug- and alcohol-related offenses.

In the first decade of McNeil Island Penitentiary's operation from 1875 to 1885, few Chinese were sent there. The fact that inmates 33 and 42 at McNeil Island Penitentiary were simply listed as "Charlie (a Chinaman)" and "Frank a Chinaman" indicates the informal nature of their identification in the early years as well as the racism of prison guards. By the mid-1880s, however, immigration restrictions against Chinese began to be enforced more vigorously, leading to an influx of Chinese prisoners on McNeil Island. On September 4, 1885, sixteen Chinese arrived at the island prison on a steamer from Seattle in what quickly became a pattern of using McNeil as an immigrant detention center. Chinese were held in a segregated hall, most serving sentences of six months while awaiting deportation. When the Chinese complained about the poor quality of their prison food, guards responded by locking them in their cells. Almost nothing about daily life of Chinese on McNeil Island was recorded, although guards noted that the Chinese were "crying."[4]

Ever since Chinese exclusion in 1882, Chinese laborers seeking entry to the United States crossed both the Canadian and Mexican border clandestinely. The first group of Chinese that ended up at McNeil Island had paid a "white man" to sneak them into the United States in late August 1885, but instead the smuggler left them to starve on a "barren" island in the chain of San Juan islands between the United States and Canada. After being discovered on the island within US territory, the Chinese were arrested and transported to Port Townsend, where they were charged with unlawful entry in a district court and ordered removed back to British Columbia "from whence [they] had come."[5] This phrase "from whence he had come" was language taken directly from Section 12 of the 1882 Chinese Exclusion Act, but just what it meant would become the subject of intense scrutiny in the coming years.[6] Having just passed their own Chinese Exclusion Act in July, Canadian officials demanded that Chinese being escorted by a US marshal pay the steep $50 head tax before entering. Since the Chinese did not have the money, the marshal was forced to return to Tacoma with the deportees. In a letter to the attorney general, US Attorney William White noted that the US government was spending $20 a day to incarcerate these Chinese. It would have been much cheaper for the US to simply pay the head tax and be done with it, but the marshal was not authorized to make such an expenditure. White urged the attorney general to come to "some arrangement" with the Canadian authorities over such cases but diplomacy failed to resolve the situation.[7] The provisions of the Canadian head tax were not supposed to take effect until January 1, 1886, but Canadian officials appeared to be implementing the policy as soon as it was passed.[8] US Secretary of State F. F. Maynard implored the attorney general that every effort should be made to return Chinese by land to Canada before the end of the year to avoid the official start of the head tax.[9]

This border dispute emerged in the context of rising anti-Chinese sentiment, especially in the western states of the United States and Canada. The US Congress passed the Chinese Exclusion Act in 1882 after a longer battle on the Pacific Coast by white-dominated labor unions and other nativists to criminalize and harass Chinese workers. Discriminatory state and local laws and racist depictions of the Chinese in the press as diseased, corrupt, deceptive, and lascivious created the conditions both for exclusion laws and for more direct attacks on the Chinese. In the 1880s, these tensions erupted in dramatic fashion as whites pillaged Chinese businesses and drove them out of scores of cities from British Columbia to southern California.[10] The most dramatic example of this wave of violence occurred in Rock Springs, Wyoming, on September 2, 1885, when twenty-eight Chinese miners were murdered and hundreds more pushed into the desert, but Chinese were also purged from scores of other towns along the Pacific Coast.

Two months after the Rock Springs massacre, white Tacoma residents rose up to expel all of the Chinese in their town, suddenly putting US Attorney White at the epicenter of anti-Chinese violence. Tacoma residents demanded that 800 Chinese residents who comprised one-tenth of the city's population leave the town by November 1, 1885. As the *Overland Monthly Magazine* put it, "An appeal to the higher law of self-preservation was determined upon, and the Chinese were asked to 'go.'" Five hundred Chinese left for Portland by the deadline, but on November 3 deputy marshals, deputy sheriffs, and the city mayor, along with a mob of 500 men, discovered 300 Chinese in hiding. The mob, led by a self-appointed Committee of Fifteen, went house-to-house, breaking down doors and dragging the Chinese residents out into the street. The Chinese were marched out of town with whatever they could carry and deposited in the middle of the night at a remote railroad station. A grand jury indicted twenty-seven Tacoma residents, including the mayor, for leading the anti-Chinese purge and violating the equal protection rights of the Chinese as well as for rebelling against US laws. The main charge was based on an 1871 anti–Ku Klux Klan act.[11] US Attorney White, who had himself heard the Committee of Fifteen threaten to blow up the houses of Chinese, led the prosecutions of the rioters. In writing to the attorney general, White declared, "No greater outrage was ever committed against the laws and government of these United States."[12] However, none of the leaders of the riot were ever convicted, and the anti-Chinese politicians won every open seat in the next election. The *Tacoma News* declared, "Free men have done this city a great service, for which its citizens are duly grateful."[13] Although White attempted to punish the leaders of the anti-Chinese purge, in the coming years, US politicians and courts would restrict the rights of Chinese laborers and criminalize their very presence in the country.[14] White found himself in a strange predicament, prosecuting the violent anti-Chinese mob at the same time he was pushing to deport Chinese stuck on McNeil Island.

As McNeil filled up with deportable Chinese, US marshals began to implement Secretary of State Maynard's plan to expel Chinese by land without the approval of Canada. In late November, a group of twenty Chinese were found on the waterfront in Tacoma and immediately arrested. *Overland Monthly* claimed that if the rest of the Chinese were still in Tacoma it would have been easy for them to blend in with the others and escape detection. However, given that almost every Chinese had been driven out of town, "their detection and detention were certainties." The twenty Chinese were brought to McNeil Island, where they remained for a short period before being taken to a judge in Seattle who put them in the custody of a US marshal and ordered them deported to Canada. The marshal marched the Chinese to the boundary line and ordered them to keep going. "The United States Customs officer at Semiahmoo explained to the Chinamen that they must not come back to this side, or the next time they would lose their queues. The Chinese seemed glad to get out of custody, and the last we saw of them they were going down the road toward New Westminster, on a dog-trot, chattering like a lot of parrots." The description by the marshal revealed the informality, brutality, and illegality of these informal deportations. Essentially, the marshal was forcing the Chinese to return to Canada illegally by clandestinely pushing them across the border.[15] One explanation is that these early deportations were improvised by local officials who had no guidance or precedent to follow. However, this case shows that the policy was designed and approved by the US secretary of state and the attorney general.[16] The threat to cut off their queues and references to the "chattering like a lot of parrots" highlights the racist discrimination faced by Chinese, particularly on the West Coast. Comparing the government's process of deporting Chinese to a foreign country to the "Tacoma method" of forcing Chinese out of the community, George Dudley Lawson, the author of the *Overland Monthly and Out West* magazine article, suggested that the latter was more humane. As Lawson put it, the " 'Tacoma method' in the abstract is an application of the principle that all of the rights of the people cannot be conditioned or defined in the statute books." The "Tacoma method" was an expression of popular democracy, Lawson contended, and it was a local application of "Abraham Lincoln's principle of a government 'of the people, by the people, and for the people.' "[17] Although some US government officials, like US Attorney White, condemned the extrajudicial purges of Chinese, both White and the vigilantes seemed united in the goal of eliminating Chinese in the Pacific Northwest.

Chinese continued to clandestinely cross the Canadian border in spite of these anti-Chinese pogroms and informal deportations. By the late 1880s, scores of Chinese were being locked up in McNeil Island prison, pending deportations to Canada that were increasingly difficult to carry out. The Chinese were literally caught between the exclusion acts of the United States and Canada, condemned to indefinite detention on a remote prison island until their cases could be resolved.

US Attorney White was concerned about the legality of indefinite detention, but he also worried about simply releasing the Chinese. In June 1888, Judge Nash warned that thirty-four Chinese being held at McNeil

Penitentiary "must be discharged unless the marshal remove them in a reasonable time." Given that the Chinese had already served their sentences under sections 1 and 16 of the amended 1884 Restriction Act, the judge gave the marshal one week to deport or release them. Frustrated by being unable to deport the Chinese and unable to continue to detain them, US Attorney White explained, "The law as laid down by the court will work a practical nullification of the restriction act."[18]

Although Chinese facing racist mobs and deportations were on the defensive with few tools with which to resist, incarcerated Chinese fought their imprisonment by suing the government. In July 1888, Num Choey's lawyer filed a writ of habeas corpus in Tacoma's district court and sued the government for not having provided Num with $15 in clothes and $5 in cash when he was previously released from McNeil in an effort to deport him. Num's lawyer argued that the law required the government to provide the clothes and the money when any prisoner was released. Upon hearing the argument, the court ordered Num Choey and the other Chinese at McNeil to be deported again; US Attorney White's view was that making such payments to deportable Chinese was against "public policy" since it was intended to help poor people reintegrate into society. Following the new deportation order, US Marshal T. J. Hamilton boarded a ship with twenty-eight Chinese and attempted to land them in Victoria, British Columbia. On the first attempt, Hamilton was rebuffed by Canadian authorities, and on the second, the Canadian authorities allowed seven of the group to land as they were recognized by a Chinese interpreter as having been in Victoria; one of the Chinese had a certificate proving his previous entry to Canada. The remaining twenty-one were returned to Port Townsend where they were immediately re-arrested for violation of the exclusion act.[19] US Attorney White anticipated their rejection in Victoria, and he wrote the attorney general indicating that he would "proceed against them under sections one and sixteen of the Restriction act."[20] This was a novel use of a new section of the exclusion act that was amended in 1884 as a way to criminally charge Chinese for unlawful presence. At this point, the Chinese had spent nearly a year in prison, their deportations to Victoria failing on two occasions, and they were back in McNeil Island prison with no end in sight to their incarceration saga.

In January 1888, US Attorney White wrote to the Justice Department about the growing number of Chinese who had completed their sentences at McNeil Island prison but could not be deported. According to Section 12 of the 1882 Chinese Exclusion Act, any Chinese person found to be unlawfully in the United States would be removed to the "country from whence he came."[21] Therefore, White reasoned, the Chinese at McNeil Island could not be deported to China since they had come from Canada, and they could not be deported to Canada because they did not have the money to pay their head tax to be admitted. "Relieve us from this difficulty," White pleaded to the State Department and Congress. As he put it, "The penitentiary will soon be full to overflowing with contraband Chinamen." The legal and moral quandary this posed was daunting. "As the subject now stands," he wrote, "they are subject to indefinite imprisonment."[22]

In the first decade of Chinese exclusion, the government and courts experimented with criminalizing Chinese unlawfully in the country even though the act itself had not specified any punishment for unauthorized presence. The 1882 Chinese Exclusion Act made it a misdemeanor, punishable by imprisonment for up to five years, for those who forged certificates of identification. Section 10 provided for seizure of ships for refusing to abide by the strict requirements to report all Chinese passengers on their manifests. Section 11 stipulated that those who helped to smuggle unauthorized Chinese into the country could be fined up to $1,000 and a year in prison. The only consequence, and it was a major one, for Chinese found to be unlawfully in the country was that they would be deported at the US government's expense.[23] Two years later, the act was amended to include Section 16, making "any violation of any of the provisions of this act" a misdemeanor punishable by a fine of up to $1,000 and/or imprisonment of up to one year. It's not clear if the vague provision was intended to criminalize Chinese found in the country without authorization, but the US attorney in Washington Territory used this provision for just that purpose. In 1892, a new provision (Section 4) mandated that Chinese who were found unlawfully in the country be imprisoned for up to "one year at hard labor."[24] From the late 1880s, federal courts in Washington Territory began to impose six-month sentences with hard labor on Chinese found in the country without authorization. In the five years between 1887 and 1892, 243 Chinese were imprisoned on the island, almost all of them for illegal immigration or smuggling.[25] Their sentences ranged from six months to an indeterminate period, and they served between one month and two and a half years.[26] Thus began criminalization of migration.

Criminalizing migration swept Chinese into the criminal justice system, which ironically afforded them more due process rights than they had simply as immigrants. If the Chinese were being charged with a crime, they had a right to a judicial trial. However, oftentimes they would simply be ordered deported by a US commissioner without the benefit of legal due process. The US attorney in Spokane, Patrick Winston, raised this concern to a congressional committee investigating Chinese immigration in 1891. Even though Winston held discriminatory views of the Chinese, claiming they were "an army of invasion" and were the "most nonassimilating people I ever knew," he was also concerned about the illegality of holding Chinese with no due process. The fact that Chinese were charged with violating the Chinese Exclusion Act without giving them an opportunity in court to deny their "intent to violate the law" struck the US attorney as unfair. "It is a common law rule that intent constitutes crime, and I do not think any statute ought to deny any man that right." Although some Chinese were formally charged in court, most were being ordered deported to China by a US commissioner without the intervention, or even knowledge, of the US attorney, much less a judicial trial. In 1891, Winston estimated that up to fifty Chinese had been held at a time in McNeil Island Penitentiary, but since he was not apprised of their cases, he could not know for certain.[27]

By the late 1880s, jailing Chinese on McNeil Island for illegal presence had become routine. In 1888, hundreds of Chinese were hauled before district court judges in Tacoma and charged with illegal entry from British Columbia in violation of the Chinese Exclusion Act. There were so many cases and the operation was so regular that the courts simply filled in the name of the Chinese defendant, the county in which the hearing occurred, the date of the trial, and the name of the judge.[28] Lawyers for the Chinese argued that the court had no jurisdiction given the absence of a criminal violation, but the Chinese were eventually deported. Among a group of nineteen Chinese whom the government had a hard time deporting to Canada was Ah Jim. On March 15, 1888, he received a six-month sentence of hard labor at McNeil Island for illegal presence in the country, but he was held for three years before being deported.[29] In the case of Ah Sing, another one of that group, the Third District Court in Washington Territory explicitly charged unlawful presence in the country as a violation of Sections 1 and 16 of the 1884 Restriction Act.[30] Judges used imprisonment not only as a means to deportation, but they imposed hard labor and prison sentences as punishment for unlawful presence. Up to 1892, Chinese at McNeil were mainly charged with "unlawful presence" or "violation of restriction act." After that point, they were charged with more specific violations including smuggling and forgery, but "unlawful presence" disappeared completely as a charge. Over time, charges would vary as new laws were passed, but the government always had a vast array of tools by which to imprison unauthorized Chinese migrants.

On June 18, 1889, Washington Territory Supreme Court Justice C. H. Hanford complained directly to President Benjamin Harrison about nineteen Chinese who had been arrested in October 1887 and two years later still languished on McNeil Island. Justice Hanford was sympathetic to the plight of the Chinese, arguing that it was unjust and unlawful that they should be deprived of their liberty for reasons beyond their control. "As in my humble opinion the spirit and letter of the Exclusion Act required such person to be taken out of the country rather than to be detained within it for the purpose of undergoing punishment for no other reason than that the officers do not know what else to do with them." For Hanford, deportation was acceptable but incarceration was not. He continued, "It is contrary to the fundamental law of this nation that any being should be subjected to repeated imprisonments, amounting to perpetual incarceration for not doing that which he is powerless to do." Nonetheless, Hanford refused to hear their cases and instead issued another Writ of Deportation. The Washington justice wrote that he did not presume to tell the president how to act, but he pleaded with him to intervene in this case to avoid the embarrassment of territory officials and to "set at liberty nineteen poor miserable captive strangers."[31] In July, the acting secretary of the State Department told the attorney general that it would be "both futile and inexpedient" to try to negotiate with the Canadians to accept the Chinese. He included Hanford's plea to the president, inquiring whether "our laws afford any relief in such a case."[32] Hanford decried the indefinite detention of the Chinese, but as he was unable to deport them and unwilling to release them, they would remain at McNeil Island for another two years.

The Chinese were unnamed in almost all official government correspondence and news articles about the case. There is only one reference to their names in a copy of a June deportation order that ended up in Canadian Privy Council minutes. The silence surrounding their names, their stories, and their backgrounds reflects the archival erasure that encourages us to see such Chinese migrants as only numbers or "poor miserable captive strangers" to be pitied. But their names should be remembered: Ah Ding, Ah Sing, Ah Sam 2nd, Ah Sam, Ha Kim, Lee Pin, Gin Chong, Hong Long, Wong Bay, Ah Ching 1st, Ah Ching 2nd, Ha Goon, Ah Jim 1st, Ah Jim 2nd, Ah Gong, Hon Ga, and Sing Hee.[33] It is unclear if the repeated names with numbers following them are relatives or whether the transliteration of Chinese names was inexact since immigration records are notoriously inaccurate in their recording of Chinese names. Furthermore, only seventeen names are listed on the deportation order even though the correspondence refers to nineteen people. While extant records do not allow for fuller understanding of these Chinese detainees on McNeil Island, the US and Canadian governments' exchanges about the case show how incarceration for non-citizens operated outside of the law.

Not until June 1891, four years after the group of nineteen Chinese were imprisoned, did Secretary of the Treasury W. H. H. Miller clarify that

Chinese should be removed to China and not contiguous countries like Canada and Mexico. Miller also emphasized that Section 15 of the 1884 amendment to the Chinese Exclusion Act made it clear that "all subjects of China and Chinese, whether subjects of China or of any other power" were to be restricted, thus clarifying that this was an ethnoracial restriction rather than one based on nationality. If a Chinese laborer had become a subject of Great Britain, then he could be deported to Canada, but if he merely landed in Canada or Mexico en route to the United States, he would be removed to China. As Miller put it, "It would be a strained construction of legislative intent to hold that Congress meant to declare that the country through which one comes shall be deemed the country whence he comes." His advice to the Department of Justice was for all Chinese found unlawfully in the country to be removed to China unless they can prove they are subjects of some other power.[34] Thus began the first deportations of Chinese to China.

Although little is known about how Chinese experienced McNeil or whether they protested their jailing, there are hints that they did not always accept their incarceration quietly. Given the rudimentary conditions and overcrowding at the prison, one might expect them to complain or resist. One historian noted that the prisoners were forced to labor during the day and then were herded "through a trapdoor into a log pit to spend the nights in mutual corruption and suffocation."[35] In September 1888, white men and Native Americans were put two men to a cell as the prison filled up, while twenty-seven Chinese were stuffed into ten cells. While there is no record of major protests by the Chinese in the prison, Chinese complained about the conditions of their incarceration and at least one Chinese man attempted to commit suicide and later escaped.

On 15 March 1888, On Gee was convicted in a district court in Tacoma of "being unlawfully in the United States" and sentenced to six months of hard labor at McNeil Island Penitentiary.[36] Eight months later, in mid-November, On Gee, referred to by the guards as the "crazy Chinaman," jumped into the water from the wharf and tried to drown himself. He was rescued by a boat and brought back to McNeil. It is not clear why On Gee was not released after his six-month sentence; officials likely continued to hold him while arranging for his deportation along with scores of others. A year and a half later, on 16 March 1890, On Gee went out after dinner, ostensibly to gather herbs. Instead, he absconded with a boat, escaping from the island prison.[37] On Gee's determination to commit suicide or escape from McNeil Island was extraordinary, but many other Chinese undoubtedly found less dramatic ways to resist their incarceration.

Beyond the more dramatic acts of resistance like that of On Gee, Chinese also petitioned US courts for relief. Although the Supreme Court eventually imposed some limitations on the nature and length of detention, it consistently affirmed the right of the government to imprison immigrants while they were petitioning for release or waiting to be deported. In the first few years after the Chinese Exclusion Act, US courts clarified how the act should be interpreted and specifically who could be detained and for how long.[38] Although the act specified that it targeted only laborers, it was not always clear who was a laborer. There were a host of other thorny questions that needed to be worked out including what legal rights detainees had while awaiting deportation. The right of the state to detain someone while awaiting deportation was held as an inviolable right of sovereignty in *Fong Yue Ting* (1893) and *Wong Wing* (1896). In *Fong Yue Ting*, the court ruled that deportation should not be considered a "punishment" and therefore there was no requirement for a jury trial. As the court put it,

> The order of deportation is not a punishment for crime. It is not a banishment, in the sense in which that word is often applied to the expulsion of a citizen from his country by way of punishment. . . . He has not, therefore, been deprived of life, liberty, or property without due process of law, and the provisions of the Constitution securing the right of trial by jury and prohibiting unreasonable searches and seizures and cruel and unusual punishments have no application.[39]

This landmark decision established the right of the executive branch to deport non-citizens without the due process that would be required in criminal cases. Furthermore, it redefined the imprisonment (referred to as detention) as a mere administrative procedure. This ruling meant that migrants had few legal means with which to fight the length of their detention or the conditions of their imprisonment.

In the *Wong Wing* decision, the Supreme Court again reaffirmed the right of the state to deport and detain someone while ascertaining whether that person had a right to be in the country, but it also limited the conditions of imprisonment. The court argued that the case raised serious constitutional issues, including Fifth Amendment due process rights and the Sixth Amendment's guarantee of a jury trial. Given that Wong Wing was sentenced to hard labor without the benefit of a jury trial or due process required by a criminal conviction, the court found the punishment to be unconstitutional. The government had the right to sentence a non-citizen to hard labor, the court opined, but not without the benefit of a judicial trial. Since hard labor was always reserved for "infamous crimes," giving a migrant such a sentence without a trial violated the Constitution. As the court wrote, "To declare unlawful residence within the country to be an infamous crime, punishable by deprivation of liberty and property, would be to pass out of the sphere of constitutional legislation unless provision were made that the fact of guilt should first be established by a judicial trial."[40] The court thus affirmed the absolute right of the state to deport and detain a non-citizen, but established limits on the harshness of detention for non-citizens who had not had a judicial trial.

The limitations imposed by the Supreme Court in *Wong Wing* served to cover with a fig leaf what was clearly a violation of the constitutional right to not be imprisoned without benefit of due process or a jury trial. And it became the precedent for legitimizing the incarceration of immigrants. The court's reasoning that immigrant detention was "not imprisonment in a legal sense" opened a loophole that allowed immigrants to be caged without due process guarantees.[41] The Supreme Court thus put its stamp of approval on the criminalization of Chinese by creating a legal fiction wherein their "detention" was not considered "imprisonment in a legal sense."[42] Nonetheless, US immigrant inspectors were constantly frustrated by their inability to punish immigrants with lengthy prison terms, and the ease with which deported migrants returned to the United States across the border. In 1907, Immigrant Inspector Marcus Braun recommended making illegal immigration a felony: "Do not deport the Chinese caught to be unlawfully within our jurisdiction; have the law amended and put the Chinaman in prison, make it a felony to come into the United States clandestinely; put him in prison to earn his passage home, and after having spent two, three or more years in prison, deport him with the money he earned in the workhouse."[43] Heeding Braun's advice, in 1929 Congress stepped in once again to criminalize unauthorized entry as a misdemeanor offense, and unauthorized reentry as a felony. The criminalizing of unauthorized Chinese migration in the 1880s and early 1890s presaged what would happen in the 1930s and beyond when Mexicans were criminalized. Mexicans accounted for 85 to 99 percent of such prosecutions in this era.[44]

The question raised by Hanford in the late 1880s of how long a non-citizen could be detained while awaiting deportation was still not clarified in the early twentieth century. In general, the rules governing deportation required the government to hold non-citizens for no longer than six months, but they allowed the state to keep them longer if they could not deport within that time limit. The longest detention at Angel Island extended for almost two years when a Chinese woman was held on suspicion that she was being brought into the country for "immoral reasons."

After filing three appeals on her behalf asserting that she was the wife of a Chinese merchant, her attorney was finally successful in August 1918 in gaining her release.[45] One Chinese man, Edgar Yuen Fong, had his deportation case drag on for twenty-one years, from 1918 until he was finally deported after exhausting his appeals in 1939. Although it appears from the criminal docket he was out on bail for most of that time, he was in detention in Ellis Island in December 1936 and remained in custody until his deportation more than two years later.[46] The lengthiest and ultimately unsuccessful deportation against Carlos Marcello, a Sicilian mob boss, limped along from 1953 until he was finally sentenced to seventeen years in prison in 1982 for conspiring to bribe a US district court judge. Marcello died in 1993 in New Orleans, having successfully fought deportation for forty years.[47] However, beyond these extraordinary cases, thousands of Chinese and others were imprisoned for months at a time on immigration charges and then deported.

When Chinese failed to fight deportation in the United States, their last hope was to appeal to Canadian courts. Ships traveling to China from Washington Territory made a brief stop in Canada, which gave Chinese deportees an opportunity to appeal for release. When four Chinese were deported on a steamship named Tacoma from that port on April 4, 1894, they simply paid the $50 Canadian head tax and attempted to disembark in Victoria. The ship captain refused to release them, claiming they were US government prisoners. Justice Drake of the Victoria Supreme Court issued a writ of habeas corpus and ordered the Chinese off the ship, arguing that although the Chinese might have violated US customs regulations, in "the ordinary sense they were not criminals and could not be treated as such."[48] While some Canadian courts refused to see undocumented migrants as criminals, in the United States unauthorized immigrants were already viewed as such.

CRIMMIGRATION AND INSANE ASYLUMS

Locking up and deporting people on immigration violations was only one part of a much larger effort to cage foreigners. The relationship between the two forms of incarceration is often difficult to discern because someone can be charged with a regular crime and then deported or can be picked up on immigration charges on pretextual grounds in pursuit of other ends, usually national security, anti-radicalism or simply racist targeting of non-white people. As today, stepped up enforcement of low-level offenses disproportionately impacts Black and Latinx people, the homeless, and the mentally ill. What one finds at McNeil Island and across the country is that most migrants were not incarcerated for immigration violations but rather for drug and alcohol charges. To understand the full story of migrant incarceration in the United States requires peering beyond immigration-related detention to other kinds of imprisonment. Looking at the whole picture, including non-immigration-related criminal offenses and detention in insane asylums and poor houses, reveals a much fuller sense that full-blown immigrant incarceration was well under way by the early twentieth century.

In the early to mid-nineteenth century, immigrants who became public charges could be held in poor houses and deported either to other states or out of the country, but these deportations were managed at the state level.[49] When federal immigration restrictions were enacted in the late nineteenth century, there was a need to hold migrants while they were being processed and underwent medical inspections. The machinery was clunky at first with most immigrants held in makeshift warehouses on docks or on ships, but by the early twentieth century, detention stations at Ellis Island and another at Angel Island were processing millions. The US Immigration Bureau also built smaller detention sheds at various foreign ports of entry, including in Canada and Cuba. In addition to their own facilities, migrants were held in a whole range of charitable and penal institutions, including federal and state prisons, local jails, and hospitals and insane asylums. Although migrants fought back through the courts and with the assistance of their home country diplomats, the deportation and detention apparatus grew over the course of the century. While only a few thousand people were formally deported each year until 1924, it was during this early period when the legal basis and bureaucratic machinery for immigrant incarceration were developed. Equally as important, the vast bulk of immigrants were imprisoned on drug and alcohol charges and other criminal offenses, as well as being locked up in insane asylums and poor houses.[50]

Documenting the growth of foreign-born incarceration is difficult because neither the Immigration Bureau nor the Bureau of Prisons consistently kept track of immigrant detention. However, in 1903, the Immigration Bureau counted 45,000 incarcerated "aliens." Just under 10,000 of these could be found in penal institutions while most were caged in insane asylums or charitable institutions, including almshouses, juvenile asylums, homes, and institutions for the feeble minded. Although non-citizens only represented one in seventy-five citizens, there was one non-citizen for every six citizens incarcerated in charitable institutions in 1903. The bulk of immigrants were incarcerated in cities like New York, but the percentages of non-citizens in charitable institutions was highest in places like Oregon and Washington, with non-citizens representing 27 percent in these institutions versus only 3 percent in the general population. Most significant, 25,000 non-citizens, representing more than half of total, were detained in insane asylums or charitable institutions for life.[51]

These statistics show that non-citizen detention occurred most frequently in charitable institutions, that most of them were held for no other reason than being poor or mentally ill, and that the vast majority of them could expect to spend the rest of their lives in detention. The report indicated the "probable period of detention," with 56 percent listed under the category "life." For those in penal institutions, almost all were being held in state or county level prisons, 50 percent being held for minor offenses and just over half could expect to spend more than two years in prison. According to the office of the Commissioner General of Immigration, in the first years of the twentieth century there were 45,000 non-citizens in penal and charitable institutions and an additional 65,000 naturalized foreigners in these institutions, meaning that about 110,000 foreign-born people were being held against their will annually.[52] Department of Commerce data corroborate this estimate, enumerating almost 100,000 foreign-born people in jails, workhouses, and prisons in 1910, or just over one-fifth of the prison population at a time when foreign-born represented about 14 percent of the general population.[53] Foreigners therefore were overrepresented in carceral institutions at the beginning of the twentieth century.

In addition to the changing demographics of the men imprisoned at McNeil Island between 1880 and 1940—the nationality shifted from mainly Chinese to mostly Mexican—by the 1920s, drug and alcohol charges began to make up the vast majority of violations for which prisoners, both foreign and domestic, were caged. Although immigration violations and criminal offenses for drugs and alcohol are often looked at as distinct phenomena, the two arenas of criminal justice and immigration worked together to lock up increasing numbers of foreign-born people in the first half of the twentieth century. Between 1875 and 1939, foreign-born prisoners comprised nearly a third of the people imprisoned at McNeil, suggesting that the link between criminal and immigration law has deeper and thicker roots than has been previously recognized.

PICTURING THE CHINESE AT MCNEIL ISLAND PENITENTIARY

When Department of Justice and State Department officials referred to Chinese at McNeil Island being captured or deported, they rarely referred to them by name, and few Chinese names appear among the 2,400 case files from the penitentiary. One of the earliest photographs of a group of Chinese inmates at McNeil Island Penitentiary from 1900 includes four Chinese men, dressed in black and white striped uniforms, standing against a brick wall. The way in which the inmates in the photograph are crudely labeled with numbers suggests the ad hoc nature of the technology at this early stage. The names on the back of the photograph indicate that they are Hop Key (1144), Chung Fung (1139), Hing Tom (1141), and Jan Jo (1142). Their sequential intake numbers suggest that they entered the prison at the same time. The first two men in the picture were convicted of forgery, the third for smuggling, and the fourth for counterfeiting. The records do not indicate how long they served, but they arrived and were released in the same year, 1900.[54] Although McNeil Island prison records contain invaluable data on individual inmates, including their place of birth, crimes for which they were convicted and intake and release dates, these statistics hide more than they reveal. However, the 4,334 photographs make real the people behind the numbers and demographic data, some locked up for just entering the United States without authorization or for helping others to do so.[55] The photographs were part of a repressive apparatus prison officials used to track and identify inmates; they could also be employed to search for escapees and in future criminal proceedings.

Figure 1.1 This photograph depicts, from left to right, Hop Key (1144), Chung Fung (1139), Hing Tom (1141), and Jan Jo (1142). Photograph of Chinese prisoners and McNeil Island prison.
Source: Photos and Records of Prisoners Received, 1875–1939, McNeil Island Penitentiary, Records of the Bureau of Prisons, NARA, Seattle, Record Group 129.

The first set of McNeil Island Penitentiary photographs from 1899 to 1906 depict almost all of the prisoners in pairs, mostly dressed in black and white striped convict uniforms; a few, however, wear their street clothes. The poses in these early photographs are not standardized. Some detainees stand, others sit either in front of a brick wall or a white backdrop. The inmates mostly stare directly at the camera and wear hardened expressions, not revealing any teeth; none are smiling. Almost all of the photographs include two inmates, although a few have three, four, or five together. It is not clear whether including more than one prisoner in each photograph was a way to reduce expenses or simply reflected the numbers of prisoners brought in on a particular day.

Immigration photography has its roots in Chinese exclusion because Chinese were the first group to be required to have a residency certificate with a photograph documenting the bearer's identity. By the early twentieth century, many European countries demanded that foreigners arrive with passports including a photographic portrait. Although the Chinese were the first, by the 1920s all immigrants were supposed to have a photographic identity document.[56] Unlike the residency certificates and passports that allowed immigrants some control over the kinds of photographs that were taken, prison mug shots are taken under conditions of almost complete control by the state. Therefore, although one might imagine seeing the agency of migrant inmates at McNeil Island Penitentiary in their expressions and gazes, they had no control over the context or framing of the photograph, nor were they in a position to withhold consent for being portrayed. If these photographs reveal the humanity of the prisoners, they show a humanity deeply constrained by the frame of the state.

In its first two decades of operation, McNeil Island Penitentiary held scores of Chinese for immigration violations ranging from forged certificates of residency to aiding and abetting smuggling of unauthorized Chinese. Wong Gong was held in McNeil between 1901 and 1902 for violation of Section 11 of the 1884 act outlawing aiding and abetting the smuggling of Chinese. Although his queue is barely visible, Tuck Gee appears to still have it, suggesting the maintenance of Chinese cultural norms even in a US federal prison. Tuck Gee appears darker in the photograph and looks more apprehensive, giving the photographer a side-eye glance while Wong Gong stares straight ahead.

Chinese relied on a well-developed network of smugglers who could either provide forged documents or could help to ferry them across the border clandestinely. Smugglers accounted for 3 percent of inmates at McNeil and generally served stiffer sentences than noncitizens who were found to be in the country without authorization. In an effort to prevent repeated crossing

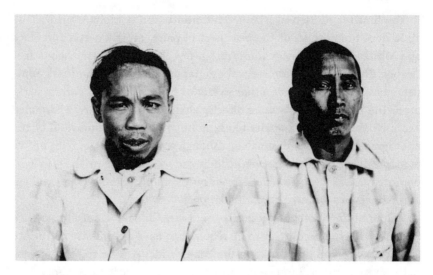

Figure 1.2 Wong Gong (inmate 1260), convicted of aiding and abetting smuggling of aliens, appears with Tuck Gee (inmate 80). Chinese at McNeil Island prison, 1901.
Source: Photos and Records of Prisoners Received, 1875–1939, McNeil Island Penitentiary, RG 129, Records of the Bureau of Prisons, NARA, Seattle.

by the same people, immigration authorities began deporting migrants directly to China. Not only was it difficult to deport Chinese to Canada because of the head tax, but such removals were also ineffective because the deportees could simply cross the unguarded border again.[57]

The story of one Chinese smuggler, Ah Jake, demonstrates the difficulties of keeping Chinese out and their willingness to return to smuggling even after being caught, jailed, and deported. Ah Jake had been deported more than four times in less than a decade, but he kept returning. In 1887, the district court found Ah Jake guilty of helping Chinese enter the United States with fraudulent papers, asserting that he had requested a certificate of travel to British Columbia to sell to other Chinese trying to enter the United States; his plan was to return clandestinely via a different route.[58] He was sentenced to seven months of hard labor at McNeil Island Penitentiary in addition to a fine of $250.[59] In 1894, he was in court again, along with three other Chinese facing the same charges.[60] The ease with which deported Chinese could return from Canada led officials to use migrant detention not only as a means to deportation but also as a form of punishment and deterrence. Even though smugglers received punishment, there is no evidence that their prison terms deterred them from their illegal activities. In the 1880s, lengthy prison sentences and hard labor were meant to keep migrants from becoming repeat offenders, but the policy failed to achieve its objective.

There are no photographs of Ah Jake, but there are several photographs of other smugglers, including the twenty-five-year-old Ng Fun (prisoner 2033), held at McNeil Island Penitentiary for smuggling Chinese into the United States. He was arrested in Los Angeles in November 1910 and arrived at McNeil in July 1911. His two-year sentence was compounded by the eight months he spent in jail awaiting his trial and conviction. The photograph depicts Ng as a sweet-looking, young man in a fedora hat, sitting in a chair. The physical description attached to the photograph indicated that Ng was 5' 2.5" tall, weighed 106 pounds, and had black hair, brown eyes, and a "yellow" complexion. In addition to this basic anthropomorphic data there was a detailed description of scars on his body, including traces from four vaccinations, dental irregularities, and one "horseshoe, burn 1 across right buttock near arms." The photograph, the biometric description, and his criminal record made it easier for authorities to track and process Ng in prison as well as to keep tabs on him once he was released. For migrants who tried to evade the gaze of the state, the mug shot was a particularly troubling technology of control. Yet even with photographs

Figure 1.3 Ng Fun served a two-year sentence at McNeil Island for smuggling Chinese into the United States. *Source:* Ng Fun (2033), Photos and Records of Prisoners Received, 1875–1939, McNeil Island Penitentiary, RG 129, NARA, Seattle.

affixed to residency and other immigration documents, Chinese routinely used other people's documents, taking advantage of the difficulty of white immigration officers to distinguish among Asians.[61]

In addition to charges of "conspiracy" and "smuggling," many Chinese were imprisoned for participating in other efforts to evade restriction laws. Forgery of certificates of residence was a cottage industry that provided "legal" papers to undocumented Chinese. Fong Sun, a forty-six-year-old Chinese man, was arrested in Santa Barbara in 1916 and eventually sentenced to two years on McNeil Island for forging a residence certificate.[62] Wearing a sports jacket, tie, and newsboy cap, Fong appears respectable. Is he frightened, impassive, or determined? Zooming in on Fong's face reveals a blurry image of the photographer reflected in Fong's eyes. This is as close as we can get to the photographers, who remain anonymous in such prison photographs, but the reflection is a reminder that at least one other person was present during the taking of this photograph.

Figure 1.4 Fong Sun was arrested in Santa Barbara in 1916 and eventually sentenced to two years on McNeil Island for forging a residence certificate. *Source:* Fong Sun, inmate 2733, Photos and Records of Prisoners Received, 1875–1939, McNeil Island Penitentiary, RG 129, NARA, Seattle.

From 1907 and beyond, McNeil Island Penitentiary photographs became more formalized with mug shots featuring the typical portrait and profile view side-by-side with a prisoner identification number superimposed on each photograph. A description of the inmate and the charges were affixed to the back of each of these photographs, thereby creating a mini-dossier on the prisoner. Prison authorities and courts could use these individual photographs much more easily since each self-contained card held the vital statistics of each inmate. The post-1907 photographs did not include black and white striped convict uniforms. Most inmates appear to have been photographed in their street clothes when they arrived at McNeil Island, many with hats on, although a few appear in dark gray prison outfits. Almost all of the prisoners photographed were men, who represent the overwhelming male inmate population; however, a few women are represented, and at least one entire family is included: father, mother, and child. John Doe Shorty was an "Indian" who received a thirty-year sentence for second degree murder in Alaska. His wife and child are not in prison clothes and there is no indication they were charged, but they seem to have been incarcerated along with him. In addition, there are at least three

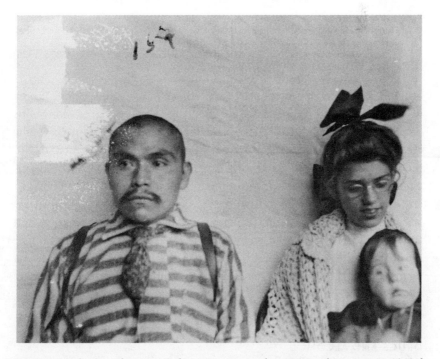

Figure 1.5 John Doe Shorty, an Indian, was sentenced in 1904 to thirty years at McNeil Island for second degree murder in Alaska. He is depicted here with his wife and child. Source: John Doe Shorty, inmate 287, Photos and Records of Prisoners Received, 1875–1939, McNeil Island Penitentiary, RG 129, NARA, Seattle.

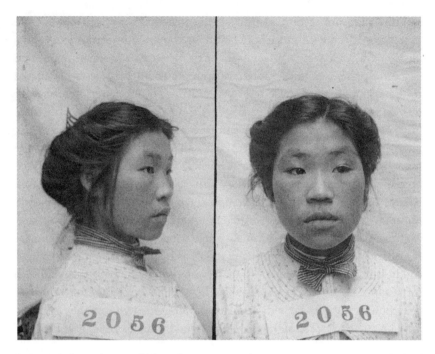

Figure 1.6 Carrie Sang, an "Eskimo," was sentenced in 1911 to two years at McNeil Island for assault with a dangerous weapon in Alaska. She was seventeen when she arrived at McNeil Island prison.
Source: Carrie Sang, inmate 2056, Photos and Records of Prisoners Received, 1875–1939, McNeil Island Penitentiary, RG 129, NARA, Seattle.

other photographs of women prisoners: a Black woman, an "Eskimo," and a woman from Alaska simply listed as "dark."[63] The photographs, along with detailed descriptions of physical characteristics and marks on the body, created an archive of the incarcerated. This archive bears the traces of late nineteenth-century French criminologist Alphonse Bertillon, who developed a scientific method for recording anthropomorphic data along with standardizing the portrait and profile views in mug shots. The profile view was meant to eliminate the inconsistencies caused by facial expression, and the portrait view was to be used by police to identify suspects as they might see them in the street.[64] Photography, like the penitentiary itself, was a technology that allowed the government to attempt to control and restrict migration at a time when border fences and walls did not exist.

DRUGS AND ALCOHOL

If the photographs provide intimate portrayals of individuals, the log of prisoners received at McNeil Island Penitentiary from 1887 to 1939 is an abstract snapshot of the 14,379 inmates who were incarcerated and their charges.[65] Although it is difficult to determine the ethnicity of prisoners from the log, place of birth was noted on most records, making it possible to calculate the percentage of various nationalities that were incarcerated on the island. Citizenship status is also unclear from these records. Some of the foreign-born Mexicans, for example, may have been naturalized US citizens. Another limitation of the data is the lack of precise notation of time served, although the intake record indicates the years inmates entered and when they were released. Finally, based on first names and photographs, it is clear that only a handful of women ended up at McNeil Island prison.

McNeil Island was perhaps the most cosmopolitan locale on the West Coast at the time, featuring people from over seventy different countries as well as those born throughout the United States. They were sent to McNeil from the entire length of the Pacific Coast, from Los Angeles, California, to Anchorage, Alaska. Considering that the total foreign-born population on the Pacific Coast from 1900 to 1930 oscillated between 18 and 23 percent, an astonishing 29 percent (4,189) of people locked up at McNeil from 1887 to 1939 were foreign-born.[66] Even more dramatic, in the decade between 1887 and 1896, more than half (54 percent) of those imprisoned at McNeil were foreign-born. McNeil was a federal penitentiary, and this may help to explain the disproportionate number of foreigners, as immigration violations were under federal jurisdiction. Nonetheless, these statistics show that immigrant incarceration was not ancillary to federal prisons but in fact was their main purpose in their early years. From 1887 to 1939, Mexicans were the largest group of foreign-born people, comprising 19 percent; next were Chinese with 18 percent, and Canadians third making up 11 percent of the foreign-born. The presence of these three groups at McNeil is disproportionate to their representation in the general population of the West Coast states from which they were drawn. Although the numbers of Europeans from individual countries was not significant, altogether they made up 35 percent of the foreign-born people.

A dramatic shift occurred in the kinds of charges Chinese received in the late nineteenth century compared to the period from the 1920s onward. Whereas almost all Chinese were held at McNeil for "being in US unlawfully" or "violation of Restriction Act" from 1887 through 1892, after that year Chinese were charged increasingly with drug and alcohol crimes; "unlawful presence" completely disappeared as a charge after 1892. From 1893 to 1939, only 6 percent of Chinese charges were immigration related, and after 1921 almost every Chinese at McNeil faced a charge of violating the Harrison Narcotic Act or other drug acts. New laws created new opportunities for criminalizing Chinese and other foreigners. We

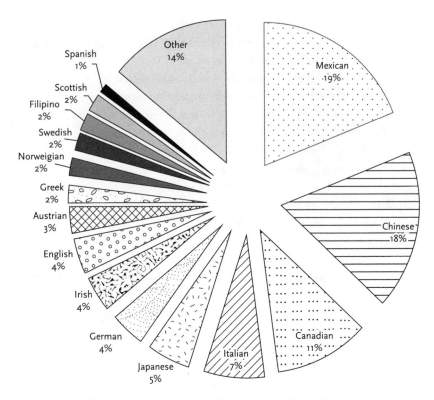

Figure 1.7 Foreign-born inmates at McNeil Island Prison, 1887–1939.
Source: Records of the US Penitentiary, McNeil Island. Washington, NARA, Seattle, 129.8. Analysis based on dataset created by archivists.

know Chinese individuals continued to cross borders illegally in the 1920s and yet immigration charges dropped precipitously in this period.[67] It was not the behavior of the Chinese that had changed but rather the tools prosecutors used to incarcerate them. The anti-immigration crusade seamlessly morphed into a war on drugs, with the Chinese being targeted in both instances.

Drug and alcohol crimes accounted for 40 percent of crimes committed by foreign-born people at McNeil, roughly divided equally between drugs and alcohol. Opium smuggling and violations for marijuana and other narcotics accounted for most of the drug charges, while violation of Prohibition and "selling liquor to Indians" made up most of the alcohol-related crimes. The large numbers of immigrants locked up for violation of drug- and alcohol-related crimes suggest that they were disproportionately targeted for enforcement. The second most frequent "crime," accounting for 21 percent of the charges, was simply for being in the country unlawfully. Immigration-related charges, including smuggling of aliens

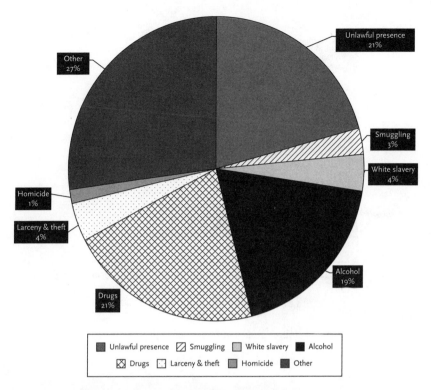

Figure 1.8 Charges for foreign-born inmates at McNeil Island Prison, 1887–1939.
Source: Records of the US Penitentiary, McNeil Island. Washington.

accounted for another 3 percent and white slavery for 4 percent. White slavery linked immigration control to moral purity by criminalizing the transport of women who engaged in sex work or who were believed to have been trafficked for "immoral purposes."[68] Many of the people imprisoned for unlawful presence at McNeil might have been held pending deportation rather than serving specific criminal sentences. Property crimes like robbery, larceny, and motor vehicle theft made up less than 4 percent of the total. Violent crimes were a very small proportion of the rest of the charges, and murder accounted for less than 1 percent. What these data show is that drugs, alcohol, and immigration charges accounted for more than two-thirds of the charges against the foreign-born at McNeil Island. Although drugs-, alcohol-, and smuggling-related crimes would have been counted by the census, a significant portion of foreign-born prisoners at McNeil Island Penitentiary would have escaped the census prison population data since only people convicted of crimes were counted.[69] The large proportion of Chinese imprisoned for unlawful presence in the 1880s and early 1890s means that their incarceration has been systematically

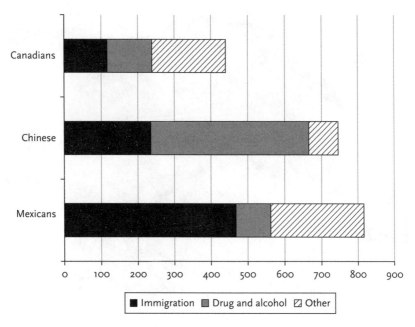

Figure 1.9 Charges for top three groups of foreign-born inmates at McNeil Island Prison, 1887–1939.
Source: Records of the US Penitentiary, McNeil Island. Washington.

underrepresented by the Census Bureau and by historians who have relied on census data.

The significance of drug-, alcohol-, and immigration-related charges, especially for Mexicans and Chinese, suggests that these groups were being targeted for enforcement. These three kinds of offenses made up a majority of charges for the three largest groups of foreign-born inmates, but Chinese and Mexicans were far more likely than Canadians to be charged with these violations. Almost all Chinese (89%) and Mexicans (69%) were in McNeil for either immigration or drug and alcohol violations, while only about half the incarcerated Canadians (54%) were locked up for these reasons. The data also reveal that Mexicans were charged more frequently with immigration-related offenses, while Chinese were charged with drug and alcohol violations. Although this is just a snapshot of one penitentiary over a fifty-year period, the data show that the federal prison was being used far more frequently to lock up non-white foreigners for victimless offenses than to punish those people for violent crimes. Although the intake lists for McNeil did not note race, the prison inmate magazine, the *Island Lantern*, published monthly census information about inmates in 1928 to 1929. These snapshots of the prison population show that even as

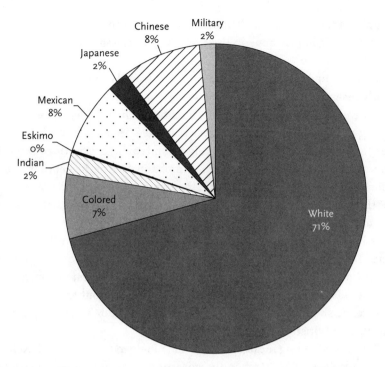

Figure 1.10 Proportion of people at McNeil Island Prison by race, 1928–1929. Averages derived from prison census in *Island Lantern* issues 1928–1929, a McNeil Island prison inmate publication from 1928 to 1980. Available at NARA, Seattle.

there were sizable numbers of Chinese, Japanese, Mexicans, and "colored" people at McNeil, in the late 1920s, well over 70 percent of the inmates were considered white. Although the prison magazine does not define what is meant by white, the other categories suggest that all people of European descent were included in that category.

INDEFINITE DETENTION ON MCNEIL ISLAND

The Chinese men who were arrested in fall 1887 and who were twice rejected for repatriation at Victoria were still at McNeil prison three years later. US State Department officials pushed the Canadian government to resolve the case, but the Canadians remained firm that there was no evidence the Chinese had come from Canada and they insisted the Chinese would not be admitted without paying the head tax.[70] In 1891, Patrick Winston, US attorney in Spokane, testified in a congressional investigation about the problem of Chinese being held at McNeil long after they had completed their sentences. "I understand that they had been sentenced say to six months imprisonment, their terms had expired, and then there was the Chinaman on your hand."[71]

Winston had taken over as US attorney from William White, who abruptly resigned in November 1890. While the reasons for White's resignation are unclear, his repeated complaints to the Justice Department about having to indefinitely detain Chinese may have been a factor. Although he was tasked with enforcing US immigration laws as a US attorney, White also defended Chinese against white mobs in Seattle in February 1886, telling the assembled vigilantes that they were "violating the law and would get themselves into trouble." It was White who rang the bell that called out the militia to restore order.[72] In 1891, White returned to court, but this time he was defending a Chinese merchant who resided in Port Angeles since 1880. The merchant frequently traveled back and forth to Victoria to visit relatives, but in 1891, an immigration officer arrested him, arguing that because he returned from a visit to Victoria without the required certificate, he should be deported for illegal entry. White's opposing counsel was Patrick Winston.[73]

The long-standing incarceration of the nineteen Chinese on McNeil was finally resolved in 1890 when the government ordered their deportation directly to China. In May 1890, three years after being incarcerated, six of the remaining Chinese were placed on a steamer that landed at Vancouver and then went on to China. One of those ordered deported, Ah Tsam, was too ill to travel. He died four days later of pneumonia and was buried on McNeil Island prison near the garden.[74] A US marshal accompanied the other six to make sure they did not disembark in Vancouver and attempt to cross the border again. This was probably the first deportation to China from Washington Territory in what would become a regular procedure in the coming decades. After this case, the policy of deporting Chinese to China rather than Canada became commonplace.

Even though the law had been clarified by the treasury secretary, in practice it still was not clear to US marshals carrying out the policy which Chinese were to be sent to China and which to British Columbia, and how to do so in an efficient manner in the absence of regular shipping lines leaving from Tacoma. In August 1890, US Marshal Thomas Brown wrote to the attorney general asking if he could charge for the expense of Chinese removals to China with the $50,000 appropriated by Congress. Even though the commissioner had determined that the three Chinese men had come in from British Columbia, Brown's orders indicated he had to send them to China.[75] With the new orders to deport Chinese to China, the number of Chinese at McNeil began to grow. In October, Brown sent a telegram to the

Department of Justice about the overcrowding at McNeil prison, where thirty-two Chinese were awaiting deportation. Rather than hold them for months while waiting for a ship to leave Tacoma for China, he wanted to send them to San Francisco for deportation.[76]

Ships left San Francisco more frequently for China than from Tacoma, but immigration officers there faced other obstacles, such as being forced to release incoming Chinese pending their hearings. In San Francisco, officials complained that Chinese would routinely claim US birth or residency upon arrival. If denied entry, their lawyers would file writs of habeas corpus and the judge would issue bail so they could be discharged while their cases were pending. In 1887, an examiner for the Justice Department found that the habeas proceedings in San Francisco were "tinctured with fraud" and "corrupt Court officials" who earned large sums of money by processing hundreds of Chinese petitions every quarter.[77] The problem was that many Chinese simply skipped bail and disappeared if they lost in court. The Collector of Customs and Special Assistant US attorney investigated the records at the District and Circuit Courts, finding 119 habeas cases involving Chinese that had resulted in a deportation order that had not yet been executed. After several notices, just over forty of these Chinese were remanded to the court, but the fact that the majority were still missing suggested that it was difficult to enforce Chinese exclusion without incarcerating the Chinese while their cases wound their way through the courts.[78] Such a conclusion, of course, meant that Chinese fighting deportation would end up spending much more time behind bars. The establishment of Ellis Island and Angel Island was in part an effort to solve the lack of detention space, but before either of these centers was built, thousands of immigrants were being held on McNeil Island. By the beginning of the twentieth century, immigrants were a growing piece of the carceral system and over 100,000 foreign-born people were locked away in jails, prisons, and insane asylums each year.

MARIEL CUBANS AT MCNEIL ISLAND PRISON

McNeil Island prison was scheduled for closure in 1980 after 135 years. Its buildings were dilapidated, those incarcerated complained about the conditions of their confinement, and the government worried about the expense of running an island prison. However, months before its closure, the Immigration and Naturalization Service (INS) requested the use of McNeil Island prison for hundreds of Cuban refugees who had arrived as part of the Mariel Boatlift with criminal records in Cuba. On June 22, 1980,

117 shackled Cubans were flown from Fort McCoy, Wisconsin, to Boeing airfield near Seattle, and bused to Steilacoom where they were put on two boats and brought to McNeil Island prison. A small group of Steilacoom residents protested the Cubans' arrival, one holding a sign reading "Go Home" and another waving a faded American flag.[79] In the end, 354 Cuban refugees would be brought to the island prison; most of them remained for a year awaiting asylum hearings.[80] The Cubans brought to McNeil had all admitted they had committed crimes in Cuba and were thus being held until their cases could be individually reviewed. One of the Cubans denied asylum, a twenty-one-year-old Havana native, commented, "I don't think I'm criminal because I stole out of necessity to survive."[81]

At the end of September, a group of thirty Cubans staged a hunger strike, fed up with their continued imprisonment after three months while the review process inched along.[82] Within a week, the number of strikers had doubled.[83] By October 1980, the government had only classified eighteen Cubans as "not dangerous" and allowed them to be released, while all of the others were labeled as "hard-core" criminals.[84] Even though Carroll D. Gray, one of the government prosecutors conducting reviews of the Cubans at McNeil, admitted that most of them had committed minor shoplifting offenses, mostly for stealing food, he granted asylum in only one-quarter of the cases.[85] The arrival of the Cubans delayed the closing of the federal penitentiary for a year, but in June 1981 Washington finally took it over as a state prison.[86]

The state prison remained on McNeil Island until 2011, when it was shuttered in what they call a "cold closure." The electricity and water were turned off and the doors closed, but the building remained frozen in time, files still in cabinets, old audio and videotapes piled in cardboard boxes in the law library. While the prison was mothballed, a Special Commitment Center for sex offenders that had been established in 1990 continued to operate on a different part of the island. By 2019 more than 200 detainees were being held on the island, many of them having been there for more than a decade after their sentences were completed.[87] In June 2019, the sole woman at the Commitment Center was released after having spent twenty-two years there, in addition to more than five years in prison for first-degree child rape. She was sixty-one years old when she was finally set free.[88] In many ways the Civil Commitment Center echoes the indefinite detention of Chinese in the late 1880s and the Cubans in the early 1980s. In all three cases, the people being held behind bars had no criminal charges pending against them, and yet the detainees faced indefinite detention. Forever prisoners can be terror suspects in Guantanamo, immigrants, or sex offenders. What links all of them is a lack of constitutional protection that allows them to be deprived of their liberty indefinitely with no criminal charges against them. What separates the sex offenders from the others is that they are US citizens.

Even though Washington State's Department of Corrections manages McNeil Island, the Special Commitment Center is run by the state's Health Department. The collaboration between prison and public health officials may seem odd, but there is a long history of such linkages, as discussed in Chapter 2.

CHAPTER 2

Nathan Cohen, the Man without a Country

In late March 1915, Nathan Cohen sat brooding in a small cabin on the steamship *Vasari* in New York's harbor. He had been on the ship for a few weeks, not being permitted to land in New York, or even to set foot on Ellis Island. Having been declared insane and rejected by Brazil, Argentina, Russia, and the United States, Cohen had become a stateless man, or as the newspapers liked to call him "a man without a country." Journalists also referred to him as the "Wandering Jew" and the "Flying Dutchman," a reference to a legendary ghost ship that can never make port.[1] Cohen had originally entered the United States at Ellis Island in April 1912, but a year and a half later he was committed to the Baltimore city hospital for the insane and ordered deported for being insane and for becoming a public charge. Thus began his 33,000 mile back and forth journey between New York and South America, unable to land at any port and not recognized by any country.

Cohen spent his long days smoking cigarettes and eating the provisions provided to him by the *Vasari*'s Captain Cadogan. Over the thousands of miles Cohen traversed between New York and South America, he had become friendly with the ship's doctor, but no amount of friendliness on the part of Dr. Davis or Captain Cadogan could eliminate the dread he felt at his seemingly endless journey. Having exhausted his appeals in New York, Cohen was about to set off for Chile as unwanted cargo on the *Vasari* in search of a country willing to accept him.[2]

Just then the thirty-five-year-old Cohen heard a knock on his cabin door. It was Dr. Davis along with a *Pittsburgh Press* reporter, James F. Taylor.

Figure 2.1 Photograph of Nathan Cohen in Hebrew Immigrant Aid Society Papers.
Source: YIVO Institute for Jewish Research.

The story of the "Sea Wanderer" and the "Man without a Country and a Mind" was widely disseminated in major newspapers like the *New York Times*, local papers from Union Springs, Alabama, to Wadesboro, North Carolina, to Bryan, Texas, and national magazines such as *The Outlook* and *The Survey*.[3] While Cohen's story had become famous, he spent his days and nights in virtual isolation, communicating with only a few of the ship's crew members at meals. Taylor's description of Cohen's time on the *Vasari* is one of two that remains. The article, which was reprinted a few weeks later in the *Boston Globe*, was splashed on the front page along with a dramatic drawing of Cohen in a long coat, disheveled hair, a bushy beard, and a hat. A larger-than-life hand was drawn in the foreground as if to say "STOP, NO ENTRY." Above Cohen's full-length portrait was a quote: "He has no address, belongs nowhere, is wanted nowhere." At the bottom of the page, there was another drawing of Cohen's face, this one featuring a dejected, downcast portrait with the caption "Nathan Cohen, whose claim to a place of refuge is still unsettled."[4] Although Taylor's description of Cohen may have served to render him as a strange and mysterious exotic, the reporter also took pains to humanize and identify with him.

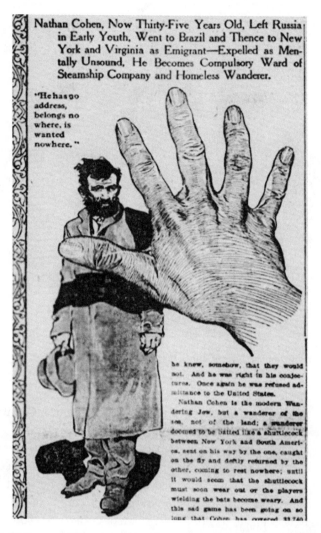

Figure 2.2 "He has no address, belongs nowhere, is wanted nowhere." Drawing of Nathan Cohen in the *Pittsburgh Press*, 18 April 1915.

Taylor's article began by inviting the reader to imagine the weariness of a passenger after a long boat journey and the excitement that he would feel after sighting land. The immigrant, Taylor wrote, would also feel a "quickening of the pulse when the New World rises slowly out of the waves." The shores of New York Bay he described as two arms waiting to embrace the immigrant. "His slate has been wiped clean," wrote Taylor in an optimistic tone; "he will write upon it henceforth in a clearer and more legible hand." This imagined immigrant experience was then likened to those of the other passengers on the *Vasari* who crowded to the rails to catch a glimpse of the Statue of Liberty. Everyone was hopeful except for one passenger, the "poor wanderer of the seas, a man without a country, a man whom the hand of fate had touched, and from whom humanity stood aloof."

It's hard to even imagine Nathan Cohen's state of mind after being shuttled back and forth across the seas so many times, but the drawings by Taylor and his description suggests that Cohen had sunk into a severe depression. According to Taylor, Cohen had once been excited to reach US shores, but "now he gazed about with the hopeless air of one who wanders in a maze and finds no exit."

When Taylor first entered Cohen's cabin, he noticed the remains of a meal and the butts of a few cigarettes. There stood Cohen, not as a dangerous "insane alien," as he had been labeled by immigration authorities, but as a meek and submissive figure, a man to be pitied and not feared. Taylor's depiction highlights Cohen's frailty, as if to question why the government would fear the entry of such a man onto US soil. "His head is large and broad, covered with brown curling hair, and a brown curling luxuriant whisker encircles his face. His eyes are brown and clear, but are more like the eyes of an affectionate dog or timid deer than those of a man." Taylor's attempt to render Cohen as not dangerous leads him to deny him his human qualities, to make him into a friendly and non-threatening animal. "His expression is pleasing and his occasional smile has something suggestive of sweetness in it. From his averted glance, from the shy, eager way he looks at one, from the smile that illuminates his face at a word or of friendliness it would seem as though he were wistfully seeking companionship and sympathy, though surprised when he found them."

Finally getting the chance to meet Nathan Cohen in person after so much had been written and said about this man's bizarre story must have been exciting for Taylor. There is no evidence, however, that Cohen said much of anything to the reporter, which is why Taylor focused his article on graphic descriptions of the cabin and Cohen's expressions. Taylor did not allow the lack of verbal communication to temper his pen. The reporter dutifully filled in the silence with his own supposition of what Cohen must have been feeling. "Who can know his thoughts in that sad mind, when evening dims the harbor, and the lights of innumerable homes begin to shed their radiance through the night?" Taylor poses the question and then answers it. "No wife to share his joys or sorrows, no children to bear his likeness and his name, no happy evening meal in the bosom of his family after the busy day's work. Poor wanderer of the seas, with no-one to love him, without a home, without even a country!" Here Taylor moves from the question of an immigrant trying to enter a country to a more deeply personal issue of a solitary man without a wife, children, or a family. In Taylor's imagination, Cohen becomes an unloved person without home or country.

Let us imagine the scene. The reporter Taylor and Dr. Davis are standing in Cohen's cabin, perhaps asking the reticent Cohen questions or merely observing, with the journalist scribbling notes and sketches in his pad. The journalist searches for something to capture the drama of the situation, a metaphor that can at once express the great hopes of an immigrant and the bizarre labyrinth in which Cohen found himself. Taylor zeroes in on Cohen's portmanteau, his stiff leather suitcase, as the object to invest with meaning. He first noticed that the leather that used to be yellow has through "time and hard usage . . . darkened . . . to a dirty brown." The leather strap is also described as "hand-blackened" to highlight the human toll connected with the dirty leather. A cardboard tag was attached to one of the handles inscribed with the name Nathan Cohen, and "under the name a dash. No address." "There is something infinitely pathetic about that bag," Taylor writes. "It is like its owner belongs nowhere, is wanted nowhere. Containing all his poor best, he picked it up joyfully when he set out to make his fortune; carried it with him when he first set foot in New York, and it was still with him when his hopes crushed, he was sent back, to begin his futile wanderings up and down the Atlantic seaboard. Like him the shabby piece of luggage is the victim of an ironical chance; and like him it has begun to look drab and abject." The blackened suitcase symbolizes for Taylor the "modern Wandering Jew," a person who is rootless, homeless, and without family ties. Cohen had begun to look like his valise, "drab and abject."

Numerous articles repeat the same story of the "wandering Jew," leaving the details of his life shrouded in mystery. More than 200 pages of documentation about Cohen's case from the Hebrew Sheltering and Immigrant Aid Society of America (HIAS) reveals a much more complex story of family feuds, betrayal, lost love, and mental illness. At the time, however, Nathan Cohen's story became a symbol of something bigger than one immigrant's story. Coming in 1915, at the height of an influx of immigrants to the United States, and also at the zenith of the hysteria about insane and criminal aliens, Cohen's story stood in for all immigrants, both what was to be feared in them and the difficulty they had navigating an increasingly restrictive immigration policy. What does Nathan Cohen's story tell us about "insane aliens" at the beginning of the twentieth century, and about the use of psychiatric evaluations to identify and deport "unfit" and "mentally defective" immigrants? To what extent was insanity understood as a hereditary trait versus the product of alienation felt by immigrants torn from their homeland, families, and culture? Cohen's story underscores the madness of being an immigrant in America rather than the madness of man without a country.

The descriptions of Cohen as lonely, dislocated, and alienated fit into an idea of what would later be described as the immigrant experience in Oscar Handlin's 1951 classic, *The Uprooted*.[5] These depictions of Cohen ignore his family connections as well as his deep affiliations with American civil society. That he ended up alienated, mentally ill, and deported is only part of his story, but it is an element of his life that sheds light on the hundreds of thousands of immigrants who were being incarcerated in hospitals at the beginning of the twentieth century. In other words, the alienation Cohen experienced and Handlin described was not an inevitable or natural response to migration, but it was the product of a society that pathologized and locked away people who were culturally different from mainstream Americans. Immigrants had deep roots in both their home countries and in the United States, but these roots were constantly being slashed by state-sponsored xenophobia and carceral regimes that isolated them from their communities. At the beginning of the twentieth century, the mental hospital was by far the carceral institution most likely to hold both immigrants and citizens, and the rate of mental hospital incarceration then is equal to the rate in the more recent era of mass incarceration in jails and prisons.

INSANE ALIENS

Nathan Cohen was not the first immigrant to end up in an insane asylum in America. Fears of "insane aliens" had percolated throughout the latter half of the nineteenth century, reaching a fevered pitch by the time of Cohen's arrival. In 1912, just three days after Cohen landed for the first time at Ellis Island, the *New York Times* published an article, the last in a series of three, highlighting the large numbers of insane aliens in New York hospitals and demanding that the federal government make its inspections stricter to exclude such migrants and reimburse the state for the expense of caring for them. The New York Lunacy Commission calculated the cost to the state of maintaining insane aliens at $25 million, and it demanded that the federal government compensate them for $9 million. An astounding one-third of New York State's total budget was devoted to incarcerating and caring for the mentally ill. According to their calculations, almost half of patients in mental institutions were foreign born, and that didn't even account for the "feeble-minded, the inmates in reformatories, and all those in prison who have perhaps become criminal because of some taint in the blood." The situation was even more extreme in New York City where 60 percent of patients in insane asylums were foreign born. Goodwin Brown, who had been hired by the Lunacy Commission to lobby Congress, argued that the problem was actually much worse than the statistics suggested since insanity was inherited from the parents. According to Brown, the population of foreign born and their US-born children accounted for three-quarters of patients in state hospitals. This was not just a financial burden on the state but also a "moral" issue for Brown, who decried the "lives and happiness that are destroyed because of some inherited defect."[6] The language of eugenics was threaded throughout the news stories on alien insanity as was the link between insanity, criminality, and immigrants. The moral panic regarding the infiltration of "defective" immigrants who would pollute and damage the nation for generations to come was already in full swing at the moment Cohen arrived at Ellis Island.

By the time Cohen was committed in 1914, politicians, journalists, and psychiatrists were well aware that foreign-born people were overrepresented in insane asylums. This had been true from at least the mid-nineteenth century. Some psychiatrists believed that immigrants from cultures distinct from what was then mainstream in the United States were not responsive to therapies they offered. Others found immigrants to be responsive but attributed their high incidences of mental illness to their poverty and cultural dislocation from home and family.[7] Whatever the causes, the numbers of immigrants committed to insane asylums in the mid- to late nineteenth century is nothing short of astounding. Immigrants were mostly locked up in the major cities where they tended to reside, but they were also present in state hospitals in more rural areas. In New York City's Lunatic Hospital on Blackwell's Island, for example, more than 77 percent of the patients there between 1847 and 1870 were foreign born. In 1846 in Boston, the foreign born comprised more than half the population of the city's hospital for lunatics. The number and proportion of immigrants locked up in asylums grew in the late nineteenth century as more immigrants arrived. For example, in 1880, 84 percent of New York City's Lunatic Hospital was made up of immigrants in a year when less than half of the city's population was foreign born.[8]

By the early twentieth century, a similar trend of foreigners being disproportionately locked up in insane asylums continued as more and more people were committed to institutions. In 1906, the US Census Bureau published a special report on this population: the "Insane and Feeble-Minded in Hospitals and Institutions, 1904." The report indicated that among the white population, foreigners were overrepresented in insane hospitals. White foreign born over ten years of age comprised about 20 percent of the general population in 1900, but they represented over 34 percent of the insane hospital population at the end of 1903. In particular regions like the North Atlantic, the percentage of foreign born in hospitals reached over 40 percent, and in the West, half of the hospital patients were foreign born. The report tried to ascertain whether the children of immigrants had similarly high rates of insanity, but it discovered that the disproportionality largely disappeared in the second generation.[9] Although there was alarm over the large numbers of mentally ill patients in hospitals, statisticians showed that if only people over twenty years of age were counted, the large discrepancies between native born and foreigners diminished, although it did not disappear.[10] Whether or not foreigners were actually responsible for the rising insanity rate, in cities with high immigrant populations, foreigners seemed to be filling up the hospitals. And newspapers like the *New York Times* fanned the flames of panic with blaring headlines such as "Too Many Insane Aliens."[11]

The hysteria about "insane aliens" may have been overblown, but newspapers were pointing to a very real explosion of people being confined in mental hospitals and other "charitable" institutions. By the early twentieth century, the number of people committed to mental hospitals was growing rapidly, peaking in 1960 at over 630,000, and then subsequently declining. Given that the US population was growing too, relative rates of institutionalization are more relevant, and they show that the peak rate

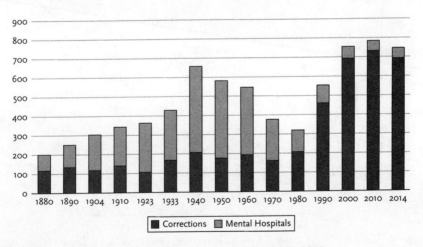

Figure 2.3 Corrections and mental hospitals per 100,000, 1880–2014.
Source: Data from 1880 to 1980 from US Census Bureau, compiled by Cahalan, *Historical Corrections Statistics in the United States, 1850-1984*, pp. 208–210. Data after 1980 from Bureau of Justice Statistics, "Incarceration Rate, 1980-2016," and Tedd Lutterman, Robert Shaw, William Fisher, and Ronald Manderschied, *Trend in Psychiatric Inpatient Capacity, United States and Each State, 1970-2014* (Alexandria, VA: National Association of State Mental Health Programs, 2014), Table 10, p. 29.

of commitments to mental institutions occurred in 1940 at 448 for every 100,000 in the population. To give a sense of perspective, in 2014, the rate of people committed to specialty mental institutions was around 54 per 100,000.[12] What this means is that Americans were locked into mental hospitals in 1940 at roughly eight times the rate they are today.

Since the 1980s, the United States has caged increasing numbers of people in prison and jails, reaching an all-time high of 2.3 million people, or a rate of 760 per 100,000 in 2007. If incarceration in mental hospitals is considered, then the mid-twentieth century rivals our present-day moment of mass incarceration. The difference is that in the past most people were locked in mental asylums, whereas today the vast majority can be found in prisons. Around the time of Nathan Cohen's commitment, there were already more than 190,000 people in mental institutions around the country. To give a sense of comparative size, the total prison and jail population at the same time was just over 128,000. Although both the prison and mental hospital populations grew in the twentieth century, it was not until 1980 that the prison population exceeded that of mental hospitals.[13]

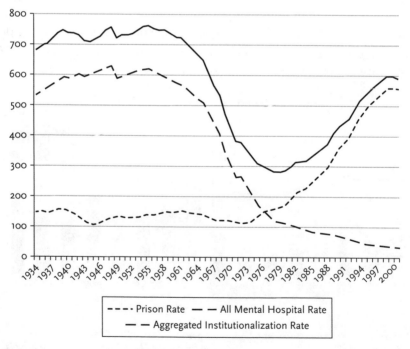

Figure 2.4 Rates of institutionalization, including jails, in the United States (per 100,000), 1934–2000.
Source: Bernard E. Harcourt, "An Institutionalization Effect: The Impact of Mental Hospitalization and Imprisonment on Homicide in the United States, 1934–2001," *Journal of Legal Studies* 40 (2011): 43.

In the study of the "institutionalization effect" in the United States, political scientist Bernard Harcourt found that only looking at state mental hospitals severely undercounted the incarceration rate for people with mental illness. He found that the aggregated institutionalization rates between 1936 and 1963 in all mental hospitals and prisons was consistently above 700 per 100,000, and reached a high of 760 in 1955. In the 1970s, the prison and jail populations exploded, and mental institutions continued to shrink.[14] In short, in the first half of the twentieth century, most incarceration was due to commitments to insane asylums, and the growth in this population correlated with the rising number of immigrants. Another cause of the rise of mentally ill patients was the transfer of older paupers to hospitals in the early twentieth century as senility was redefined as a mental illness. One incentive for localities to shrink their almshouses and shift patients to hospitals was that the state was responsible for funding hospitals, whereas local governments paid for poorhouses.[15] Taken together, the levels of mass incarceration in the mid-twentieth century are similar to those of today, but the population from mental hospitals and other charitable institutions has simply shifted to jails and prisons. In addition to incarceration, in the early twentieth century, a growing number of immigrants were being deported or debarred (that is prevented from entering) due to mental illness, reaching a high of over 2000 in 1914.

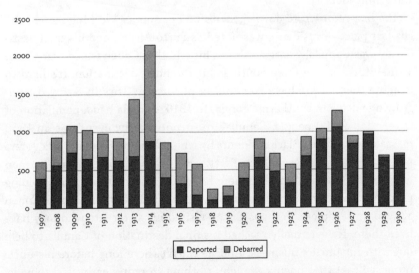

Figure 2.5 Total aliens deported for insanity or mental disorders, 1892–1930.
Source: Culled from Annual Commissioner of Immigration Reports, 1892–1930.

When Nathan Cohen first arrived at Ellis Island on 4 May 1912 on the steamer *Vasari* from the port of Santos in Sao Paolo, Brazil, he was one of thousands of immigrants arriving in New York every day. Cohen was thirty-five years old and unmarried when he landed. His race appears in the ship's manifest as "Hebrew," while his nationality was listed as Hebrew and then crossed out with "Ruso" (Russian) written above it. Perhaps when asked his nationality, Cohen responded in Portuguese, "Russo," meaning Russian. One can imagine the confusion of the immigrant inspector when it came to Cohen's nationality. He was a Jew arriving from Brazil, but he was born in the town of Bausk in Kurland, a region that was under the control of Russia, but very much still a contested borderland 50 km from the German border. During the First World War, Cohen's town of around 6,000 inhabitants, most of whom were Jewish, would pass back and forth between the Russians and the Germans before becoming part of newly independent Latvia.[16] The crossing out of Hebrew for nationality may have suggested a mistake by the bureaucrat, but it also represented the liminal position of Jews born in Central Europe who had lived in third countries. Historian Tara Zahra makes a similar point about the inhabitants of the Bohemian region of Central Europe whose "national indifference" has been overlooked by historians who assume the nation-state as the most salient identity.[17] The confused immigration inspector's scratch marks may ultimately have been the most accurate registry of Cohen's complex national and ethnic identity.

The inspector wrote down Cohen's occupation as "clothing merchant." His last place of residence was noted as Porto Alegre, and his final destination was Camilla, Georgia.[18] It is a bit odd that Cohen would name such a small town in the Deep South as his intended destination. It's hard to imagine there was a large community of Russian Jews in a tiny cotton-growing village in southern Georgia. In 1910, Camilla had a population of fewer than 2,000 people; Camilla's most noteworthy event was an 1868 massacre of a dozen Black residents by whites who bristled at Black voters rallying behind the Republican Party.[19] But Nathan's uncle Israel Berman happened to live in Camilla, where he was a wealthy landowner, holding property worth over $75,000. Two days after landing at Ellis Island, Cohen arrived in Baltimore. Perhaps Cohen visited his sister Itte who may have lived there. He eventually reached his final destination of Camilla to help out with his uncle's business. And he wasn't there long before his uncle proposed that they open a women's clothing store in nearby Jacksonville. Fewer than 200 miles separate Camilla from Jacksonville. Uncle Israel took the fresh off-the-boat Cohen, who barely spoke English at the time, to the local bank in Camilla and had him withdraw $3,000 that he had saved while in Brazil.[20]

Israel Berman appears in the 1910 Census in Camilla with his wife, his eight children, and his niece. Like the immigration inspector who puzzled at how to fill in Cohen's nationality, so too the census taker was confused by Israel's birthplace. He originally wrote Kurland for place of birth, perhaps based on Israel's own response. Maybe after he brought the form back to the office, a more seasoned officer recognized that Kurland was not a country, so scratched out Kurland and wrote Russia above it. Perhaps the two of them debated whether Kurland was really in Russia. Maybe it was in Poland. To cover their bases, in addition to Russia, the bureaucrat scribbled Pol (for Poland) to the right side. As with nationality, the language box only gave space for one. Israel and his wife Sarah were listed as German speakers, but they surely also spoke Yiddish.

There is no mention on the passenger list that inspectors noticed anything strange about Nathan Cohen when he arrived in 1912. Cohen wove his way through the labyrinthine lines with thousands of other passengers navigating Ellis Island's inspection system on that day. Immigration inspectors were on the lookout for mentally unstable patients coming through ports of entry like Ellis Island. In 1903, the Bureau of Public Health and Marine-Hospital Service (PHMHS) published guidelines to help immigrant inspectors, who were not trained psychiatrists, to detect the "insane," "feeble-minded," and "mentally defective." The instructions indicated that it required two medical inspectors to certify an immigrant as "insane" or what they termed an "idiot." The definitions of what constituted an insane and idiotic person were vague. An insane person, for example, was defined as someone who was "deranged and abnormal" and who suffered from "delusions, or hallucinations or illusions." "Idiots" were those who had a mental defect that did not allow them to take care of themselves. The line between physical and mental conditions was often blurred— for example, people suffering from delirium tremens due to alcoholism were automatically defined as insane. Inspectors were encouraged to adjust their diagnoses to be sensitive to different cultural norms. For example, the instructions stated, "In the case of immigrants, particularly the ignorant representatives of emotional races, due allowance should be made for temporary demonstrations of excitement, fear, or grief, and reliance chiefly placed upon absolute assurance of the existence of delusions or persistent refusal to talk or continued abstinence from eating."[21] In other words, expressions of excitement, fear, and grief that might be suspect in some would be perfectly normal for "ignorant representatives of the emotional races." Although these guidelines did not spell out who constituted the emotional races, subsequent instructions made it clear that the Irish, Jews, and Italians were seen as particularly voluble and emotional.

At its peak in 1907, 10,000 immigrants filed through Ellis Island every day. With only sixteen physicians to inspect 900,000 immigrants each year, the inspections were necessarily cursory. Medical inspectors stood at one of four lines and observed the immigrants as they passed, paying special attention to signs of contagious disease, chronic disabilities, and "mental defects." By the summer of 1912, Binet and Simon's scale intelligence testing was launched at Ellis Island to try to classify immigrants as "idiots," "imbeciles," or "feeble-minded," or what Ellis Island Surgeon Howard Knox called "morons."[22] In 1917, the surgeon of the Public Health Service, E. H. Mullan, published guidelines for the mental examination of immigrants at Ellis Island. Mullan noted, "Many inattentive and stupid-looking aliens are questioned by the medical officer in the various languages as to their age, destination, and nationality. Often simple questions in addition and multiplication are propounded." This cursory interrogation determined whether the immigrant would undergo further scrutiny. If the immigrant appeared "stupid and inattentive" and a mental "defect" suspected, an X was chalked on his right shoulder. If the immigrant seemed to have a definite mental "defect," then an X in a circle was written with chalk on the shoulder. After the first examiner, the immigrant passed before the second inspector, known as the "eye man" who did an eye inspection and asked further questions to determine mental acuity. Approximately 15 to 20 percent of immigrants were chalk marked and had to undergo a secondary medical inspection. Passing the inspection line could take several hours, and if an immigrant were held for secondary observation, that could take several days or longer. Nine out of every 100 immigrants were typically identified for secondary inspection, and out of those nine, one or two would be held for a thorough mental examination lasting anywhere from one day to a week. The ones identified with a circle X were immediately sent to the psychiatric hospital.[23]

Mullan emphasized the importance of understanding the particular "racial characteristics in physique, costume and behavior" during this first inspection where conversation, style of dress, and any "peculiarity" were being keenly observed. The characteristics used to determine "active or maniacal psychosis" were so vague they could potentially have been applied to any immigrant: "Striking peculiarities in dress, talkativeness, witticism, facetiousness, detailing, apparent shrewdness, keenness, excitement, impatience in a word or manner, impudence, unruliness, flightiness, nervousness, restlessness, egotism, smiling, facial expression of mirth, laughing, eroticism, boisterous conduct, meddling with the affairs of others, and un-common activity." The fact that peculiar dress, witticism, and uncommon activity were imagined as signs of psychosis said more about the expected cultural norms of the medical inspectors than it did about the mental health of the immigrants. Depression could be diagnosed if the inspectors noticed "slow speech, low voice, trembling articulation, sad facies, tearful eyes, per-plexity, difficulty in thinking, delayed responses, [and] psycho motor retar-dation." Alcoholism, paresis, and dementia were suggested by "surliness, apprehensiveness, untidiness, intoxication, apparent intoxication, confu-sion, aimlessness, dullness, stupidity, expressionless face, tremulousness, tremor and twitching of facial muscles, ataxia, stuttering and tremulous speech, great amount of calmness, jovial air, self-confident smile, talkative-ness, fabrications, grandioseness, sullenness, fussiness, excessive friendli-ness, defective memory, misstatement of age, disorientation, difficulty in computation, pupil symptoms, and other physical signs." Even some phys-ical ailments like deafness or blindness were attributed to mental defects. Mullan warned that "immigrants afflicted with defective hearing, defec-tive vision, and fever frequently assume peculiar attitudes and do strange things, all of which are suggestive of mental disease."[24] In short, whether they were talkative or responded slowly, laughed or had sad expressions, expressed excitement or sullenness, all of these could be construed as evi-dence of a mental defect.

Racial profiling was an important part of the medical inspector's job. According to Mullan, an inspector could "tell at a glance the race of an alien." Determining the race was so crucial because the diagnosis of mental imbal-ance depended on considering the norms of different cultures. Inspectors believed they understood the typical reactions of each race while waiting on the inspection line, and they had to calibrate "peculiar" behavior according to their understandings of cultural difference. As Mullan put it, "On the line if an Englishman reacts to questions in the manner of an Irishman, his lack of mental balance would be suspected. The converse is also true. If the Italian responded to questions as the Russian Finn responds, the former would in all probability be suffering with a depressive psychosis." The testing for mental defects was rudimentary and was also adjusted to racial and class expectations. A northern Italian, Irish, Scandinavian girl, or a male Greek would be asked more difficult math addition problems, while an illiterate man from southern Italy would be asked simpler problems, and a southern Italian or Greek girl and children under twelve would be asked to solve the simplest problems: $6 + 6$ or $3 + 3$.[25]

In his guidelines, Mullan included the inspectors' notes indicating why particular immigrants were sent to the psychiatric hospital. The first one appears to come from Nathan Cohen's file since it matches exactly his story. It reads: "Deported by the United States; insane. Refused admittance by the Brazilian authorities at Santos." The list of other notes suggests how arbitrary and capricious the inspectors could be in their diagnosis of mental illness:

> Insane. Loves America and wishes to defend America. Will go into Army; delusions of patriotism.
>
> Speech defect; coarse voice; repeats words that are spoken to him without any attempt at answering examiner's questions.
>
> Alien returned from the board with statement that she acted queerly before board.
>
> Wanderer and traveler. Trouble with a woman several years ago.
>
> Alien has peculiar affected manner.
>
> Emotional, talkative.
>
> Silly facial expression. Appears to be thinking of something foreign to the examination.
>
> Irritable, claiming that it is her privilege to do as she pleases; went back to Ireland last December with her sister who was deported from Ward's Island (hospital for insane); another sister was deported 4 years ago; paranoid view of life; ship surgeon reported that patient would burst out into laughter without cause; also get up from dinner table and play the piano to the annoyance of other passengers.
>
> Alien sent to island by boarding officer with the notation that she has been depressed since last December; alien is still depressed; says its due to death of her mother; some clouding of consciousness present.
>
> Position of inattention while talking.
>
> Talkative and flighty.
>
> Baby 2 years old; unable to walk; observe.[26]

The observations in these notes indicate that any sign of not comprehending questions, which may have been asked in a language the immigrant did not understand, could be construed as a mental defect. Disabilities such as "speech defects" or deafness also made the immigrant suspect. Facial expressions set off alarms, anything from having a "silly" expression to having an "affected manner" or being "talkative" or inattentive. Perhaps the most shocking diagnosis was based on one immigrant's indication of loving America and wanting to join the army. The inspector decided that this immigrant had "delusions of patriotism" and sent him for observation as a potentially "insane" or "feeble-minded" alien.

Although this elaborate inspection system seemed to suspect feeble-mindedness or insanity of many people who were just exhibiting normal reactions to arriving in a new country after a long journey, very few immigrants were ultimately excluded based on these diagnoses. From 1892 through 1930, only 7,785 immigrants were excluded and deported for insanity or mental disorders, which meant that in an average year just over 200 immigrants were barred from entering and deported for reason of mental unfitness. Up through the early twentieth century, the numbers remained fairly low, below fifty per year, but then hundreds began to be deported for mental illness, reaching a high in 1914. Coincidentally, that was the year Cohen was deported for insanity, when over 1,200 were diagnosed with insanity or declared feeble-minded and deported. By the mid-1920s, the numbers begin to decline, and by the late 1920s only a handful of immigrants were being deported for mental illness.[27] The categories used to classify these people shifted over time, but the most consistent labels were idiot, imbecile, feeble-minded, insane, and constitutional psychopathic inferiority. Epileptics were also lumped together with the insane.

To put these numbers in perspective, more than 22 million immigrants arrived from 1892 to1930, meaning that only three of every 10,000 immigrants were deported for mental illness during this period. A snapshot of inspection data from three months in the summer of 1916 at Ellis Island reveals the large number of immigrants being questioned and subjected to inspections as well as the relatively few cases of people declared insane or feeble-minded and deported. In those months, 30,711 immigrants were inspected, just over 3,000 were sent to secondary inspection, but only 610 were detained in the hospital. And of those 610, only 108 were certified, almost all of them for being "feeble-minded."[28]

Behind the concerted efforts to identify and exclude the mentally "defective" was the eugenicist idea that such people would "infect" and destroy the nation. In 1913, Ellis Island assistant surgeon Howard Knox published an article in the *Journal of the American Medical Association* in which he warned of the dangers of allowing people with mental illnesses into the country. As Knox put it, "A drop of ink in a barrel of water does not make ink, but the greater the number of drops of ink in that barrel of water the more inky it becomes." While Knox believed the insane immigrant could be easily detected, he was much more concerned about the "moron [who] will not be recognized and will immediately start a line of defectives whose progeny, like a brook, will go on forever, branching off here in an imbecile and there in an epileptic."[29]

In the 1910s, Ellis Island became an important testing ground for eugenicist ideas. Knox was clearly influenced by the eugenics movement, was a member of the Eugenics Research Association, and published an article in its journal entitled "How the Public Health Service Prevents Contamination of Our Racial Stock." Other key figures in the eugenics movement like Harry Laughlin and Henry Goddard visited Ellis Island, consulted with Public Health Service (PHS) doctors, and used evidence from Ellis Island to advocate immigration restrictions based on race.[30] Nonetheless, medical historian Amy L. Fairchild and John T. E. Richardson, Knox's biographer, both argue that the PHS doctors at Ellis Island resisted the most extreme eugenicist ideas about the heritability of defects among particular races. They show that these doctors often debated whether physical and mental defects were the result of inherited traits or the product of poor conditions for immigrants, both in home countries and in the United States.[31] In the end, however, presumptions about the racial inferiority of particular races clearly influenced Ellis Island medical inspectors, and their medical observations were used to impose racially restrictive national origins quotas in the early 1920s.

FAMILY FEUD IN JACKSONVILLE, FLORIDA

When Nathan Cohen first landed in New York on May 6, 1912, he appears to have passed through inspection without any special notice. Cohen was arriving from Brazil as a merchant, had $90 in cash with him, and apparently had $3,000 in the bank that he had earned in Brazil. Since Cohen arrived on a $45 second-class ticket from Brazil, he would have been inspected on board the ship and perhaps not even have been sent to Ellis Island if the shipboard inspection did not reveal any suspicions of disease.[32] After going to Camilla, Georgia, he moved to Jacksonville and opened a "ladies cloak and ready made garment" store with his uncle.[33] Newspaper stories contain contradictory information about where Cohen first landed (some indicating the port of entry was Baltimore), and they muddled some key facts about his life. But after arriving in New York, he went to Camilla, Georgia, to meet his uncle, Israel Berman, and within a few months he had moved to Florida.[34]

Cohen's life in Jacksonville was off to a promising start. Within four months of landing in the United States, he and his uncle signed a formal business partnership to which each was supposed to contribute $2,000.[35] At some point in that first year, Cohen also married a "beautiful young woman" from Jacksonville.[36] Cohen was quickly becoming a well-respected member of the community in his new home, and he was invited to join the fraternal order, the local Knights of Pythias. This fraternal organization was founded in 1864 in Washington, DC, but quickly spread across the country and by 1880 even had African American lodges. It's not clear if the Jacksonville Lodge was founded by African Americans.[37] The Jacksonville Davis Lodge No. 15 vetted candidates based upon their character as well as their physical and mental condition. When lodge member A. S. Metzner of the Investigating Committee interviewed Cohen, he "did not notice any mental condition" or "abnormal mental trouble"; Cohen was elected to the order.[38] The Knights of Pythias would later become instrumental in defending Cohen and helping him to fight his deportation order.

At some point between signing the partnership with his uncle in September 1912 and July 1913, Cohen's business started to fall apart. According to the agreement, the uncle could draw a monthly salary of $100 as a married man, while Cohen, then single, would only draw $70. Cohen started noticing that the uncle seemed to be drawing more than his allotted $100 from the business and was also mixing up his personal and business expenses. When Cohen asked to see the books, the uncle refused and kept his nephew in the dark. What's more, the uncle had not paid some of the business creditors, and thus Cohen's reputation had been sullied. Finally, the situation became so bad that Cohen filed a lawsuit in Duval County, Florida, on July 26, 1913, asking the court to appoint a third party to run the business and liquidate its assets. The brief filed by Cohen's Jacksonville lawyer F. D. Brennan was unearthed by the Pythian Lodge and sent to Samuel Littman, the HIAS representative at Ellis Island, to try to show that Cohen was not insane when he arrived in 1912.[39] This legal brief is the most detailed description of Cohen's time in Jacksonville and reveals why Cohen may have become mentally unstable.

The lawsuit paints a picture of a conniving uncle taking advantage of his naïve nephew to defraud him of his money. Cohen alleged that in addition to keeping the business accounts hidden from him, his uncle never invested the agreed upon $2,000 in the business and had additionally taken a personal loan of $1,000 dollars from Cohen that was never repaid. Furthermore, Israel Berman transferred the lease of the store into his own and his son Abe's name and in this way attempted to substitute Abe for Cohen as a business partner. When Cohen complained, the uncle "harassed, annoyed and misled" him, claiming the business had large debts, and tried to "force" Cohen to sell "at a great loss." Cohen finally agreed to sell his stake in the business for $1,750, but when the uncle took over the store he refused to pay Cohen. In the meantime, his uncle had begun to sell the goods below cost and double-locked the store to prevent access by Cohen. When Cohen managed to enter the store, the uncle insulted him, ordered him arrested, and paid a hired private security guard to watch over him. The money from the business was kept in a safe to which only the uncle had keys. Cohen also feared that Berman was in the process of "selling the business to some dummy buyer so as to oust and defraud" him.[40]

In addition to portraying Berman as a deceptive business partner, Cohen depicted him as someone who took advantage of his familial relationship and Cohen's lack of experience doing business in America. "Being unfamiliar with such matters [Cohen] relied upon his uncle," the lawsuit claimed, and that is how Cohen was swindled out of $3,000. Cohen demanded that the court take over the business, liquidate the stock, pay creditors and divide the assets proportionally among the two partners. He also sued Harry Gerbert and Abe Berman (Israel's son), whose shoe store was next to Cohen & Berman's ladies clothes store, asserting that they had illegally purchased a stake in Cohen's business.[41]

It's not clear what happened in the intervening months, but suddenly on October 22, 1913, Cohen wrote a terse letter to his lawyer directing him to drop all pending law suits against his uncle (Israel), the uncle's son (Abe), and Abe's business partner (Gerbert). Cohen further drafted an agreement to sell his interest in the business partnership for $50.[42] We don't know why Cohen gave up his fight for the business and accepted an almost total loss of the $3,000 he had invested. Cohen's brother-in-law, Gabriel, would later recount a story he heard from a friend who was in Jacksonville around this time suggesting that Cohen had stopped eating and was a "nervous wreck." It was at this moment of vulnerability that Cohen's uncle asked him to sign the agreement "relinquishing all his right to the business."[43] In addition, sometime in the midst of his business falling part, Cohen's young wife apparently ran off with his best friend. Perhaps it was the combination of betrayal by his uncle, his wife, and his friend that led to his severe depression and mental imbalance. Jacob Pincus, who claimed to be "intimately acquainted with Nathan Cohen" in Jacksonville, gave a sworn affidavit indicating that he spoke with Cohen in mid-July 1913 and that he was "very much worried over his losses."[44] After this series of betrayals, Cohen decided to return to Brazil.[45]

This was not the story of immigrant success in America. In September or October 1913, the dejected and depressed Cohen left Jacksonville and went to visit his brother-in-law in Baltimore to say goodbye before he departed.[46] Cohen's sister's husband, Gabriel Jaffe, also known as Zeje, had come from Russia to Baltimore in 1910.[47] According to Gabriel, his wife, Itte or Ide, was still in Kurland, Russia, taking care of her ailing father, Israel Judolowicz, along with their six children in June of 1915.[48] However, Gabriel appears to have been lying in order to protect his wife from the trauma of hearing about her brother's predicament. Nathan Cohen's hospital record indicates that his sister was living with Gabriel in Baltimore in early December 1913, when Cohen was committed.[49] It's possible that his sister returned to Russia with her six children to care for her father, and then returned in 1915, but that is highly unlikely given the difficulty of transportation to Russia in the midst of the war. In March 1916, Gabriel would reveal that his wife, Cohen's sister, had also been temporarily committed to an insane asylum.[50]

There are three accounts of what happened to Nathan Cohen in Baltimore: Martha Rezenstein's letter to HIAS based on her interview of Gabriel, an anonymous unpublished typescript in the HIAS archives, and the minutes of Nathan Cohen's deportation hearing in which Gabriel testified. The three accounts match, but each provides different details. According to Rezenstein's account, Gabriel indicated that Cohen always had a "very nervous temperament" and while in Baltimore he would "often get in moody spells when he refused to talk." Cohen had been treated at several hospitals in Baltimore according to Gabriel. The brother-in-law did not seem to know much about Cohen's life in Jacksonville and was unaware that he had been married. He also had never met Cohen before their encounter in the fall of 1914 in Baltimore.[51]

The typescript narrative of Cohen's life story suggests that it was Gabriel who had Cohen committed to the Baltimore Public Hospital when he started acting erratically. According to this narrative, "Cohen was still worrying over his bitter wrongs, and is often the case when one broods incessantly with nothing to divert the mind from its morbid fancy, his reasoning power became weakened; it finally gave way. Insanity characterized by melancholy and loss of speech followed." Cohen had become paranoid, "obsessed with the idea that all men were his enemies," and it's then that he refused to speak. Since he refused to speak, this author concluded, the hospital could not ascertain whether he was a US citizen. As an immigrant who had only arrived two years earlier, he was declared a public charge and ordered deported back to Brazil.[52] Immigration law allowed people who became public charges within three years of arrival to be deported.

The most revealing account of Cohen's descent into madness and commitment to the Bay View Hospital and Asylum in Baltimore comes from the minutes of Cohen's deportation hearing in which Gabriel was the only person to testify. The hearing minutes indicated that since Nathan Cohen was "unable to speak," his brother-in-law, Zeje (Gabriel) Jaffe was given a chance to testify. Apparently Zeje didn't speak English but the immigrant inspector spoke Zeje's "mother tongue." It was not indicated which language that was, but it was probably either Yiddish or Russian.

Gabriel responded to Inspector Doyas's questions like he was on trial, and at one point seeming frustrated, he insisted, "I am telling you the truth." Gabriel said he had arrived in America four years earlier, but was not a US citizen. He was a tailor by trade but had been without work for the last sixteen weeks, and he had no property or money in the bank. He also claimed his wife and six children were living in Russia. Gabriel knew very little about his brother-in-law's life in the country, responding "I don't know" to questions about how long he had been living in Jacksonville, how long he had been in Bay View hospital, and who was paying for his care there. In Russia, Gabriel had heard about Nathan from his mother, who said that he left Russia for Brazil at the age of seventeen, but since they never received any letters from him, they "thought he was dead." The first time Gabriel heard from Nathan was through a letter he received when Nathan was with his uncle in Camilla, Georgia, in 1912. Gabriel indicated that there was no sense from the letter that Nathan was sick or mentally unstable.[53] This line of questioning by Doyas was intended to show that Cohen was mentally unstable when he arrived to the United States, which would provide justification for deportation. Gabriel's testimony, however, did not corroborate this story at all, and in fact it proved that Gabriel had not even met Cohen until after the traumatic bankruptcy in Jacksonville.

Three weeks before Cohen turned up in Baltimore, he wrote his brother-in-law, saying that he would be visiting him. Instead of going to Gabriel, Cohen went to straight to a mutual friend's house, Mr. Isaacs, who was a "ladies tailor." Gabriel described the scene when he arrived at Isaac's house and saw a deranged man in the parlor "throwing paper money in every direction." Gabriel immediately left the room, looking confused. Isaacs then turned and told Gabriel that the crazy man in the next room was his brother-in-law, Nathan Cohen. Gabriel responded, "Is that possible because I never saw the man in my life." Gabriel returned to the parlor and shook his brother-in-law's hand, asking him what he was doing with the money. Nathan said, "Go ahead and take this money." Gabriel refused, not wanting to even touch the money. At Cohen's deportation hearing, Gabriel testified about this encounter, noting, "I immediately saw that his mind was not sound."[54] The image of Nathan Cohen wildly throwing money around and telling his brother-in-law to take it makes sense given the financial troubles he had been experiencing and his state of distress. This was the only brief encounter between Gabriel and Nathan, and yet Nathan's defense rested entirely on Gabriel's testimony.

Cohen remained in Isaacs's home trying to convalesce, with a doctor coming to see him there. After a couple of weeks, caring for Cohen became too much for Isaacs, and Cohen was transferred to the Hebrew hospital for treatment, which was paid for by Isaacs. After four or five weeks, the Hebrew hospital transferred Cohen to Bay View hospital, Baltimore's main hospital to care for poor people suffering from physical and mental ailments.[55] In 1904, there were over 1,300 patients in the hospital, mostly elderly people; 625 of these were in the "insane" ward. Bay View received "pauper patients" from the other city hospitals as well.[56] The census report on *Insane and Feeble-Minded in Institutions 1910* listed 438 patients in Bay View's insane hospital, of which the foreign born represented just under 20 percent.[57]

When the inspector asked Gabriel whether he was in a position to care for his brother-in-law, he said, "No, I can't help myself." The inspector asked whether he would like to hire a lawyer to represent his brother-in-law, but Gabriel responded that he had no money, not even money to send for his wife. When the inspector asked whether Gabriel had any objections to Cohen being deported, he asked for a break in the hearing to consult with his friends. When Gabriel returned at 3 P.M., he was asked again whether there was any reason that Nathan Cohen should not be deported. Gabriel responded, "What shall I say? I have nothing more to say. The matter is in the hands of the government and I trust that it will do what is right."[58] And with that, Nathan Cohen's brief hearing ended, with Cohen having said nothing, and his brother-in-law leaving Nathan's fate in the "hands of the government." It would not be long before Cohen received his final order of deportation.

DEPORTATION

Three days after the hearing at which Gabriel testified, Acting Secretary of Labor J. B. Densmore issued a warrant for Nathan Cohen's deportation to Brazil. Inspector Doyas found Cohen in violation of the 1907 Immigration Act because he was "insane" and had become a "public charge" at Bay View Insane Hospital within three years of entry. Section 20 of the Act also made transportation companies liable to pay for return of all deportees within three years of their arrival.[59] Determining whether insanity was a preexisting condition or a result of the trauma of migration was hard to prove. Immigration officials, physicians, psychiatrists, public health experts, and academics developed their own theories to explain the high numbers of insane aliens showing up in hospitals. Some argued that the decision to migrate was itself the act of a crazy person, while others claimed that the hardships for immigrants caused them to go insane.[60] While it was difficult, if not impossible, to prove that Cohen was insane when he arrived, especially based on the limited evidence the Bureau of Immigration had, there was no doubt that he had become a public charge in under three years.

Once the deportation order was rendered, things moved quickly since the hospital staff had been preparing for such an outcome. A day before the hearing, the chief physician at Bay View Hospital, Kenneth B. Jones, recommended to the Immigration Bureau that Cohen be accompanied on his way to New York "as there is a probability that he might commit some act that would jeopardize his own personal safety."[61] Finally, on March 6, 1914, Nathan Cohen was escorted by the doctor on a train to New York.[62] The very next day, he was placed on the *Vandyck*, a ship of the Lamport & Holt line, and shipped off to Para, Brazil.[63] Although this should have been the end of Cohen's tragic chapter in America, it was just the beginning of a much longer nightmare.

When the *Vandyck* landed in Rio de Janeiro, the Brazilian authorities refused to allow Cohen to land, claiming that there was no way to prove he was a Brazilian citizen. It's not clear from the record whether the US immigration authorities returned Cohen's Brazilian passport to him, and whether he was a Brazilian citizen, but Cohen's inability or unwillingness to speak did not help matters. The *Vandyck* continued on to Buenos Aires, but the Argentine authorities were also unwilling to land the taciturn Cohen, and so he remained on the ship and returned to New York.

In attempting to return Cohen to Brazil, albeit unsuccessfully, the Lamport & Holt Company believed it had satisfied its legal requirements. Cohen remained on Ellis Island in the psychiatric hospital from May 8, 1914, until January 8, 1915.[64] In the intervening months, the Immigration Bureau and lawyers for Lamport & Holt exchanged a series of letters in which each side argued that the other side was responsible for taking care of Nathan Cohen and removing him from the United States. On July 25, 1914, immigration officers again presented Cohen at the steamship *Vauban* for deportation, but the shipping line refused to accept him, and so he was returned to Ellis Island. Negotiations dragged on for six more months between the two parties, and finally, seeing no resolution and without alerting Lamport & Holt, officers managed to place Cohen on the *Vasari* on January 9, 1915, the original ship on which Cohen had arrived in 1912.[65] Cohen made the long journey back to Brazil, and again, the Brazilian government refused to accept him; he returned on the same ship back to New York.

At this point, the US attorney general, the secretary of the Department of Labor, and the commissioner general of immigration were all involved in this case. Fearing that Brazil would once again refuse to accept Cohen and he would be returned to New York, the US attorney's office in New York advised the commissioner of immigration at Ellis Island to refuse Cohen permission to land, even to prevent him from setting foot on Ellis Island. The attorney recognized that once Cohen was in the hospital on US soil, it would be harder to make Cohen the shipping line's responsibility. Leaving him on board the *Vasari* put the onus on Lamport & Holt to resolve the case.[66]

Busk & Daniels, the general agent for the shipping company, negotiated with US authorities in the Cohen case. The agent held steadfastly to the idea that the shipping company should not be responsible for an insane alien as long as it had made a good faith effort to return him to the country from which he had arrived. The agent argued that they had attempted to enlist other shipping companies to return Cohen to Russia, but they had all declined. Furthermore, in Rio de Janeiro, they even contacted the Russian minister and begged him to accept Cohen, but the minister argued that unless they could prove that Cohen was Russian, they would not take him.[67] The fact that Kourland was at that very moment the center of battles between German and Russian forces, with Russians trying to push Jews out of the region, made it unlikely that the Russians would want to accept a Jew, especially one who had been labeled insane.

The Lamport & Holt shipping line was worried that if it accepted responsibility for Cohen, it would be taking on a virtually limitless liability, for Cohen's indefinite care and for future cases where it was impossible to deport immigrants. So the company pressed its case and dug in its heels. Busk & Daniels wrote plaintively to Secretary of Labor Densmore in early February 1915: "We respectfully beg to ask in what respect we can protect ourselves against a person becoming insane after he has been duly landed and passed by the immigration authorities at this port; and if it is possible to put such an interpretation on the law that would make the party a perpetual burden on our hand on board of our steamers, neither allowed to land in this country or in Brazil."[68] From the shipping line's perspective, the government, not the shipping line, should have shouldered the burden of maintaining Cohen.

In mid-February, the agents for Lamport & Holt reached out to New York senator James A. O'Gorman to enlist his help with the Cohen case. It appears as if Senator O'Gorman interceded and asked the Bureau of Immigration for an explanation.[69] The commissioner of immigration explained it would not be possible to hold Cohen at the "psycopathic ward at Ellis island," and that the only possible solution would be to detain Cohen in a private hospital at the shipping line's expense.[70] The agent replied that if they agreed to these terms, they would then be responsible for immigrants who were deemed immoral, diseased, and likely to become a public charge, thereby their "liabilities would always be an unknown quantity."[71] Densmore responded with his last offer, which he viewed as a "concession," that the government would allow Cohen to land if Lamport

& Holt paid for his expenses. If they did not accept this offer, the commissioner of immigration at Ellis Island would refuse to allow Cohen to land.[72] By the end of February, Busk & Daniels had received word that the Brazilian government had once again not allowed Cohen to land, and he was now on the *Vasari* heading back to New York. Given Densmore's ultimatum, the lawyers asked whether they would permit Cohen to land under a $500 bond if the shipping line would pay for his expenses in a private institution. They also reiterated their objection in principle to assuming liability for Cohen. "We do not think that the fact of our Company's agents abroad having sold in good faith a ticket furnishing transportation carries with it a liability to become permanently responsible for the personal welfare and custody of a passenger or that our own company or any other commercial corporation is obligated to this extent."[73]

In March, a law firm representing Lamport & Holt wrote to the commissioner of immigration at Ellis Island, Frederic C. Howe, to once again lay out their objections to holding the shipping line responsible for a situation beyond their control. The lawyers wanted to bring the case to court to resolve the issue of responsibility. However, a handwritten message at the end of the typed letter proposed the idea of the shipping line paying for the bond and maintenance of Cohen until he could be deported to Russia.[74] On March 18, the Bureau of Immigration accepted Lamport & Holt's proposal but reiterated that they were "extending a privilege" in doing so and that the "law does not vest the Secretary authority to land an insane alien."[75] The crisis seemed to have been averted, but when Cohen arrived in New York, he was refused landing. It's not clear if Lamport & Holt decided to retract its offer, but Cohen found himself stuck on the *Vasari* in New York's harbor.

DEFENDING NATHAN COHEN

By the time Cohen arrived back in New York, his story of being transported on one $45 ticket for more than 33,000 miles had become a national news story. The story reached H. M. Sasnett from the Knights of Pythias lodge in Jacksonville, who then wrote to Max Kohn of the New York Lodge No. 154 asking him to determine whether the Nathan Cohen being held on the ship was the same one from their lodge. "If he is our brother Knight," Sasnett wrote, "we want to do what we can to help him."[76] There was urgency to find out more about Cohen's time in Jacksonville and obtain affidavits from people there to prove he was not insane when he arrived in the United States but rather developed his disturbance afterward. Initially it appears as if the Knights of Pythias coordinated the efforts to defend Cohen, sending urgent telegrams to the Jacksonville Pythians to enlist their help. A day after his initial missive to Kohn, Sasnett wrote a telegram to William Grossman, a New York lawyer and fellow Pythian brother, explaining that they could not put together the requested information on such short order.[77] "Impossible for us to act by time boat leaves will make effort to solve difficulty upon return."[78] On April 6, Sasnett suggested that Grossman contact some "influential men of [Cohen's] race," perhaps from HIAS, to take up Cohen's case. Samuel Littman, the HIAS representative on Ellis Island, had already been involved in Cohen's case since at least March.[79] The HIAS representative on Ellis Island, I. Irving Lipsitch, appealed the Special Board of Inquiry's decision to exclude Cohen.[80] Cohen's hearing before the Board of Special Inquiry occurred at 2:25 P.M. on March 31, 1915, at Ellis Island. Two immigration inspectors were present at the hearing. While the schematic hearing minutes don't reveal much, they include a previous exclusion order on December 26, 1914. Cohen was reexamined by three surgeons at this new hearing and found to be "afflicted with INSANE." The decision was rendered at the bottom of the page in bold capitals: "EXCLUDED AND ORDERED DEPORTED."

In April, Littman, who also happened to be a fellow Pythian, started coordinating Cohen's defense with the Knights of Pythias and the HIAS representative in Baltimore, Martha Rezenstein. In the meantime, the Jacksonville Pythians set about gathering eight affidavits from fellow lodge members to help with Cohen's defense. The members of the committee that vetted Cohen for membership provided affidavits, and even Abe Berman, Cohen's nephew, and his partner, Harry Gerbert, both of whom were sued by Cohen over their business dealings, wrote on Cohen's behalf to say he had been a respected member of the mercantile community in Jacksonville. As Berman and Gerbert put it in their duplicate statement, Cohen was regarded "as a successful, competent, capable and good businessman and fully capable in every way of transacting and handling the customary duties incident the said mercantile business."[81] Whatever animosity had existed between them, Berman and Gerbert must have recognized that Cohen's being locked up in an asylum and deported was an unjustified punishment for someone who had suffered so much trauma. Perhaps they felt guilty that his mental instability seemed to stem from their own efforts to take over Cohen's business.

Rezenstein managed to obtain the hospital record for Cohen in Baltimore, which noted that he was admitted on November 1, 1913, and discharged "unimproved" on December 5 of that same year. The doctors diagnosed Cohen with dementia praecox and he also tested positive on the Wasserman test for syphilis. The dementia praecox diagnosis had become common in the early twentieth century to describe hopeless and incurable insanity. German psychiatrist Elim Kraepelin first described the term dementia praecox in his foundational 1896 textbook *Psychiatrie*. Symptoms included a "deadness of emotional experience, a flatness of affect, an eerie remoteness that evoked an uncanny 'praecox feeling' in physicians who evaluated such patients." The "praecox feeling" was an intuition that clinicians had that enabled them to make a diagnosis within a few minutes of meeting a patient. At the beginning of the twentieth century, alienists and doctors in the eugenics and mental hygiene movement identified dementia praecox as the primary disorder in the field of mental health. For a long time doctors believed that dementia praecox was linked to schizophrenia, a link that psychiatrists have since rejected.[82] The descriptions of Cohen refusing to speak and being in a listless or catatonic state of depression fits the characteristics of dementia praecox, but such behavior can also be attributed to "selective mutism" stemming from a traumatic event or extreme social anxiety.[83] Whatever the limitations or accuracy of the diagnosis, in 1913, such a diagnosis was prima facie evidence of "insanity" or having a "mental defect," both causes for deportation for immigrants.

At the end of March, Samuel Littman traveled to Washington to meet with immigration officials and plead Cohen's case.[84] HIAS was trying to get the authorities to allow Cohen to land temporarily and to remain at a private sanitarium at the expense of HIAS and the Knights of Pythias until he had become more stable and could be deported to Russia. Littman tried to get the shipping line Lamport & Holt to agree to pay for Cohen's eventual deportation to Russia, arguing that they were legally obligated to cover these costs anyway.[85] Lamport & Holt's agents sent a dismissive reply to Littman, stating, "We of course feel sorry for any passenger over our line that meets with misfortunes and from a charitable standpoint are not [averse] to aiding any society like yours to meet such emergencies. As a steamship company furnishing transportation, we alas feel that we do not commit ourselves to look after passengers for life." They further argued that their legal requirement ended when they deported Cohen to Brazil.[86] The agents at Lamport & Holt must have discussed the matter and realized that by taking up Littman's offer they were getting off cheaply. Lamport & Holt's lawyers had already told the government they would pay for maintaining Cohen in a private hospital, but if HIAS was willing to take on that expense, they were happy to be relieved of the burden. The shipping line promptly sent HIAS a check for $60 to pay for Cohen's eventual deportation to Russia, thus ending their legal exposure in this potentially expensive case.[87] Nonetheless, even after Lamport & Holt had paid HIAS to wash their hands of Cohen, the government continued to pursue the shipping company for expenses related to Cohen's lengthy stays at the psychiatric hospital at Ellis Island.

The day finally arrived on which Nathan Cohen's future depended. On Saturday, March 27, 1915, at 9 A.M., Samuel Littman met with the solicitor general of the department of labor, John B. Densmore, to argue on behalf of Cohen. Littman laid out all the evidence gathered to show that Cohen was not insane when he landed but became mentally unstable in the United States as a result of his business losses and personal calamities. Littman also raised the possibility that Cohen may have become a naturalized US citizen at some point. Finally, Littman appealed to Densmore's humanity and railed against the "injustice of shuttling Cohen up and down the seas continuously." Even if the laws did not permit Cohen to land permanently, Littman implored Densmore to allow for his temporary release to a sanitarium so he could be treated and deported at a later date. Littman later recalled, "Mr. Densmore without a moment's hesitation picked up the telephone receiver and calling Ellis Island, ordered, 'Take Cohen off Vasari—Hold him on Ellis Island until the Knights of Pythias and the Hebrew Sheltering and Immigrant Aid Society of America make suitable arrangements to place him in a Sanitarium.'"[88]

At the time of Densmore's call to Ellis Island, the *Vasari* had already raised steam, the gangplank had been pulled, and the sailors were casting off. Cohen was being held below decks in the ship's hospital, forbidden to go above until the ship was out in the harbor. At that point, Cohen must have been contemplating another lengthy journey thousands of miles through the seas to Chile. As one narrative of his story put it, "He had lost all hope of ever setting foot on land again; life seemed to offer him nothing but doom of the Flying Dutchman to boat back-and-forth on the seas, but never to find a haven of rest on terra-firma." Although Cohen was unaware, the captain had ordered the sailors to pause in their preparations for sailing as a tugboat from Ellis Island came "puffing up along the *Vasari*." Suddenly three immigration officers appeared in front of Cohen who looked up at them with wonder. "'We have orders from Washington to let you land,' one of them said. 'Come right along; the tug is waiting to take you to Ellis Island.'"[89]

There are various descriptions of Cohen's reaction to the news, but they all portray him as shocked and in disbelief. One narrative noted, "Cohen did not understand. He remained listless and unstirred by these words of liberation."[90] A newspaper article indicated that when he was brought up to the deck and a rope tied around his waist, he showed "fear he was about to be killed." A few moments later he was lowered over the side of the ship to the waiting tugboat that ferried him to Ellis Island.[91] He remained in the psychiatric hospital there for a few days until Samuel Littman enlisted a wealthy New York Pythian, Louis S. Barnard, to post the bond for him. At the same time, Littman signed a contract requiring HIAS and the Knights of Pythias to each reimburse one half of the amount in the event of the loss of the bond.[92] By April 10, Nathan Cohen was transferred to Holbrook Farms, also known as MacFarland's Sanitarium, at Green Farms, Connecticut, where he was admitted as a patient.[93]

MACFARLAND'S ASYLUM

Nathan Cohen's time at MacFarland's Sanitarium is somewhat of a mystery. Samuel Littman was in regular contact with the doctors at the institution, but most of their correspondence revolved around payment for Cohen's stay there. McFarland's was a private mental health institution located near Westport. Just after Cohen arrived, Dr. McFarland agree to lower the rate charged to Cohen from $10 to $7 per week because Cohen was a "ward" of the Free Synagogue. HIAS paid McFarland's directly, but then got reimbursed for half of the expenses by the Knights of Pythias.[94] Along with his reports on Cohen's health, McFarland would ask Littman to send provisions for Cohen. "The patient is sadly in need of clothing, please send some shorts, underwear, socks, collars, hat, a pair of shoes and a pair of trousers."[95] A few days later Littman sent a package of clothes to the sanitarium, and over the course of the next few months, Littman sent tobacco and a pipe and paid for Cohen to be fitted for eyeglasses.[96]

Dr. McFarland indicated that Cohen's health was improving, but the vagueness of his reports make it unclear why he was still being held at the institution. By mid-May, just a month after being admitted, McFarland wrote to say, "Nathan Cohen is doing as well as can be expected under the circumstances in fact he begins to show signs of improvement."[97] Two months later, on July 4, McFarland wrote again to say that Cohen was eating and sleeping better. "Mentally, he appears bright, and does little odd jobs around such as sweeping his room. He is still mentally deficient at times and has a tendency to stay in one position for a long time if allowed."[98] These periodic updates were then forwarded to the Knights of Pythias representative in New York, William Grossman.[99] In November, McFarland sent news that Cohen's physical and mental outlook had improved, but he also argued that he needed to remain at the sanitarium for a full recovery. "While the improvement is not a decidedly great one, Mr. Cohen can now answer questions more intelligently than when he was first admitted here. There is still improvement needed to make him a most useful member of society." This report suggested that Cohen had begun speaking and answering questions. One possible reason that McFarland would recommend keeping him at the sanitarium in spite of his improvement would be to continue to get paid for his institutionalization. At the end of the letter explaining Cohen's lackluster improvement, McFarland politely requested payment: "We would very much like to have a remittance from you."[100]

From very early on, Littman tried to enlist Knights of Pythias members living near Westport to visit Cohen.[101] While it is not clear that ever happened, Littman decided to pay Cohen a visit on Thanksgiving. Littman described Cohen as "improved considerably," and he was even able to discuss his "financial troubles as well as his domestic troubles which brought on his present condition." It is clear from this meeting that at this point Cohen wanted to be released from the sanitarium. He emphasized to Littman his reputation for "honesty" and indicated that he had never "harmed anyone." Littman wrote, Cohen "expressed a desire to be released from the Sanatarium so that he could find some employment outside so that he may not be dependent on anyone for assistance." Dr. Henersey told Littman that, although Cohen was better, it would "take quite a long time before he could take his place in Society."[102] For whatever reason, the doctors at McFarland's wanted to retain Cohen, even though he was lucid, had improved both physically and mentally, and expressed a desire to leave the institution.

Littman wrote to Dr. Henersey on December 28 asking to allow Cohen's brother to visit him in the sanitarium.[103] It is not clear who this brother is, whether it was Gabriel Jaffe, the brother-in-law, or one of the Knights of Pythias "brothers." In any case, there is no further reference to such a visit. The Knights of Pythias were busy in the next few months gathering evidence to allow Cohen to be released and transferred to Baltimore so he could be put in a hospital there. There were no more reports from McFarland's after early December 1915 and apparently no visits from HIAS or the Knights of Pythias. The last page of an undated letter from HIAS to an unknown recipient provides one more clue about Cohen's state at McFarland's. Someone from HIAS, perhaps Littman, reported on Cohen's paranoia. "It seems that he is still very much in fear of something unknown. He spends a great deal of his time walking and at farm labor."[104] And then suddenly on March 3, 1916, Littman received word from the sanitarium that Nathan Cohen was dead.[105]

Upon learning of Cohen's death, Littman immediately sent a telegram to the Knights of Pythias in Jacksonville asking if they wanted Cohen's body shipped there or would rather he be buried in New York City.[106] The Davis Lodge wrote back to say that they would prefer a New York funeral.[107]

According to the Pythians, Cohen died from pneumonia, although the death certificate lists pulmonary related disease as the secondary cause of death.[108] The Pythians wanted to make Cohen's case and his funeral an example of the fraternal order's benevolence. Even though Cohen had long ceased paying his dues, they recognized him as a fellow brother and agreed to share in the cost of his maintenance as well as his funeral expenses. As one New York Pythian wrote to the Jacksonville Lodge, "It is indeed too bad that when on the road to recovery he should have passed away so quickly. However, your Lodge can proudly have the conviction that it has acted in true Pythian spirit toward our late brother Cohen."[109]

After Cohen's death, Martha Rezenstein, the HIAS representative in Baltimore, reached out to Gabriel, Nathan's brother-in-law, to inform him of Nathan's death and to ask him to share the sad news with Cohen's sister. Gabriel pleaded with HIAS not to tell his wife about her brother's death because "She is still *very* nervous and any little excitement might cause another flare up."[110]

FUNERAL

Nathan Cohen's body arrived by train at Grand Central station in New York City. Judge Leon Sanders, president of HIAS, was at the station to meet the body and accompany the casket to the Richmond Cemetery in Staten Island. Several newspapers ran lengthy stories about the funeral and Cohen's life, portraying Cohen as a pitiable person, while recognizing that he had achieved a status as a kind of ur-immigrant. A *Tribune* secondary headline declared ironically, "Jew All Nations Scorned Now Sure of Place in Land He Longed For." The story described Cohen as an isolated wanderer, but one who had found sympathizers. "Without a home to miss him and without a relative to shed a tear at his grave, the shuttlecock of the sea was committed to the friendly earth with what was far from a pauper's funeral." The absence of family and friends suggested Cohen's loneliness; even so, in attendance at his funeral were sixty people from HIAS and the Knights of Pythias, some of whom were fairly prominent citizens. The superintendent of HIAS emphasized the absence of Cohen's relatives in attendance or even anyone who knew Cohen before his onset of insanity. At the same time, he noted that it was a dignified burial. "There were about sixty of us, officers of the society, immigration authorities and sympathizers. We took the body to Richmond Cemetery where we had made arrangements to bury him just as his folks might have done." In his eulogy, Judge Sanders spoke about everything that HIAS and the Knights of Pythias had done for the "unfortunate wanderer," but he also mentioned "what more could have been done for him had he lived." Sanders asked for "pardon of the dead for aught that we overlooked that we might have done." The Rabbi I. L. Siegel emphasized the idea of the wandering Jew who fought to "find a home in free America." The ironic idea of his grave being a home highlighted the struggle he had to make a home in "free America." The rabbi told the sixty congregants, "At last he had found a final abode in the land that had so often closed its door in his face." " 'The wanderer . . . had found at last his rest.' "[111]

Millions of immigrants like Nathan Cohen chose to come to the United States to seek a better life, but the reality they found did not always match their fantasies. Hard work, misfortune, and discrimination, particularly against Jews, Italians, Mexicans, and others not considered white, or white enough, made it hard to settle in this new land. The very process of migration, together with the obstacles of integrating into a hostile society, may have led to depression and other forms of mental illness. That so many immigrants ended up behind bars in insane asylums in the first half of the twentieth century suggests not only the difficulties faced by immigrants but also the inability of US society to deal with cultural difference. The insane asylum was supposed to be a therapeutic environment to rehabilitate people and make them healthier, but these institutions were often just prisons where people could be locked up indefinitely and disappear.

From the beginning of the twentieth century up to the 1960s, the insane asylum was a much larger part of the carceral regime than prisons or jails. Both immigrants and citizens were locked up in such institutions at rates that rival the rates of incarceration in jails and prisons today. Far more significant than the low numbers of immigrants held in detention facilities in this era, the insane asylum was the carceral institution where most foreigners could be found. Therefore, to the extent that scholars have focused on immigration detention facilities and glossed over mental hospitals, they have dramatically underestimated the size of alien incarceration in the first part of the twentieth century. During World War II, tens of thousands of other foreigners, some of whom had not come willingly to the United States, would be deemed "enemy aliens" and find themselves locked up in immigration detention facilities.

CHAPTER 3

Japanese Peruvian Enemy Aliens during World War II

It was a cramped hole dug into the ground beneath the floor planks in the bedroom, barely enough room for a cot, a small table, and a short-wave radio. For more than year, Seiichi Higashide secreted himself away in this underground cubicle for an hour at a time whenever anyone suspicious entered the house. His young daughter Elsa remembered, when she opened the plank, "that smelly dirt smell, very musky and very kind of damp smell would come up."[1] Higashide was hiding from the police who had issued a warrant for his deportation in March 1942. After several months with no visits from police or strangers, Higashide began to let his guard down. On January 6, 1944, Seiichi, his wife, and four young children, along with his wife's parents, two nannies, and some company employees, went for a picnic next to the spectacular green waters of Lake Huacachina, in southwestern Peru. The family returned late that evening to the coastal town of Ica and settled in for their evening meal when they heard a knock at the door.[2] Their leisurely Sunday family outing at a natural oasis in the middle of the desert would be their last respite from years of incarceration in prisons spanning the Americas, from Peru to Panama to Texas and New Jersey.

Four Lima police officers and one local detective burst into the house and announced that Seiichi Higashide was under arrest. In this incredibly tense moment, Higashide calmly asked the police to wait outside until he finished his meal and changed his clothes. In his autobiography, Higashide noted this small act of non-compliance. "It is said that even rats in desperate circumstances fight back; I also needed to put up some resistance."[3]

In a 2012 interview, his daughter Elsa remembered how her mother carefully labeled all of the linens with her husband's name so that he could have fresh sheets in jail. "It was a turmoil. And I remember feeling scared, but we didn't know what war is or was. It's just that here these strange people are coming to get Father, and he didn't do anything bad. But it was being done." Elsa was traumatized seeing her father, who had home-schooled her and who she describes in Japanese as *otokorashii* (very manly), abducted from the family home. More than sixty years later she still recalls how she cried into the thick velvet drapes when her father was arrested. That traumatic experience turned her into a gloomy child.[4]

Seiichi Higashide was not an agent of the Japanese emperor or a pro-Axis immigrant. In fact, having dodged the military draft in Japan, authorities there considered him a wanted criminal. And yet he and more than 1,800 other Japanese Peruvians got caught up in a wave of anti-Japanese hysteria that led to their kidnapping, forced migration, and incarceration in hastily erected camps in Texas and New Mexico.[5] Higashide and his family ended up incarcerated in an Immigration and Naturalization Service (INS) detention facility in Texas alongside thousands of other foreigners in numerous camps spread across the US Southwest. Although they were deemed "enemy aliens" by the US government, the Japanese, Germans, and Italians kidnapped from Latin America were not placed in War Relocation Authority (WRA) concentration camps with the 120,000 Japanese and Japanese American residents in the US West. Rather, these Latin American residents were incarcerated as "illegal aliens" in immigration facilities. Higashide's story reveals the intersection between US empire, national security, and immigrant detention. Immigration laws provided the legal justification for an international kidnapping program.

Once arrested, Higashide spent the night in a local jail, but he refused to be transported in a paddy wagon, choosing instead to hire a taxi to bring him and his armed escort to Lima. His wife and four children watched as his taxi left Ica. A young Nisei (born in the Americas of Japanese descent) employee of Higashide's store grasped his hand through the taxi window and began to "cry unabashedly." It was this same employee who inadvertently opened the door to the Higashide's home the night before, allowing the police to enter while the family was dining. As Higashide's taxi drove off, he could hear the small group in front of his shop shout out "Adiós, sayonara." Even though Higashide was a prisoner, he continued to make demands, insisting that his driver stop so he could bid farewell to a few friends and even have his photograph taken at a studio so his family could keep his portrait in his absence.[6] Elsa still treasures this photograph of her father who looks younger than his thirty-five years as he stares directly at the camera.

Figure 3.1 Seiichi Higashide, photograph taken the day of his arrest just before he was taken to Lima.
Source: Courtesy of Elsa Kudo.

"No matter what angle you looked at him," she said, "he looked like he was looking at you."[7] When he arrived at the police headquarters in Lima, he was told, "You will be held here for a while," but he was given no further explanation about why he was arrested. The police placed Higashide in a bare cell without a toilet; prisoners were forced to urinate and defecate on the floors where they slept. The prison food had "an indescribable odor" that made him want to vomit, but fortunately someone in the Japanese community arranged for the Japanese prisoners to get Japanese-style lunch boxes delivered every day.[8]

After almost two weeks, on January 18, 1944, Higashide was taken to the port of Callao and forcibly marched up a gangway flanked by armed American soldiers to a US military ship. Although Peruvian police made the initial arrests, this was a US government operation. Once aboard the ship, passengers were strip-searched and all of their belongings were examined. An officer read a lengthy list of rules and regulations in Spanish and explained that any violation would result in severe punishment. Then they were ordered down into the hold of the ship, the heavy doors clanging shut behind them. At this point, Higashide finally realized that he had become a prisoner of war. "Locked within its hold," he wrote, "I suddenly became very angry. I had earlier felt a deep hatred toward wars, but now I grew angry at the cowardliness of the Peruvian government." Higashide's fury was directed at the United States as well for this violation of his "human rights." Higashide had admired the nation, but this experience soured him. "Where was the spirit of individual rights and justice that had filled the Declaration of Independence and the US Constitution?" Higashide asked. "If I termed Peru, even provisionally, a 'third rate country,' was not America, in this instance, no different?"[9]

ADIÓS TO TEARS

In 1981, Seiichi Higashide, then living in Hawaii, wrote his memoirs at the urging of his children. In 1993, they had the manuscript translated from Japanese into Spanish and English, appearing under the title *Adiós to Tears: The Memoirs of a Japanese-Peruvian Internee in U.S. Concentration Camps*.[10] Although there are voluminous records about the Japanese Peruvian internees in the US National Archives and in Peruvian archives, none of those government records provides a window into the subjective experience of being kidnapped and forcibly placed in a detention camp. Higashide's memoir and interviews with his daughter Elsa Kudo, along with the legal and bureaucratic records relating to the incarceration of Japanese Peruvians during World War II, reveal how this group of people was rendered stateless, unwanted by Peru, distant from war-torn Japan, and seen as "enemy aliens" by the United States. Some of them were Japanese citizens who had resided in Peru for decades; others had married Peruvians and become naturalized Peruvian citizens, and many of the children, like Elsa and her siblings, were natural-born Peruvian citizens. As stateless people, they, and the families who followed them, found themselves locked in indefinite detention in isolated camps in the US Southwest, unsure if or when they would ever regain their freedom.

Historians who have written about the Japanese Latin American and German Latin American internees during World War II tend to place the Latin American enemy alien program in the context of diplomacy and for-eign relations during the war; internees and their families, however, have written their own accounts or given interviews about their experience, presenting it from a very different perspective.[11] While the diplomatic context is crucial for understanding this program, and the personal ac-counts reveal what detention felt like, this chapter focuses on the ways in which Japanese Peruvians were criminalized as immigrants, albeit as forced immigrants. Even though none of them chose to come to the United States, they were charged with illegal entry. Since the Japanese

Latin Americans were not US citizens, they have generally been relegated to footnotes in the history of Japanese American internment and are almost completely absent from the histories of US immigration because they do not fit the profile of the typical immigrant. Putting the Japanese Latin Americans back into immigration history reveals the limits of freedom for people who were forcibly brought to the United States, and then denied redress in courts or by legislative action because they had been labeled "illegal aliens."

Unlike the Chinese locked up on McNeil Island and Nathan Cohen's endless purgatory on a ship, the Japanese Peruvians were declared enemy aliens, and national security was invoked as the underlying reason for their detention. However, war was also an issue in Cohen's plight since it was the shifting borders between Russia and Germany during World War I in addition to his mental illness that rendered Cohen virtually stateless. Wartime has a way of creating stateless people who are then exposed to arbitrary and absolute state power to cage such people indefinitely. The case of the Japanese Peruvians is unique in that they had not chosen to come to the United States like the other migrants in this book; instead, they were forcibly removed from their homes and shipped to the United States at gunpoint.

SEIICHI ESCAPES POVERTY IN JAPAN

In a photograph before he left Japan, Seiichi Higashide, then twenty years old, has a soft, youthful face, wears his hair carefully cropped, and sports a natty bow tie and a light-toned suit. Five years earlier, he had left his small village in Hokkaido to escape the grinding poverty of the countryside. His village was so remote that doctors barely visited. Higashide's two elder brothers succumbed to illnesses when they were still babies. While parents toiled in the fields, they bound their infants to baskets and left them for hours at a time without milk or water. Higashide describes seeing snow falling on the half-naked bodies of Korean laborers constructing irrigation embankments; his father explained that the workers were not allowed to wear clothes to motivate them to work harder. These young Koreans had been deceived by promises of high wages, and they found themselves barely making a living and confined to "detention huts." "They had been robbed of their freedom," Higashide would later write. The memory of these laborers tormented Higashide and motivated him to leave his hometown at the age of fifteen and move to Sapporo.[12] It would not have occurred to him that fifteen years later, he would be the foreign laborer toiling in the field and confined to a detention camp surrounded by barbed wire. He went halfway around the world to escape the exploitation he saw in his hometown, only to be subjected to it himself.

After a couple of years studying and working in Sapporo, Higashide traveled to Tokyo with his sister, who had been convalescing from a difficult pregnancy in their village. In Tokyo, Higashide toiled all day in manual labor jobs and studied at a technical school at night, hoping to one day become an engineer or an architect. He dreamed of going to the United States, but Japanese immigration had been banned since the early twentieth century, and so his remaining options were emigrating to China, Southeast Asia, or South America. Having read about the success of the Japanese community in Peru, the largest outside of the United States, he began studying Spanish and set his sights on the South American country. With a 150 yen gift from one of his professors, Higashide was finally able to purchase a ticket on a steamer bound for the port of Callao.[13]

Seiichi Higashide arrived in Peru alone, with few savings and with a passport he managed to obtain by forging a job offer from the Japanese Overseas Development Corporation. When he disembarked from the *Heiyo Maru* at the busy port in Callao, he was met by a contact in the Japanese community who brought him to Cañete, where he found employment as a "working guest" with the Araki family. The Araki family imported lumber from North America and sold food supplies to the Chinese and Japanese contract workers at the large haciendas in the region. Higashide worked a variety of jobs for the Araki company, including delivering vermicelli noodles to the haciendas, doing unskilled carpentry, and drafting architectural drawings. Although he was not a low-paid "contract laborer," neither was he entirely free, having tied himself to the Araki family business.[14] This working guest category lay somewhere between indentured servitude and free laborer.

Several months after arriving in Peru, Higashide was summoned to appear before the Japanese Consul in Lima. The consul informed him that he would be sent back to Japan for the crime of evading military service. Higashide begged the consul not to send him back and miraculously, the consul agreed. The consul simply told Japanese authorities that he hadn't been able to locate the draft dodger. Higashide later learned that local police in Japan had questioned his neighbors and searched for him in his hometown for several years. Given his neglect for one of the three obligations of Japanese subjects, Higashide had, in his own words, become a "'noncitizen' and a felon."[15]

Within a decade, Higashide rose from being a working guest, to teacher, manager of a business, and finally a successful clothing store owner in Ica, a coastal town 300 kilometers south of Lima. In 1938, he was elected president of the Japanese Association in Ica. His prominence there as a merchant, and especially his friendship with the local police chief, provided a modicum of protection for him and his family. His daughter Elsa could not remember facing any discrimination as a person of Japanese descent in Ica.[16] All signs pointed to a prosperous future in Peru.

Then on December 24, 1941, Higashide's name suddenly appeared in Peru's two leading newspapers as one of thirty Axis nationals on the Proclaimed List, a black list compiled by the US government. By the middle of March 1942 he was ordered deported, but he was told to remain in the local area until the order could be executed.[17] The Proclaimed List of Certain Blocked Nationals was first issued by the State Department in July 1941 as part of economic warfare on businesses that were perceived to be pro-Axis. Compiled based on information from US diplomats, Rockefeller's Office of the Coordinator of Inter-American Affairs, and the British government, the list was recognized, even at the time, as notoriously inaccurate. Although Higashide did not appear on the first 1941 roster, his name showed up on the first supplemental blacklist a few months later.[18]

On February 22, 1943, a friend in Lima called Higashide to let him know that detectives were headed his way. "Please be careful," the friend warned. Higashide ran around Ica to let his friends know they were in danger, and then he returned to his shop. When the detective arrived, Higashide pretended to be a customer, and his wife told the detective that he wasn't there. In spite of threats to arrest her, she held fast to her story when the detective returned later in the evening. The local police chief had seen Higashide enter his house that day, but the police chief kept his silence and did not inform the detectives from Lima. The detectives eventually left that night with two other Japanese men who were on their list.[19]

Higashide remained in hiding in his own house, with his wife and children telling neighbors that he had gone missing the night the detectives showed up. After almost a year in hiding, Higashide believed the danger had passed. Even though everything seemed to have returned to normal, Higashide always had the threat of deportation in the back of his mind. And then on January 6, 1944, detectives knocked on the door of his house while his family was eating their Sunday dinner. This time he could not escape.[20] By the time of his arrest, Higashide had been living in Peru for fourteen years, was married to a natural-born Peruvian citizen, and had four children, with another on the way, all Peruvian citizens.

Higashide's wife, Angelica Shizuka, was born in Cañete, Peru, to parents who had emigrated from Japan. Higashide met the thirteen- or

Figure 3.2 Seiichi Higashide and Angelica Shizuka wedding, March 7, 1935, Cañete, Peru.
Source: Courtesy of Elsa Kudo.

fourteen-year-old Angelica when he was delivering noodles to the sundry shop owned by her family on the Arona hacienda in Cañete.[21] The Cañete valley was the epicenter of the worst massacre of Chinese in the Americas, when Black and mestizo peasants brutally killed up to 1,700 Chinese laborers in 1881 during the War of the Pacific (1879–1893).[22] Even several decades after the massacre, it's hard to imagine that there would not be lingering tensions between people of Asian descent and other Peruvians. Seiichi began to date Angelica, who was known in the Japanese community as a "very attractive and likable young girl." Her protective parents sent a chaperone on their dates. A few years later, Seiichi and Angelica got married. Their wedding reception without alcohol was such a novelty that newspapers in Peru and Japan carried the story.[23]

Unlike Seiichi whose autobiography provides a detailed description of his perspective, his wife Angelica left no journal or memoir to explain how she experienced life in Peru, her husband's arrest and deportation, or her own journey to a detention camp in Texas. Angelica's daughter Elsa describes her mother as tremendously resourceful and creative, bleaching her baby's diapers and reusing them to make dresses for her older daughters.[24] Although Angelica was principally a homemaker in the United

States, in Peru it was she who welcomed people to the family store while Seiichi educated the children at home.[25]

ENEMY ALIENS

In the 1920s, Argentine author Manuel Ugarte cited a Central American newspaper that quipped that a US-led pan-Americanism would be like "a congress of mice presided over by a cat."[26] In the mid-1930s, Franklin Delano Roosevelt's Good Neighbor policy sought to shift an overtly interventionist relationship with Latin America to a partnership for the defense of the hemisphere. The cat might have put on new clothes, but for Latin Americans, it was still the bad neighbor they knew quite well. Thus, in spite of the United States' efforts to move away from the historically imperialist role it had played in Latin America, the hegemon continued to dominate the hemisphere, supporting friendly dictatorships and opposing regimes that pushed for national self-determination. Even before World War II broke out, US officials had begun to discuss issues of hemispheric security with Latin American governments, in particular the potential dangers posed by foreign nationals working and living in Latin America. After the bombing of Pearl Harbor on December 7, 1941, the United States felt an increased urgency in tracking and detaining Axis nationals throughout the hemisphere. When Franklin Roosevelt issued an executive order to move all people of Japanese ancestry from the West Coast to internment camps, US diplomats also requested that their allies in Latin America keep an eye on their Japanese, German, and Italian residents, some of whom had acquired citizenship in the countries where they lived, and to identify potential "enemy aliens."[27] While they did not dictate to Latin American governments what they should do, US hegemony made it hard for many Latin American countries to refuse a request from their neighbor in the North.

The Pan American Union (the precursor to the 1948 Organization of American States) emerged in the late nineteenth century just as the United States began to extend its power beyond its own borders. This hemispheric political body convened the first meeting of the Emergency Advisory Committee of Political Defense on April 15, 1942, but efforts to round up Axis nationals were already well under way in Panama, Peru, and elsewhere before that meeting.[28] The Committee's Resolution XX, passed in May 1943, provided for "the continuous detention, for the duration of the present emergency, of all dangerous nationals of member States of the Tripartite Pact . . . who reside within their territories." The agreement not only authorized setting up camps for "dangerous nationals" but it also legitimized "expulsion or deportation" to other countries where detention camps could be established. The same committee report recognized that 6,500 such detentions had already occurred in sixteen American countries, and another 2,000 people had been deported to the United States.[29] Peru in particular jumped on the deportation bandwagon, receiving $29 million in US armaments and munitions and import-export credits for its coopera- tion.[30] In addition to the money, anti-Japanese sentiment in Peru gave the government an added incentive to accede to US wishes and expel Japanese Peruvians. In other words, this is not just a story of US power but also of how Latin American countries had their own nationalist and internal pressures to expel people of Japanese, German, and Italian descent. In the case of the Japanese, racist stereotypes of Asians as diseased, thrifty, and conniving were fertile ground to sow the seed for mass deportations.[31]

By 1940, there were more than 25,000 Japanese citizens in Peru, 21,000 in Lima alone. Japanese were visible in Lima because they tended to congre- gate in particular neighborhoods, and even though they became the largest group of foreigners in the country, they still represented less than three- tenths of 1 percent of Peru's total populace. In spite of these small num- bers, native white Peruvians exaggerated the numbers, and Peru responded by restricting Japanese migration in 1927 to those invited by Japanese residents already in the country. In 1936, Peru issued a supreme decree that capped foreign-born people in the country at 16,000 per country, thus effectively ending new Japanese migration since the Japanese community already exceeded that limit. Peru also began charging high reentry fees for Japanese residents who left and then returned to Peru and prohibited the entry of "racial groups," an ambiguously worded clause that was under- stood to refer to Asians.[32] In addition to limiting Japanese immigration, the government prohibited the selling of Japanese newspapers in Spanish translation. By 1940, only one of five Japanese language newspapers was still published in Peru.[33] Although the Nikkei (Japanese diaspora commu- nity) had been contract workers in the earlier part of the twentieth cen- tury, by 1940 most were merchants or exporters of raw cotton. By many accounts it was a thriving community.[34]

The economic success of the Japanese community combined with a rising tide of nationalism in the 1930s led to growing anti-Japanese senti- ment in Peru. Peruvian president Manuel Prado supported anti-Japanese policies and gave Washington his full support in combating the supposed fifth-column threat. Meanwhile, the leftist and formerly anti-imperialist Alianza Popular Revolucionaria Americana (APRA) Party began to court US support after 1938 by touting their anti-Japanese sentiments. APRA's party newspaper ran headlines such as "We do not want to be Japanese" and argued that the Germans and Japanese in Peru were forming a fifth column.[35] In 1943, former senator and anti-Japanese activist Manuel Seoane expressed his distrust for Japanese Peruvians, claiming they were inassimilable. "Even Peruvian-born children of Japanese immigrants," Seoane wrote, "were in reality 'Japs' in their spirit, their organization, will and customs."[36] US war diplomacy must be understood within this context of Peru's restrictions on Japanese migration, disenfranchisement of Japanese Peruvians, and popular xenophobic attacks on the Japanese community in Lima.

In addition to restricting entry of new Japanese immigrants, the government moved to strip Japanese Peruvian children of their citizenship and to limit the Japanese ability to acquire naturalized citizenship. A year after the 1936 decree, the government passed another restriction, preventing children born to Japanese parents after 1936 from becoming citizens. In 1940, minors who returned to their parents' home countries for education or military training lost their Peruvian citizenship. This particular restriction only applied to *jus sanguinis* (blood citizenship) countries, in this case only Japan. Furthermore, the state began to recognize only Peruvian marriages as legal. Although Peru was still a country that recognized *jus solis* (birthright citizenship), it tried to deny children of Japanese descent this privilege. This series of laws and decrees were all designed to strip Japanese Peruvians of their rights and thus force them to leave. Japanese diplomats fought these restrictions and particularly the exorbitant fees charged to Japanese Peruvians who were returning to Peru, but the Peruvian government was unmoved.[37]

At the same time the government was restricting the rights of Japanese Peruvians, popular anti-Japanese sentiment erupted into a massive outburst of violence against the Japanese in Lima and Callao as well as a couple of agricultural centers. The incident was provoked in May 1940 when the Japanese consulate attempted to repatriate a Japanese Peruvian, Tokijiro Furuya, who had been involved in a power struggle within the Japanese Barber's Trade Association. A Peruvian woman, Marta Acosta, was badly beaten and later died during the attempt to kidnap and expel Furuya, provoking Peruvian teenage students to stage an anti-Japanese march in Lima. The student-led protestors attacked and looted 600 Japanese businesses and homes in downtown Lima. Hundreds of Japanese were injured and ten were killed in the riot in which police refused to step in to stop the violence. The Japanese consul estimated the damages at several million US dollars, but more than the property destruction, the violent outburst left a permanent mark on the memory of the Japanese Peruvian community.

Seiichi Higashide was living in Ica at the time, and he toured the town with the local police chief to ensure the peace after hearing reports of violence. Although Ica remained peaceful, Higashide noted that in Lima "the destruction was so complete that there were no targets left. . . . Almost all Japanese-owned shops in the city were destroyed." As a result of the riots, 54 families comprising more than 300 people were forced to return to Japan.[38] Anthropologist Ayumi Takenaka described the violence, known as *el saqueo* (the pillaging), as the "worst rioting in Peruvian history."[39] The *saqueo* was thus motivated by racial antipathy against the Japanese as well as "yellow peril" discourses about Japanese military aggression.[40] By the time the United States began to lobby Peru to round up its dangerous Japanese residents for deportation, Peru was happy to comply. By deporting Japanese Peruvians, the government both appeased anti-Japanese nationalist sentiment and placated a major foreign benefactor.

In November 1942, when the Pan American Union's Emergency Advisory Committee advocated removing citizenship from those Axis nationals who had fraudulently obtained their citizenship, the Peruvian government eagerly obeyed.[41] In addition to their effort to strip Germans and Japanese of their Peruvian citizenship, Peru also facilitated the deportation of many naturalized and native-born Peruvian citizens. Seiichi Higashide's four children and wife, for example, all Peruvian citizens, ended up in US detention camps during the war. Adult males were almost always the ones who were forcibly deported, while the wives and children joined their husbands "voluntarily." As Elsa Kudo said, the word "voluntary" was very questionable. "I mean you volunteered because your father was taken."[42] About half of the 2,118 Japanese Latin Americans who ended up in US detention camps were forcibly taken, and the other half were family members who joined their fathers or husbands later.[43] All told, more than 6,400 Japanese, Germans, and Italians living in twelve other Latin American countries were detained under the wartime Enemy Alien Control Program.[44] While there were legitimate though usually overblown fears of Nazi infiltrations throughout the Americas, there was little evidence that Japan had sent nearly the same number of its agents to the Americas.[45] In any case, it is clear that the vast majority of people who were deported or detained in Latin America were not working for Axis powers but were simply prominent people within their communities.

Seiichi Higashide had a flourishing business, had been named president of the Ica Japanese Association, and importantly had established contacts within the Peruvian elite. Higashide was surprised to see his name on the initial black list of thirty "dangerous Axis nationals" published in Peruvian newspapers *El Comercio* and *La Prensa*. Higashide did not consider himself so important that he would be one of ten Japanese on the list, but he later surmised that he was included because of his contacts with the local Peruvian establishment. Later blacklists included more businessmen, but this initial group seemed to target people who were presumed to have political influence.[46] While the United States used its hegemonic power in the hemisphere to push such policies on its neighbors, Peruvians had their own domestic reasons for wanting to eliminate and marginalize the Japanese Peruvian community. Deep-seated racism and economic competition led many Peruvians to denounce their neighbors to the police.[47]

The enemy alien program in Latin America ended up incarcerating 8,500 people of Japanese, German, and Italian descent in local detention centers, and deporting to the United States 4,058 individuals of German descent, 2,264 of Japanese descent, and 287 of Italian descent.[48] US officials screened suspected enemy aliens and recommended deportation for those for whom there was supposedly "sufficient" evidence based on their intelligence reports. Others would be detained in Latin America, and if evidence later emerged, they too would be deported.[49]

The Latin American program was only a small part of a much larger effort to incarcerate Axis nationals in the United States. The Enemy Alien Internment Program (1941–46) imprisoned more than 31,000 suspected enemy aliens. Unlike the internment of over 120,000 Japanese and Japanese Americans, which was overseen by the War Relocation Authority, the Enemy Alien Internment Program was led by the Immigration and Naturalization Service (INS) and administered by Border Patrol agents.[50] The key distinction between those caught domestically and placed in internment camps versus those who were transported from Latin America is that the people in the latter group were labeled "illegal aliens" and were incarcerated by the INS, a bureau under the Department of Justice. Although neither the Japanese Americans in War Relocation camps nor the Japanese Latin Americans in INS camps received due process protections of the US Constitution, in 1988 the US government admitted that it had violated the rights of Japanese Americans while still maintaining that the Japanese Latin Americans had no such rights.

The Latin American enemy alien program reaffirmed the absolute power of the president to conduct foreign affairs as he saw fit. Although constitutional protections applied within the United States, even for undocumented immigrants, the Supreme Court held that no such protections extended to the exercise of state power beyond its own territory. In *US v. Curtiss-Wright Export Corp.* (1936), the Supreme Court upheld the idea of sovereignty as extra-constitutional and a byproduct of nationality itself.[51] The president, therefore, according to this ruling, was not bound by the

Constitution in matters of foreign affairs. In contrast to the president's acts in foreign affairs, the executive cannot violate individual rights in the domestic context; these protections apply to all people in the United States, not just citizens. In 1800, James Madison articulated this principle, arguing that since aliens are bound by the law and the constitution, these individuals "are entitled, in return to their protection and advantage."[52] The question about whether constitutional protections applied to refugees who had entered the country but were deemed to still be on the country's threshold would be a source of controversy for the next fifty years and the subject of intense litigation. There was no question, however, of whether US law allowed the government to kidnap, jail, or kill people in other countries. According to the courts, that was entirely an executive prerogative over which they had no jurisdiction. Extraterritorial killings are usually carried out in the context of a declared war, but there is also a long history of CIA peacetime assassinations prior to a 1976 law prohibiting such acts, and even afterward.[53]

Wartime executive authority is perhaps the strongest of executive sovereign powers, and it was precisely this power that was invoked in the case of the Japanese Peruvians. The 1798 Alien Enemy Act granted broad authority to the president to arrest, detain, and deport foreign nationals of countries with which the United States was at war. President Woodrow Wilson had also invoked the act to intern "enemy aliens" during World War I. Although courts indicated that the government had the burden of proving the suspected people were enemy aliens, they also refused judicial review in such cases. Thus, by the time of the seizure of Japanese Peruvians, the principle that "enemy aliens" could be incarcerated without any judicial procedure was well established.[54]

Even though the 1798 Enemy Aliens Act gave the president wide latitude, he would still need to assert that the people being detained were, in fact, dangerous enemies. Japanese American internees were not specifically accused of subversion, nor were they aliens within the United States and thus should not have been considered enemy aliens. In the case of Japanese Peruvians, the act did not authorize the United States government to seize people abroad, nor did it allow for the arrest of people who were not nationals of an enemy nation. Given that many of the Japanese Peruvians were in fact Peruvian citizens, a friendly nation, the Alien Enemy Act should not have applied to them. The courts turned a blind eye to the legality of the arrests of Japanese Peruvians and other Axis nationals in Latin America, calling the question of how they arrived in the country "neither important nor controlling."[55] The presumption was that the "constitution can have no operation in another country," and even in US colonies or protectorates controlled by the United States, courts ruled in the Insular Cases that the Constitution does not "follow the flag."[56] Edward Ennis, chief of the Alien Enemy Control Unit, argued in a 1942 memo that the government's authority to intern alien enemies "is [no] less over those brought here involuntarily from another country than over residents." Not only did the courts affirm Ennis's interpretation but they also noted that such action taken under the Alien Enemy Act was unreviewable by the court.[57] Finally, in addition to being subject to the Alien Enemy Act, Japanese Peruvians were also detained under immigration laws once they landed in the United States, being determined to be illegally in the country since they lacked passports and visas.[58] As one INS official commented at the time, "Only in wartime could we get away with such fancy skullduggery."[59] In short, Japanese Peruvians were abducted from Peru under the aegis of the Enemy Alien Act, but then incarcerated in the United States for violating US immigration law.

Notwithstanding the tortured legal arguments for kidnapping and then detaining Axis nationals and Latin Americans of Japanese, German, and Italian descent, the US government had a secret ulterior motive, which was to use the detainees as pawns in a prisoner-exchange program with Axis powers.[60] In October 1942, Secretary of State Cordell Hull referred to the plan to exchange German and Japanese Latin American internees for US nationals in Europe. However, he was reticent to accept all 50,000 Japanese Peruvians due to the expense and logistical problems of incarcerating such a large number of people.[61] So while intending to use the Japanese Peruvians and other Axis nationals as bargaining chips, Hull didn't want to end up with too many chips in storage. Roosevelt's chief of staff, George Marshall, sent a coded secret message in December 1942, explaining that 1,000 Japanese and 250 Germans detained in Latin America were intended to be "used for exchange with interned American civilian nationals."[62] The level of cooperation differed among the Latin American nations; Mexico and Venezuela were loath to hand over Axis nationals without strict guarantees that they would be repatriated, whereas Central American and Caribbean countries seemed happy to follow US directives. As one memo from the Special War Problems Division put it, "We could repatriate them, we could intern them or we could hold them in escrow for bargaining purposes."[63]

The deportation program in Latin America was run out of US embassies, with the help of FBI agents whom Congress had authorized to do nonmilitary investigations in the Western Hemisphere.[64] The head of the FBI, J. Edgar Hoover, helped to spread rumors of a 6,000 man Japanese "suicide" squad that intended to attack northern Peru. Believing these reports, President Roosevelt and Vice President Henry Wallace claimed that the "impenetrable" Japanese Peruvian community "live and work like an organized Army."[65] In Peru, third secretary in the US Embassy John K. Emerson, a diplomat with expertise on Japan, and the only US official who spoke Japanese, led the deportations. At the time, Emerson believed that the Japanese Peruvians represented an underestimated fifth column in the hemisphere, but thirty-five years later he admitted that they had found "no reliable evidence of planned or contemplated acts of sabotage, subversion or espionage."[66] However, given that Peruvian businessmen had an interest in denouncing their economic competitors, many of the Japanese Peruvians who ended up on the list of deportees had no record of pro-Axis activities. The bad information used to create the deportation lists meant that the deportation program was failing to identify and deport dangerous enemy aliens and instead was largely rounding up Japanese Peruvian merchants. In addition, to the forced deportations, there were others who applied to return to Japan voluntarily to escape the anti-Japanese hysteria sweeping Peru. US Ambassador Norweb assessed a list of 978 Japanese who filed applications with the Spanish embassy for voluntary removal and found that, aside from three of them, there was not a single individual "who is either important in the Japanese colony or a dangerous alien."[67] In the end, neither the deportation nor the voluntary removal program was working as the US government intended.

By 1943, US government officials began to realize that many of the people being deported from Latin America and incarcerated in US camps were neither pro-Axis agents nor did they pose a danger. Raymond W. Ickes and James D. Bell of the Alien Enemy Control Unit went to Costa Rica in March 1943 to investigate the enemy alien program there and discovered that there was flimsy evidence against many of the people on the deportee list. As they put it in their memo, "Experience has indicated that in too many instances we have had to accept for internment an inordinately large number of apparently harmless individuals disliked for one reason or another by the local government."[68] At the same time, another report suggested that deporting only the male head of the household left the wives in the country who became "a very dangerous focus of anti-United States propaganda," and therefore the author recommended removing the wives as well.[69] Thus even though women were not generally considered dangerous spies, the US government recognized that family separation would turn the families who remained in Latin America against the United States. In spite of caution about the feasibility of transferring so many non-dangerous Axis nationals north, the program continued moving many more men and their families to detention camps. Once the deportations began, it became difficult to limit the program.

After being held in a Lima jail for eleven days, Higashide and other deportees were suddenly marched onto a US military transport ship at gunpoint. Although Seiichi did not describe the conditions aboard the ship in detail, a group of Germans who were deported from Costa Rica provided a lengthy report about shipboard conditions on similar deportation ships. According to their report, men were crammed into rooms, leaving one or two square meters for each, while women and children were housed in cabins. The air, they noted, was stifling, especially since they were required to keep portholes closed at night to avoid detection. Men were only provided two meals a day, which some had to eat in the bathrooms given the crowded conditions. Women received three meals a day, but the authors of the report were particularly offended that women were forced to "sweep the deck in front of negro members of the ship's personnel who seemed to take a particular delight in littering up the place first and then watch white women clean up." They also complained about the officers' "unwarranted bullying" of passengers. One of the officers was even overheard saying "it would be best to throw them all (the men) overboard and to chuck the women and children after them."[70] In short, detainees were treated like prisoners on the deportation ships.

After three days in the hold of the ship not knowing exactly where they were headed, Higashide and the other prisoners emerged to find themselves in a hot, tropical climate. They were in the US-controlled Panama Canal zone. In addition to twenty-nine Japanese, five or six of whom were naturalized Peruvian citizens, and one or two were Nisei who had been born in Peru, there were also a number of people of German ancestry who were on the ship with Higashide. In the US military camp in Panama, they were forced by military police with bayoneted rifles to raise and salute the US flag, recite the "Pledge of Allegiance" and clear underbrush. Demanding that "enemy aliens" pay ritualistic homage to the United States was a form of humiliation. Given the advanced age of most of these men and the fact that they were all merchants, the manual labor work routine also took its toll. Higashide described the detainees as being "physically and spiritually exhausted."[71] One Japanese Peruvian merchant from Higashide's town of Ica went mad one day and ran barefoot in his pajamas toward the fence. Guards opened fire with their machine-guns, almost killing the man.[72] Higashide tried to keep his fellow prisoners' spirits up by telling them jokes, but they were so exhausted that by the time they returned to their cots, they "were again wrapped in a heavy silence." On one occasion, Higashide, desperate for fresh vegetables, stole a few onions and divided them among his fellow prisoners. For one meal at least they savored the taste of fresh vegetables.[73]

John K. Emerson, the US diplomat who orchestrated the Japanese deportations from Peru, claimed that Japanese people were so eager to leave Peru that they voluntarily agreed to be shipped to US detention camps. While it is true that Japanese people faced hostile attacks in Peru, including the devastating 1940 *saqueo* and anti-Japanese legislation, the putative voluntary nature of the deportations takes on a different hue when looked at from the perspective of the deportees.[74] Higashide explained how he told his family definitively not to join him in detention when he was leaving Peru. However, after a month away from them, and facing the prospect long-term detention, he sent a telegram from Panama that simply stated, "When ship comes in board all family, Leave even all assets. This is last chance."[75] Higashide's daughter made a similar point questioning the use of the word "voluntary" for what she experienced as a forced deportation.[76] Thus, while it's true that many family members chose to join their husbands and fathers in detention, this decision was made under great duress and in an effort to keep their families together in a time of increasing hostility toward the Japanese.

Before Higashide's family could join him in Panama, he was shipped out on the USS *Cuba* along with other Japanese Peruvians. Given the presence of German submarines in the Gulf of Mexico, the eighteen-ship convoy took a circuitous route from Panama to Cuba and finally landed in New Orleans two weeks later.[77] US consuls in Latin America followed instructions not to issue visas to the deportees, and once aboard, deportees had their passports seized. In this way, when they landed on US soil, the INS claimed each new arrival had the status of an "undocumented illegal alien entering the country at a time of war."[78]

It's hard to imagine the confusion and disorientation of the deportees who were arrested by Peruvian detectives, ordered onto ships by US soldiers, and now found themselves being herded into detentions stations in the port of New Orleans. Like the Mexican guest workers being brought to the United States under the federal Bracero program at the same time, the Japanese Peruvians were ordered into large shower rooms where they were sprayed with DDT, a carcinogenic white powder that was intended to destroy any contagious microbes they might be carrying. Having had their passports seized, they were identified by small tags they wore around their necks that indicated their names and the seat they would occupy on the train.[79] Through the long road from seizure in Peru, forced labor in Panama, and criminalization in the United States, Higashide was slowly having his identity as a Japanese Peruvian shopkeeper stripped away; he was becoming a prisoner.

Higashide described the two-day train trip to the Texas detention camp as feeling like a "luxurious trip to North America by a tour group of Japanese from Peru," except for the armed MPs posted between the railway cars who reminded them they were headed to prison and not a resort. This tour ended abruptly in a small country train station in South Texas where Higashide and the rest of the single men were ordered off and taken to Camp Kenedy. Others continued on to Crystal City, to a "family camp."[80] A census of Camp Kenedy at the beginning of November 1942, two years before Higashide arrived, shows that there were already 338 Germans, 315 Japanese, and a handful of others from Italy, Chile, Danzig, France, Guatemala, Hungary, Nicaragua, Panama, Peru, Romania, Russia, Sweden, and Switzerland in the camp. By 1942, INS camps held more than 600 people from Latin America, mainly Germans and Japanese. These internees had come from thirteen Latin American countries: Costa Rica, Guatemala, Honduras, El Salvador, Costa Rica, Nicaragua, the Dominican Republic, Haiti, Panama, Colombia, Ecuador, Bolivia, and Peru; about half of these prisoners were sent from Peru.[81]

The Kenedy Camp, named for a large Texas landowner, Captain Mifflin Kenedy, was just one of twenty-seven camps mainly in the US Southwest that held "enemy aliens" during the war. The site had been a Civilian Conservation Corp (CCC) camp in the 1930s; during the war, it was quickly expanded from twenty to forty-seven acres and turned into an "enemy alien" detention facility with 200 prefabricated huts. The town, whose carpenters, electricians, and plumbers were eager for work, welcomed the detention center, but townspeople had a decidedly negative view of the Japanese Peruvian detainees. The *Kenedy Advance* newspaper described the Japanese as "small, unshaven and insignificant looking," while they viewed the Germans as "young and smart looking." These racist views prevailed inside the camp as well, as the Japanese were housed in the decrepit CCC barracks while the Germans resided in the newly built quarters.[82]

Camp Kenedy was surrounded by barbed-wire fencing. Although their lives were not as regimented as they had been in Panama, there was no mistaking that this was a prison and they were prisoners. As Higashide put it, "The US government agencies formally called it a 'relocation camp,' but we simply perceived it as no more than a 'concentration camp.'" Unlike in Panama, they were not forced to work at Camp Kenedy, so they passed the time talking, gambling, and playing sports to fend off the boredom.[83]

Higashide describes himself as a model prisoner, who was even viewed as pro-American by some of his fellow prisoners because of his willingness to obey orders. Some of the internees attempted to resist their caging though a "war of attrition." The internees would drop their dishes and cups after each meal in a coordinated effort to break as many as possible, thereby decreasing the enemy's resources and their ability to carry out the war. Higashide disdained such acts as childish and unbecoming of represent-atives of "a great civilization" who were "obligated to behave in a higher, more civilized manner." Prison officials, however, didn't seem bothered by the broken dishes and simply replaced them without comment. As Higashide expressed it, "It seemed to be a case of tiny frogs attempting to make crazed resistances against a large water buffalo."[84]

Work opportunities at the camp were offered to the detainees at the rate of 20 cents a day, but Higashide refused. The camp also had a program to allow prisoners to work on farms on the outside at prevailing wages. Some Japanese fretted over the option, wondering whether they would be seen as aiding the "industry of an enemy country," meaning the United States, but Higashide counseled his fellow prisoners that such work could be carried out with pride if they felt so inclined.[85] Although many of the Japanese Peruvians did not necessarily take Japan's side in the war, others saw America as the enemy.

Six months after Higashide's internment, his wife Angelica and their five children, one of whom was just four months old, boarded one of the last ships to leave Peru with Japanese passengers. Angelica had packed milk containers for the baby, but they were confiscated at the port. Unable to breastfeed because only blood trickled out of her breasts, she begged an American soldier to give her milk, but he pretended not to understand her. Finally, a Filipino soldier provided her with milk for her baby.[86] Most of the women and children were placed in the stifling hold of the ship, but because of the age of the baby, the Higashide family was given a cabin on the deck. Angelica had converted all of her cash and almost all of her possessions into jewelry because they were restricted in the amount of cash they could carry. As she boarded the ship, officers confiscated her jewelry pouch, but she was relieved to have it returned to her on board. Most of the family property, including their store and the inventory, had to be left in Peru and entrusted to a friend. The ship traveled the same route that Higashide had taken through the Panama Canal, finally landing in New Orleans. The family boarded the train to Crystal City where they were incarcerated in a camp that had been established for families. On July 2, 1944, Seiichi Higashide was transferred from Camp Kenedy camp to Crystal City and was finally reunited with his family.[87] Elsa has few memories of life inside the camp, but the feel of her father's hands is seared into her memory. His hands had always been smooth, but now they were rough and calloused from the hard, manual labor he had been forced to do in Panama.[88] She also remembered that when the Germans left the camp they were finally able to move in to the better-quality houses.[89]

The Higashides were the fortunate ones. Many families remained separated for years if they were not able to join their relatives in US detention camps. After the war, the Peruvian government invoked its 1940 immigration law to refuse the return of Japanese Peruvians. In 1946, Peru finally agreed to allow seventy-nine people, those with Peruvian citizenship and their families, to return.[90] Although the United States was trying to negotiate the return of Japanese Peruvians, the US ambassador in Peru, William D. Pawley sympathized with Peruvian recalcitrance that reflected his own racist views. Pawley characterized the Japanese as "this alien population in Peru [that] has reverted to its non-moral Asiatic cunning, unchecked by self respect."[91] It was also difficult for wives and children to join their husbands and fathers who had been incarcerated because after the war these former prisoners were still considered "illegal aliens." This fiction of illegal entry provided grounds for the United States to issue orders of deportation against all of the Japanese Peruvians after the war. In addition, President Truman issued a proclamation on September 8, 1945, in which he ordered the removal of all enemy aliens, not only outside the country, but outside the entire Western hemisphere.[92] In 1946, internees of German descent brought a series of *habeas corpus* cases to prevent their deportation, arguing that since they had been transported to the United States against their will they could not be deported as illegal immigrants. Although the Germans won the right for voluntary departure, the government retained the right to deport Latin American internees who did not voluntarily depart.[93] Even though many had been released on parole after the war, lived for years in the country, had established families in the United States, and had children who were US citizens, the US government kept trying to deport them. Higashide noted the irony of being labeled "illegal aliens" because it was the US government that had "illegally and unreasonably forced the matter upon us."[94] The illegal alien label had many consequences after the war, including preventing some from paying in-state tuition in universities in spite of having lived in the country for years.[95] The only choice left to the Japanese Peruvians was to return to war-torn Japan, a country in which many had never lived or had not lived in for decades.

Angelica's mother, father, and sister were among the Japanese Peruvians who returned to Japan after the war. They believed the rumor that Japan had actually won the war, and in any case, Angelica's elderly parents wanted to return to their homeland to die there. While not everyone believed that

Japan had won the war, the majority of detainees returned to Japan after not being allowed back to Peru and being labeled as unwanted illegal aliens by the United States. Angelica's family tried to persuade their daughter and son-in-law to return with them to Japan, but Seiichi was determined to stay in the United States. In the end, only 364 of the 2,118 Japanese Peruvians remained in the United States.[96]

SEABROOK FARMS

As the War Relocation internment camps closed down, Crystal City became the repository for special cases of Japanese who still remained in custody after the war. A group of Japanese Americans who had renounced their US citizenship during the war but then wanted to regain it afterward were moved from Tule Lake to Crystal City, but by the middle of 1946, Crystal City was emptying out. The remaining Japanese Peruvians were granted the status of "restricted parole," which meant they could leave the camp if they found a guarantor for them. In September 1946, Higashide and his family along with most of the other Japanese Peruvians at Crystal City moved to Seabrook Farms in New Jersey, which acted as a sponsor.[97] Like the Kenedy Camp, Seabrook Farms had been a CCC labor camp in the 1930s, and the agricultural industrial complex eventually grew to employ 3,000 southern Blacks, Appalachian whites, and Caribbean workers in what *Life* magazine in 1955 called the "world's largest farm and food business."[98] During the war, hundreds of Japanese American families came to Seabrook; this work-release program was a way to alleviate crowding at WRA camps and also put the Japanese American internees to work. When the Japanese Americans left Seabrook after the war, their lawyer Wayne Collins negotiated with the farm to import 110 Japanese Peruvians who were still being detained at the Crystal City camp. By the fall of 1946, over 200 Japanese Peruvian internees were working at Seabrook, scores were living on California farms under parole, and fewer than 100 remained at Crystal City. Although Higashide and others preferred Seabrook to Crystal City, this work release program did not allow them complete freedom. They were essentially confined to a minimum-security, privately operated plantation until they could resolve their immigration status either by gaining permission to remain in the country legally or by leaving.[99]

Although they were released on parole and no military police guarded their train en route to Seabrook, Higashide recognized that "the strings still attached to us had been transformed into invisible restraints." Nonetheless, he described his train journey from Texas to New Jersey in optimistic terms, being struck he said, "by the vastness and bountifulness of America." "It is good," Seiichi commented, "that we chose to remain in America." In St. Louis, he had a hard time communicating with a taxi driver until he finally found someone who spoke Spanish who could bring him and his family to the zoo for a visit. From a prisoner in a detention camp to a tourist visiting animals in cages was a complete reversal. It felt strange for the "prisoner of war" to suddenly be released on his own recognizance and not be followed by guards.[100]

The freedom Higashide experienced on the train came to an abrupt end upon arrival at Seabrook Farms. He and his family found themselves in rudely constructed barracks sharing a bathroom with other families much

Figure 3.3 Higashide children at Seabrook Farms, 1946. Elsa, Carlos, and Irma (back row); Martha and Arthur (front row).
Source: Courtesy of Elsa Kudo.

like they had in Texas, but it was colder in New Jersey. Higashide noted, "Ice even formed in the cracks in the walls." Although they had "voluntarily" chosen to "live in this town of chain-linked fences," they were not free. "The transfer to this place from our former life behind barbed wire fences in Texas was no more than a shift from complete confinement to partial confinement." Higashide recognized one major difference; at Seabrook they were "completely responsible for their own survival."[101] Elsa remembers the family living in a tiny three-room house, five children crammed into two single cots, a bunk bed, and a bed for her parents.[102] Another Japanese Peruvian matriarch described the conditions of the barracks at Seabrook as "appalling," with no running water, no bathroom, and no shower.[103] The ease with which Seabrook moved from a farm for poor unemployed people to a private farm with war prisoners and foreigners of ambiguous legal status reflects the connections between the vulnerability of poor citizens and that of political enemies and undocumented migrants. Poor citizens, war prisoners, and illegal aliens all shared a common susceptibility to incarceration. Seabrook Farms was happy to employ a semi-captive labor force whatever the source.

The work routine at Seabrook Farms was harsh. Both Seiichi and his wife Angelica worked in the factory for twelve-hour shifts; he earned 50 cents an hour and she earned 35 cents an hour. If they were late or had to leave due to sickness, they had their salaries docked at five-minute increments. There were no paid holidays or sick leave, and they got only one day off every two weeks. Seiichi and Angelica took opposite shifts so that one could take care of the children while the other one worked. The company stores on the farm charged exorbitant prices, but without a car, they were forced to shop on the farm.[104] Even though the Higashides were no longer confined to an enemy alien detention camp, they felt just as trapped on the farm. In some ways, it was worse because now they were forced to work to maintain themselves.

Higashide experienced industrial factory work for the first time at Seabrook, and he began to identify as a worker and not a boss. He described how the employer would flood the factory with huge quantities of lima beans to be processed. Given the pace of the work, nobody could keep up, and occasionally the beans would spill out onto the factory floor. On the first few occasions this happened, he would rush over to help pick up the beans. No other workers would follow his lead, which seemed strange to him until another worker explained that these accidents allowed workers a brief rest, and that no matter how efficient they were, their wages would not be increased. Therefore, if one helps another worker, Higashide realized, that person "strangles oneself." Having inculcated these "weapons of the weak,"

Seiichi learned to not lift a finger to help when he saw beans piling up on the floor.[105] These kinds of lessons in workplace resistance helped Seiichi and the other workers survive Seabrook Farms.

Given the difficulties trying to support their family, and their feeling of entrapment at Seabrook farms, the Higashides realized they had no future there and after three years, he began to plan what he called their "escape." While this was not a barbed-wire encircled prison like Kenedy and Crystal City camps, he experienced the farm as a prison, and so leaving the farm felt like an escape. During the winter months when Seabrook laid off its employees, Higashide moved to Chicago to look for work. He eventually rented an apartment and moved his entire family there.[106]

WAYNE COLLINS AND THE FIGHT TO REMAIN AFTER THE WAR

Although Japanese Peruvians had all been released from the INS camps by 1946, and almost all had moved on from Seabrook by the early 1950s, they still faced pending deportation orders based on immigration status. At the same time Peru refused to accept them and many were unwilling to go to war-torn Japan. In 1945, Wayne Collins, a lawyer based in San Francisco, heard about the Japanese Peruvians when he visited Japanese American Tule Lake renunciants at Crystal City detention center. The renunciants were a group of more than 5,000 Japanese Americans who had renounced their US citizenship while incarcerated. In a class action lawsuit, Collins argued that because renunciants were coerced into renouncing their citizenship, it should be reinstated. He also took on more than 300 cases of Japanese Latin Americans who petitioned for their right to remain in the United States after the war. Collins had established the Northern California branch of the American Civil Liberties Union (ACLU) in 1934 and, along with Ernest Bessig, led Fred Korematsu's legal challenge to the internment of Japanese Americans. His radical approach and zealous defense of constitutional rights of Japanese Americans and Japanese Peruvians occasionally conflicted with the more reformist stance of the national ACLU and the Japanese American Citizens League (JACL). Ultimately, Collins prevailed in the renunciant cases and prevented deportation for almost all of the Japanese Peruvian internees.[107] Like Samuel Littman of HIAS and the Knights of Pythias members who were instrumental in helping Nathan Cohen get released from the ship, Wayne Collins was central to the legal battle for Japanese Peruvians.

Collins's involvement with the Japanese Peruvians' case began at the end of April 1946, when the spokesman for the internees from Peru,

Hajime Kishi, sent a telegram to Collins from Terminal Island immigration station in Los Angeles asking for help.[108] The next day Collins indicated that he would be sending Tetsujiro "Tex" Nakamura to speak with them. Nakamura, a Japanese American who was interned at Tule Lake, was instrumental in the Tule Lake Defense Committee that sought to regain citizenship rights for renunciants.[109] Collins wrote that he would personally meet with them at Terminal Island, and he reassured him, "There is no need for any of you to be worried."[110] Thus began Collins's work, not only for the Japanese Peruvians held at Terminal Island, but his defense of the entire group of kidnapped Japanese Latin Americans.

Collins immediately began reaching out to Japanese at other detention camps, and within a few days he received a letter from Koshiro Mukayama from the Crystal City detention camp explaining that they too would like to be represented by him.[111] Mukayama enclosed a newspaper article from Peru's main newspaper, *El Comercio*, indicating that the government there had decided not to accept the return of Japanese Peruvians unless they were naturalized Peruvian citizens. Japanese nationals who had married Peruvians would be evaluated on a case-by-case basis.[112] In the summer of 1946, the Peruvian government approved the return of only twenty Japanese Peruvians. Over the next year another fifty-seven were given permission to return from Crystal City and Seabrook Farms, and one was even repatriated from Japan.[113] Given the strict criteria and the unwillingness of Peru to embrace its former residents, return to Peru was not going to be an option for most Japanese Peruvian internees.

Collins's strategy was to try to negotiate with the Peruvian consul to take back all of the Japanese Peruvian internees, but he recognized the official's recalcitrance was going to make this difficult. Failing in negotiating a return to Peru, Collins intended to file a lawsuit on behalf of all Japanese Peruvians at Crystal City to prevent their deportation. In the meantime, he would also negotiate with the Department of Justice to see if the internees could be released pending the outcome of negotiations with the Peruvians.[114]

Higashide was also represented by Collins, and he credits Collins for single-handedly defending the Japanese Peruvian in court.[115] Although Higashide's legal documents are not available, the case of Hajime Kishi's case is very similar in that he had Peruvian-born children who accompanied him in the detention camp. Kishi's pathway to legalization provides an appreciation for the roadblocks faced by families such as the Higashides, who were similarly situated. Collins succeeded in gaining parole for Hajime Kishi and his Peruvian-born sons, but four years later in 1950, his sons received a letter from the INS asking them to report to a hearing about their deportation. Collins had succeeded in temporarily suspending their deportation and garnering permission for them to live and work at Seabrook Farms, but their deportation orders were still pending. Hajime wrote to Collins after his sons received the INS letters asking for advice on how to proceed.[116] Collins responded that they should not worry because the deportation proceedings had to first be concluded before they could apply for other forms of relief. The two main forms of relief Collins outlined were waiting for seven years to have elapsed since their entry or having an American-born child. Both circumstances, Collins assured, would make them eligible for a suspension of deportation.[117] Elsa Higashide did not even realize that she had been declared an "illegal alien" until she was a junior in college and was applying for her citizenship papers. She remembers the judge holding her FBI file with the words stamped "Illegal Entry." She grew indignant and asked the judge, "What is this? Why is my file stamped 'illegal entry'? We didn't come illegally. You folks knew we were coming in; you brought us here."[118]

Hajime's two sons, Masao and Katsumi, faced a more dire legal situation than their sister. Both were brought in for deportation hearings in which they were asked a series of questions, including whether they had entered the country without a visa and a passport. Although they had initially wanted to return to Peru, having established themselves in the United States, they now desired to stay.[119]

Like the Higashides, Hajime and his sons had lived for several years in Seabrook after the war. They eventually moved to San Diego in 1951 as their immigration case slowly wound its way through the courts. In the meantime, one of Hajime's sons had married a US citizen; that alone allowed him to apply for suspension of deportation. Collins believed the US government would not attempt to deport his Peruvian citizen children to Japan, but if they did, he was prepared to sue.[120] Collins's arguments were rejected on a number of occasions by courts that refused to grant a suspension of deportation for Japanese citizens. However, there was a final means of gaining relief, which was a special appeal to Congress to grant residency, notwithstanding the attorney general's rejection.[121]

In his appeal to the Immigration Board's decision to deny Masao Kishi relief, Collins laid out a searing indictment of the whole "enemy alien" program in Latin America. First, he established that Masao was a natural-born citizen of Peru and yet could not return there because the Peruvian government denied his readmission.[122] In his brief, Collins argued that the seizure of Hajme Kishi in Peru was illegal and denied him any judicial or administrative hearing. As he put it, "This criminal kidnapping of innocent persons was carried into execution under *lettres de cachet* despite the fact that the

5th amendment acts as a guarantee against such letters. They were enacted under the fictitious plea that they were dictated by Western Hemispheric security reasons, ie. extra-constitutional reasons." Collins did not mince words, arguing that acting in this way showed the "barbarism" of the US government. Furthermore, "This ruthless action of the United States and Peruvian governments was unlawful from the viewpoint of international law and the common principles of justice." Collins concluded by writing, "The appellant did not enter the US of his own free will and desire. The forced entry of his father compelled him to consent to his own entry as a voluntary refugee from Peru."[123] The brief went on to argue that there was no evidence whatsoever that Hajime Kishi, Masao's father, posed a danger. Furthermore, Masao was merely a "voluntary detainee allowed refuge and asylum in this country for political reasons." Beyond the question of deportation, Collins pointed to a 1946 change in the law that had expanded naturalization to include indigenous races of North and South America, Filipinos, Indians, and Chinese, arguing that children of Japanese ancestry born in Peru should be included.[124]

Collins was the only lawyer who remained steadfast in his defense of the Japanese Peruvians. He offered to negotiate with Peruvian authorities to take back Peruvian citizens and also lobbied US officials to suspend their deportation orders. In one of his letters to President Truman in February 1948, Collins wrote, "Our government, acting in concert with the Peruvian authorities, kidnapped several hundred Peruvian Japanese from their homes in Peru. . . . Our troops transported them to this country where they were incarcerated in concentration camps [under the auspices of] Western Hemispheric security grounds."[125] Collins's efforts finally paid off later that year. In July, Congress passed Public Law 863 revising a section of the 1917 immigration law. The revised statute allowed for suspension of deportation in cases where ineligibility for naturalization "is solely by reasons of his race" or if such deportation would cause "economic detriment" to a citizen or legal resident alien who is a spouse, parent, or minor child of the deportee. Congress would still have to act in these cases to affirm their rights.[126] In other words, the Japanese Peruvians would be eligible for suspension of deportation through an act of Congress.

In 1952, the bar preventing Japanese from attaining naturalized citizenship was finally dropped as part of a new immigration law, the McCarran-Walters Act. That act removed one of the barriers to adjusting their status in the country, but the ostensibly "illegal" manner in which the Japanese Peruvians entered was a condition that prevented them from gaining residency. On July 14, 1953, almost a decade after being forcibly removed from Peru, the US government recognized that it would be unrealistic to continue to wait for Peru to accept back the Japanese Peruvians and unfair to deport them to Japan, a country they had not lived in for more than three decades. Given these special circumstances, an immigration judge ruled that Hajime Kishi should be granted suspension of deportation.[127] However, this suspension did not resolve the long-term issue of permanent residency.

In 1954, bowing to Collins's incessant lobbying, Congress passed Public Law 751 that amended the US Refugee Relief Act of 1953, specifically giving people "brought from other American republics for internment" the right to apply for permanent residency.[128] Relief for Japanese Peruvians still required a special act of Congress for each individual, but at least there was a pathway to legal status.[129] In November 1954, Congress suspended Masao Kishi's deportation, allowing him to gain legal residence and eventually naturalized citizenship.[130] Seiichi Higashide and his family found relief in a similar fashion. As Higashide put it in his autobiography, "the large stamp, 'Illegal Entrant,' no longer appeared on our documents." For the first time, "we had finally been freed from a lingering fear of possible forced deportation."[131]

CITIZENSHIP IN-BETWEEN

Seiichi and Angelica became US citizens in 1958. This was the final act of their long journey from prisoners to citizens. For the teary-eyed and emotional Seiichi, that day marked the "end of our detention period." In their retirement, Seiichi imagined they would return to Japan, but on a visit there, Seiichi just didn't feel right. He and Angelica ended up moving to Hawaii, a space midway geographically and culturally between Japan, the United States, and Peru.[132]

In the final chapter of his memoir, Seiichi mused about the commonalities and differences between Polynesian, Japanese, and Western cultures. As an amateur architect, he focused on architecture, noting that in spite of cultural and architectural differences, there was a commonality in all houses in that they contained spaces at the boundary or edge. The traditional Japanese home has areas with earthen floors and *engawa*, or walkways that extend outward from the home, while Polynesian and Western homes had sunrooms and atria, both representing "in-between" spaces. In his conclusion, Higashide pointed to aspects of the hybrid culture in Hawaii, such as the adoption of Aloha shirts and sandals, to suggest that Westerners adapted to indigenous and Japanese cultural norms. Whether we accept the implicit assumptions in each of these cultural artifacts, Higashide was clearly trying to work out what he experienced and felt as contradictions in his life. The in-between spaces in houses reflected his own feelings of being betwixt and between countries, with his citizenship called into question for so much of his life. Waxing poetic, Higashide ends his memoir with the Hawaiian word "aloha," which he translates as love for the earth and an acceptance of human emotions.[133] Finally, under the tropical sun of Hawaii, Seiichi found a place to rest that was a central node of US empire, but one where people of Japanese descent could feel accepted.

Elsa also moved to Honolulu, where she still lives with her Japanese Peruvian husband. However, her story of finding a home there is less about love than hate on the mainland. She and her husband lived for a couple of years in Japan, but they ultimately chose to move to Hawaii to escape the racism they experienced in Chicago. One day her daughter Eimi came home from elementary school crying. Two girls pushed her against a tree and pinched while pulling her hair. "Jap, go home," they yelled. When Elsa's husband overheard what had happened, he immediately said "We don't have to take this. Let's go to Hawaii."[134] Hawaii had a blend of cultures, but more important, Japanese people had a large enough presence in Hawaii that they were somewhat protected from the kind of anti-Asian harassment that was common on the mainland.

CONCLUSION

The story of Japanese Peruvian abduction and detention in US camps is somewhat unique, but it fits into a pattern of non-citizens being subject to incarceration with almost no legal protections. While Congress eventually passed specific legislation to recognize the plight of the Japanese Peruvians and allow those remaining in the United States to legalize their status, during the war and for years afterward these individuals had no way to challenge their detention. Less than 20 percent of Japanese Peruvian internees were able to remain in the country after the war. Had war continued, as some wars do these days, Japanese Peruvians and others labeled enemy aliens might have faced decades in detention. Even so, the uncertainty of not knowing when their detention would end and their status after the war as "illegal entrants" who could not return to Peru left them in a state of limbo.

The decision by Congress to address the situation of the Japanese Peruvians in 1954 and provide a pathway to citizenship came at a moment when the US government made a conscious policy decision to stop detaining asylum seekers, and instead to parole them into the country while their cases could be heard by an immigration judge. The 1953 Refugee Act that opened the door to more than 200,000 refugees from Western Europe and communist countries did not even mention detention. Although more than 150,000 people, most of whom were US citizens, were interned during World War II, by the mid-1950s, the United States declared its intention to move away from mass detention. However, detention did not end but merely shifted to the southern border where the government rounded up hundreds of thousands of Mexicans and pushed them across the border in a program they called "Operation Wetback."

Although the legal battles for Japanese Latin Americans to remain in the United States ended in the 1950s, the battle for acknowledgment and reparations continues. In 1996, the Campaign for Justice was founded as a collaboration between activists and civil rights organizations, including the ACLU, Nikkei for Civil Rights and Redress, and the Japanese Peruvian Oral History Project. The principal activists were Japanese Latin American internees, their children, and grandchildren. Grace Shimizu, the principal activist behind the Campaign for Justice, is the daughter of formerly incarcerated Japanese Peruvians. Her father's first wife died in the camp in Crystal City due to the trauma of imprisonment and inadequate medical care. Her uncle and his family were deported from the camp to Japan after the war, but Shimizu's father was able to stay under the sponsorship of his relatives in northern California.[135] Although the efforts of the Campaign for Justice for redress by the US government have failed, in spite of congressional hearings, legislation, and civil law suits, Shimizu is not giving up.

In 1980, the US Congress established a Commission on Wartime Relocation and Internment of Civilians to review the history of Japanese American internment and make recommendations for redress. The commission held twenty hearings across the country, listening to testimony from 750 witnesses, including detainees, public officials, and historians. In addition to documenting the history, the Commission also recommended reparations of $20,000 for each of the surviving Japanese American internees, and the establishment of a $5 million fund to benefit Aleuts impacted by the evacuation of their islands.[136] The commission was unsure how to handle Japanese Latin American internees. A ten-page appendix at the end of the commission's report summarized the experience, concluding that "their history is one of the strange, unhappy, largely forgotten stories of World War II."[137] Japanese Latin Americans were not even mentioned in the commission's recommendations, and they received no compensation as part of the 1988 Civil Liberties Act that restricted compensation to "citizens and permanent resident aliens of Japanese ancestry."[138]

Since the Japanese Latin Americans were left out of the apology and reparations under the Civil Liberties Act, in 1996 the Campaign for Justice sued the US government to receive compensation. Three years later, the Federal Claims Court acknowledged the "tragic experiences of Latin Americans of Japanese descent who were interned here during World War II" and established a judgment of $5,000 per person for those who were interned, or for their surviving family members.[139] In total, almost 800 Japanese Latin Americans received payments and apology letters, 152 of them received $20,000 due to retroactive permanent residency, while 645 received the $5,000 payment. Seventeen of the internees opted out of the settlement arguing that the amount offered was an insult and put them in a secondary status in relation to Japanese Americans.[140]

Following their rejection of the settlement, four different lawsuits attempted to gain reparations equal to those received by Japanese Americans, but all of those lawsuits were dismissed on technical grounds. Finding no justice in the US courts through legislative action, three brothers who were abducted from Peru and locked up in a US detention camp for more than two years filed a case in 2003 with the Inter-American Commission on Human Rights (IACHR), an arm of the Organization of American States. The Shibayama brothers asserted that their rights under the American Convention on the Rights and Duties of Man had been violated.[141]

In March 2017, the IACHR held a public hearing on the Shibayama case at which internees, their relatives, and scholars testified. Isamu Carlos Arturo (Art) Shibayama was the only detainee to testify. He was taken from Peru when he was thirteen years old, along with his eleven-year-old sister and his parents. His grandparents were also seized, but then later they were exchanged during the war for American prisoners and sent to Japan. The Shibayamas followed the same pathway as the Higashide family had: through Panama to the Crystal City camp in Texas and Seabrook farms in New Jersey. In spite of serving in the US Army in the early 1950s, Art Shibayama did not gain his US citizenship until 1970. At the hearing, the commissioners apologized to Shibayama for what one described as a "clear, fraudulent act." The United States government refused to participate in the hearing. Sixteen years after the case was first filed with the IACHR, it still remains pending. Art Shibayama did not live to see the outcome; he died on July 31, 2018, at eighty-eight years of age.[142]

The surviving Japanese Peruvian former internees are now scattered around the globe. The ones who returned to Japan after the war would meet regularly to trade stories, but they kept these meetings private and allowed only internees to attend. As the former detainees aged, these meetings became more infrequent. However, over the years, the diasporic community, Peru-kai, has organized sixteen larger reunions, in the United States, Japan, and also in Peru. In 2014, they met in Honolulu to remind younger generations of their history and to recount traumatic stories of being snatched from their homes in Peru and being sprayed with DDT. Most of the elderly attendees had been children when they were imprisoned in Crystal City. Mitsuaki Oyama, the leader of the Japanese Peruvians from Kawasaki, Japan, wanted to attend the reunion, but he was too infirm to travel.[143] Oyama has since died, and the Peru-kai has not had another meeting.[144] One of the reunion attendees, Libia (Maoki) Yamamoto, now gets around Richmond, California, with the help of a walker. She recalled the sadness when her neighbors were getting ready to leave the internment camp at Crystal City. The Japanese Peruvians gathered around and sang an old cowboy song:

> From the valley they say you are going.
> We will miss your bright eyes and sweet smile.
> For they say you are taking the sunshine
> That brightened our path for a while.[145]

The end of Japanese Peruvian internment came at exactly the moment the INS was shifting its policy away from long-term immigrant detention in 1953. By the early 1980s, however, a new group of immigrants from Haiti and Cuba led the government to shift course yet again, creating mass detention sites in the United States and elsewhere for these asylum seekers.

CHAPTER 4

"We Have No End"

Mariel Cuban Prisoners Rise Up

In May 1980, a group of Cuban refugees arrived by airplane to Fort Chaffee, an army post on the Oklahoma-Arkansas border. Right before the first refugee plane landed, a man in a white Ku Klux Klan hood broke through a line of state troopers and stood on the tarmac chanting: "Don't let them Cubans in!" and "Hoodlums! They're gonna come in here and get welfare, gonna get a free ride for everything." The KKK man, Mac McCarty, was a retired Marine who had used his identification to get onto the base.[1] Robed Klansmen lined the street holding signs reading: "We do not support communist criminals," "Fight Jewish communism," and "Today Miami, tomorrow U.S.A."[2] It's not clear if the Cubans ever saw the Klansmen, but when they landed they erupted in cheers in Spanish, "Down with Castro" and "Long live Carter!"[3] Neither the Cubans' anti-communism nor their pro-American sentiment assuaged the fear of the townspeople, who marched armed through the streets and staged Klan protests in white robes at the front gate of the army base.[4] Klan activists were blinded to the Cubans' anti-communism by the blackness of the refugees. White supremacy and anti-immigrant sentiments erupted in this remote corner of Arkansas, linking the long history of the Ku Klux Klan from the nineteenth century to the 1980s.

What were these Cubans doing in a remote part of Arkansas and why were townspeople so upset? The Cubans were part of a mass exodus of more than 125,000 from Cuba in the spring and summer of 1980. The boatlift, dubbed the "Freedom Flotilla," was sparked when a bus smashed through the gates of the Peruvian embassy in Havana so the passengers could request asylum. Fidel Castro decided to use the opportunity to rid the country of what he referred to as *escoria* (scum). Within a week more than 10,000 Cubans were camping out on the embassy grounds after Castro removed surrounding guards. Several South American countries accepted hundreds of Cuban asylum seekers, and President Carter agreed to take 3,500. By the end of April, Castro announced that he would allow anyone who wanted to leave to depart from the port of Mariel, just outside Havana, prompting one of the largest boatlifts in history.

With thousands of Cubans arriving on boats in Florida each day, the US government set up INS processing centers at the Orange Bowl in Miami and at a nearby former missile base on Krome Avenue; other processing centers were established at Elgin Air Force Base in Fort Walton Beach, Florida, and then in Fort Chaffee, Arkansas; Fort Indiantown Gap, Pennsylvania; and Fort McCoy, Wisconsin. However, these makeshift camps were deemed unsecure for those who were believed to be mentally ill or criminals, and so the high-risk Cubans were transferred to fourteen prisons throughout the country run by the federal Bureau of Prisons (BOP), including McNeil Island Penitentiary. In 1981, the Cuban detainees were concentrated at the Atlanta Penitentiary in order to manage them more effectively and keep them segregated from the rest of the prison population. However, by the mid-1980s, overcrowding in Atlanta led authorities to turn the Federal Alien Detention Center in Oakdale, Louisiana, into a center to hold Cuban detainees who had been approved for release.[5] By the mid-1980s, all Cuban detainees, except for those serving criminal sentences in state and federal prisons, were locked up either in Atlanta or Oakdale. This collaboration between the BOP and the INS was not the first between immigration and federal prison authorities; it had occurred at McNeil Island Penitentiary back in the 1880s. However, given the size of the Cuban refugee population, this round of lockups would require a massive investment in prison infrastructure. In 1986, both the Department of Justice and the INS pointed specifically to the large number of Mariel detainees to justify requests for millions more in funding.[6]

In the spring of 1987, Armando Sanchez, one of more than 3,000 Cuban Mariel refugees imprisoned in federal prisons across the country, wrote a poem entitled "We Are." Sanchez expressed both his sadness and frustration at being seen as "scum" as well as his desire to be understood as a victim.

> You see our faces
> . . . look really mean

We are scum.
We are worse.
We have no end.
But look deeply inside us . . .
What do you see?
Are they hard faces?
Are they full of hate?
You know better than that!
It is pain and sadness.
It is crying and hurting.
It is the resentment of a victimized people,
and ones suffering, weeping and hopefully waiting!

The poem referred to how the Marielitos were seen in the United States as criminals. Sanchez invited his readers to see them not as hardened criminals but as suffering victims. The line that best captured his feelings of powerlessness induced by being caged indefinitely was "we have no end."[7] The unbounded nature of their imprisonment was a particular type of torture, one that had been experienced by other immigrants over the previous century, the Chinese on McNeil Island, Nathan Cohen on a ship, and the Japanese Peruvians in Crystal City, but in this case the Cubans rebelled. In spite of their condition of rightlessness and being shackled and locked behind thick bars and walls, the Cuban Marielitos fought back.

A few months after Sanchez wrote his poem, thousands of Mariel detainees at two prisons rose up to demand liberty. By the time the Cubans released their hostages and surrendered in Atlanta on December 4, 1987, it had become the longest prison takeover in US history. All told, close to 2,400 Cuban detainees in prisons in Oakdale and Atlanta rose up, seized 138 hostages, and destroyed over $64 million in property. In addition to the $50 million the federal government spent to quell the protest and transfer the detainees, this two-week uprising cost the government well over $110 million.[8] Remarkably, only one Cuban detainee, José Peña Pérez, was killed in Atlanta. Hostages were taken violently and a few guards and detainees suffered minor injuries during the lengthy standoff, but the takeover could have ended in a bloodbath. Nonetheless, more significant than the loss of life and property, this rebellion would usher in an era of dramatic escalation of immigrant imprisonment. In that sense, the Mariel detainees might have won the battle, but they and all other immigrants lost the war. The story of the uprising reveals how law and order politics, emphasizing a heavy-handed policing of crime, merged with immigration restrictions in the 1980s to produce mass immigrant incarceration.

Figure 4.1 Cuban detainees in Atlanta Penitentiary in 1987 prison uprising.
Source: Atlanta History Center.

Several protagonists in the event recorded their versions of what happened, including Gary Leshaw, the lead legal aid lawyer representing the Cuban detainees, and Earl Lawson and Renaldo Smith, both prison guards in Atlanta at the time of the takeover.[9] What is absent from all of the newspaper, magazine, memoir, and academic accounts, however, is the perspective of the Cuban detainees themselves. One detainee, Enrique González Sarasa, who participated in the uprising in the Atlanta Penitentiary and was eventually deported to Cuba, penned a memoir about his life in the United States as an "excluded one."[10] This chapter attempts to add the views of Cuban detainees through the hundreds of letters they wrote to their lawyers and the two women at the center of a support group called Coalition to Support Cuban Detainees. Even today, the Mariel Cuban detainees who participated in the prison takeover are reluctant to talk about their experience for fear that their tenuous immigration status may be compromised.[11] Although approximately 1,400 of those involved in the takeover were ultimately paroled into the United States, their immigration status is still that of excludable aliens who may be deported if Cuba agrees to accept them. Recent Supreme Court decisions have also affirmed the right of the government to indefinitely detain immigrants eligible for deportation due to even minor past criminal offenses; such immigrants have no right to judicial review for their incarceration.[12] The Mariel Cubans continue to live in fear.

Although the immediate cause of the prison rebellion was the threat of being deported back to Cuba, detainees were also protesting against the torture of living under the threat of indefinite detention and horrific conditions inside the prison. The Bureau of Prisons claimed that there were no problems with food, housing, and medical care, and instead blamed the uprising on what they called "external" factors.[13] However, a congressional investigation into conditions at the Atlanta Penitentiary a year before the uprising revealed a litany of complaints from prisoners including being locked down for two years, having inadequate light and recreation, lack of access to personal property, poor and unsanitary food, limited access to showers, lack of Spanish-speaking staff, and discrimination against Cubans in housing and work assignments. Detainees also noted the high levels of violence at the prison, with an average of fifteen inmate-on-inmate assaults each month, and between eleven and forty-one inmate-on-staff monthly assaults. The levels of desperation experienced by detainees facing indefinite imprisonment for no reason other than their bizarre immigration status also led to sky-high rates of self-mutilation and suicide. In five years, there were 4,000 incidents of self-mutilation, half of them serious; 158 attempted suicides, seven of which were successful; and nine homicides. In 1986, a congressional committee described the living conditions in the Atlanta Penitentiary as "intolerable," "brutal and inhumane."[14] Although conditions at Oakdale may have been slightly better given the campus-like design of the prison, the basic fact of incarceration in spite of having been approved for release was a kind of torture. The high number of suicide attempts revealed the levels of desperation directed inward by the detainees. When this same frustration was directed outward, it led to rebellion.

It was not only the fact of being locked up for no reason other than an inability to be deported but the horrendous conditions they were forced to endure in prison that led the prisoners to rebel. In the mid-1980s, before the uprising, detainees wrote dozens of letters to defense lawyers complaining about cramped living quarters, lack of recreation, humiliating treatment by guards, and assaults both by other detainees and by staff members in the various prisons where they were being held. Cosme Damian Rodriguez explained that he had been at the Atlanta Penitentiary for two months and had had no change of clothes or underwear, no ability to buy toothpaste, and no access to medical care.[15] Leondro Gandaria wrote to a federal public defender about his cellmate slicing Gandaria's face, neck, and ears with a razor. The violent attack requiring fifty-two stitches occurred when a guard left Gandaria handcuffed and defenseless in his cell. This was the third assault Gandaria had suffered in prison, but this time he decided to sue in court.[16] In his memoir, Enrique González Sarasa admitted that on two occasions he had stabbed fellow Cuban detainees who had crossed him.[17] Roman Jaime, who served time in a Cuban penitentiary for having worked in Batista's military, wrote that some detainees had put themselves on the list of voluntary repatriates "because they do not support the torture inside the wall of the federal penitentiary in Atlanta, Georgia." Jaime went further, explaining, "Our situation is the worst one in the world. We are living in such ways that we never live when we were in the Cuban penitentiary."[18] For a former Batista soldier to state that conditions at the Atlanta prison were far worse than in Castro's Cuba was a stinging indictment of US prisons.

The prison chaplain in Atlanta understood that the uncertainty and grim prospects for release put the Cuban detainees in an untenable and potentially explosive situation. The Reverend Russ Mabry counseled a Cuban whose wife in New Jersey had just had a hysterectomy and whose daughter was hospitalized with pneumonia. The prisoner's wife wrote to him to say that she did not have enough money to get through Christmas. Mabry, who would later be seized as one of the hostages, said, "I had never before confronted that much pain. American inmates know why they're in prison, how much time they have and about when they'll get out. This Cuban didn't know when he was getting out or—if he got out—whether he would go live with his wife and kids or be deported. Underneath his pleasantness there was real rage. He had no control over his life."[19] At its heart, the prison uprising was an expression of this rage, a thirst for freedom, a desire to gain control over one's life in a nightmare of unending imprisonment.

DUE PROCESS

At the center of the uprising was the indefinite detention faced by Cuban detainees who were imprisoned because they were deemed too dangerous to release and yet could not be deported back to Cuba. As a 1986 congressional committee put it, "These detainees—who are virtually without legal rights—are worse off than virtually all other Federal sentenced inmates." Since none of the detainees were facing criminal charges, they had no right to government-paid legal counsel and no due process protections. In 1986, the INS estimated that 300 of the 1,840 Cuban detainees at the Atlanta Penitentiary had been locked up since they arrived in 1980.[20] The rest had been paroled into the community and had committed some infraction that resulted in their incarceration by the INS after they had served their criminal sentences. The INS characterized the "vast majority" of detainees as violent criminals who had committed "arson, rape, aggravated assault, murder and narcotic related crimes" on US soil. In its written response to Congress, the INS indicated that "all but 300" of the approximately 1,800 had been convicted of serious crimes while in the country. However, the actual number of detainees convicted of serious violent crimes was much smaller. In 1986, the INS submitted a list of all of the "serious crimes" committed by Cuban detainees as part of their appeal of a case in the 11th Circuit Court, a list whose total amounted to less than 1,200. It included many low-level property and drug crimes; almost one-third of the INS's "serious crimes" were drug possession or distribution charges. All told, only five detainees had been convicted of murder, eleven of rape, and 150 of assault.[21] While a handful of detainees had committed violent offenses, the INS grossly inflated the seriousness of most of these crimes. By focusing on the most extreme cases, the INS tried to stigmatize the entire group.

The question of whether some of the detainees had committed serious crimes overlooked the fact that all of the detainees in Atlanta and Oakdale had already served their sentences for those crimes and would have been released if they had not been in the unique position of being un-deportable aliens. Their immigration status as "entrants," meaning technically on the threshold of entering, led to their being declared "excludable" due to their offenses, and to be put in prison pending deportation. The bizarre "entry fiction," as it is called, meant that even though the Cubans had been living in the United States for seven years—some had even married and had US citizen children—they were considered legally to still be waiting somewhere outside the country. This entry fiction allowed the government to deny them certain due process claims and made it easier to deport them than if they were acknowledged to have been inside the United States. At congressional hearings, an exasperated Representative Robert Kastenmeir responded, "We cannot stick our heads in the sand, hiding behind the legal fiction that the Mariel Cubans are not really here and therefore not due any legal rights."[22] But stick their heads in the sand they did. The detainees' status as awaiting entry was critical because it allowed the government to deny them due process and legal protections afforded to other migrants who had entered the country legally or illegally. Throughout the 1980s and all the way up to 2005, the entry fiction was used to deny any due process rights to Cubans and other refugees in similar circumstances.

As a result of this lack of due process, many detainees were held simply because they lacked legal entry papers or the INS had erroneously labeled them as criminals and they had no form of legal redress to adjudicate their claims. The legal precedent for the absence of due process for people entering the country stretched back to 1950 when the Supreme Court affirmed the right of the government to deny due process to all aliens seeking entry to the country. In a case involving the denial of entry to a non-citizen wife of a US citizen (*Knauff Shaughnessy*), the court declared, "Any procedure authorized by Congress for the exclusion of aliens is due process, so far as an alien denied entry is concerned."[23] In other words, since aliens had no right of entry, they also had no right to a hearing to determine whether those non-existent rights were violated. At a congressional hearing following the prison uprising, the US District Court judge from the Northern District of Georgia, Marvin Shoob, who heard class action lawsuits by detainees held at Atlanta's prison, pointed out that many of the individuals he reviewed should never have been in detention in the first place. One medical student from Havana who had spent thirteen years in a Cuban prison for his political activities was detained for over a year for lacking entry papers. Even after Judge Shoob ordered him released from the Atlanta Penitentiary, the prison refused until the judge called the prison and threatened to send federal marshals to pick him up. According to Shoob, 381 other individuals with no criminal record had been detained for over a year just for lacking legal entry documents. Other detainees at the Atlanta Penitentiary included three teenagers who were sent there after their halfway house was closed due to lack of federal funding. The INS responded to Shoob's concerns with comments like, "Oh, judge, that man slipped through the crack." Judge Shoob insisted that detainees should be afforded due process so that they would be able to question their incarceration, have a fair hearing, and not slip through the gaping holes in the system.[24]

Given the 1950 *Knauff v. Shaughnessy* Supreme Court ruling regarding due process, the INS established their own hearing process for detainees. There were multiple problems with these hearings, including the lack of right to legal counsel, no advance notice of charges, and no opportunity to call witnesses or cross-examine government witnesses. The fact that INS agents, who were not neutral in these proceedings, were the judges rendered the whole process a kind of kangaroo court. The hearings officers were often Border Patrol agents who had received one day of training. After the prison uprisings, the government agreed to an appeals process run by the Justice Department, but these appeals panels would only review the written record, allowed no questioning of evidence or witnesses, and provided for no legal counsel. In other words, in the estimation of Gary Leshaw, the new process was "less than full, fair and equitable."[25]

At the time of the uprising, Gary Leshaw was a thirty-five-year-old staff attorney for Atlanta Legal Aid. Leshaw had been representing Cubans at the Atlanta Penitentiary since 1980, but he was initially focused on prison conditions. When Deborah Ebel, who had been the attorney representing

Mariel Cubans left Legal Aid in 1986, Leshaw inherited the cases. Leshaw's class action lawsuits about prison conditions in the penitentiary landed in front of Judge Marvin Shoob, a Carter appointee in the federal Northern Georgia District Court. Shoob, a Jewish southerner, was liberal and active in Democratic Party politics. During World War II, five frightened German soldiers surrendered to a solitary Shoob. When Shoob confided to an American lieutenant that he didn't know what to do with the Germans, the lieutenant summarily executed the five men with a spray of machine-gun fire. Shoob would later recount this incident as the reason he always sought to do what was right rather than what was simply expedient.[26] In his decisions regarding Mariel Cubans, Shoob steadfastly defended the rights of the detainees to due process and condemned the government's insistence on holding them indefinitely in the brutal and inhumane conditions at the Atlanta Penitentiary. As Judge Shoob put it in congressional hearings following the uprising, "You cannot give a man a fair hearing when he doesn't understand what's going on, doesn't speak the language, is not aware necessarily of the charges against him—even if they are presented to him—has no attorney to represent him, and doesn't know how to marshal the evidence to disprove the charges against him."[27] Although the appeals court ultimately reversed many of Shoob's rulings, he remained a strong voice in favor of due process for all. Two decades later, the Supreme Court would echo Shoob's reasoning when they put some limits on indefinite detention.

US courts had addressed questions of indefinite detention and excludability prior to the arrival of the Marielitos, but the Cubans' unique situation posed fundamentally new legal issues. Since the late nineteenth century, courts held that excludable aliens, even those who had lived in the country for years, had few due process rights. As early as 1892, the Supreme Court ruled in *Nishimura Ekiu* that prospective immigrants had limited due process rights and had no right to judicial review. As the court put it, "The decisions of executive or administrative officers, acting within powers expressly conferred by Congress, are due process of law."[28] Subsequent decisions, including *Ju Toy* (1905), upheld the idea that as long as people seeking entry were being adjudicated by the procedure set up by immigration officials, they were receiving due process.[29] The issue of indefinite detention was once again addressed by the Supreme Court in *Shaughnessy v. Mezei* (1953) in which a Hungarian citizen who was a legal US resident traveled to Hungary and on his return was excluded and detained at the port of entry. The attorney general asserted, based on secret information, that Mezei's entry would be "prejudicial to the public interest for security reasons." Since no other nation would accept Mezei, he remained detained at Ellis Island for nearly two years. A Federal District

Court ruled that Mezei must be paroled into the United States pending his deportation, but the Supreme Court ultimately reversed that decision asserting that Mezei had no constitutional or statutory right to due process or to enter the country.[30] Therefore, from the 1890s through the 1950s the courts had firmly established the principle that the executive branch had sole authority over determining what was due process for prospective immigrants seeking entry. Furthermore, these decisions affirmed the right of the government to indefinitely detain migrants pursuant to deportation. Simply put, migrants standing at the gates to the country had no rights.

The law was clear, but just as the court affirmed the right to detain prospective immigrants indefinitely, the government shifted away from the practice of detention. Although the Supreme Court issued its *Mezei* ruling in 1953, the very next year the government closed Ellis Island, a place where many aliens had been held pending deportation, and the INS began paroling all immigrants who were deemed excludable but could not be deported. However, even as the Supreme Court in the *Leng May Ma v. Barber* (1958) case critiqued the idea of detaining migrants, it also affirmed the right of the government to treat parolees as having never officially entered the country.[31] The result was that although long-term immigrant detention was not generally practiced from 1954 until the late 1970s, the legal basis for indefinite detention remained firmly in place, even for those who had lived for years within the United States.[32]

What happened in the 1970s that would lead the government to reverse course and start detaining masses of migrants seeking entry? The most significant factor was the influx of tens of thousands of predominantly Black Cubans and Haitians, who were feared to be criminals and mentally ill. The policy toward Haitians fleeing the island had already begun to change in the 1970s as they were routinely detained, denied their asylum claims, and deported. Historian Carl Lindskoog found differential treatment of Cubans and Indochinese versus Haitians applying for asylum. More than 600,000 Cuban refugees (1962–1979) and 200,000 Indochinese (1965–1979) were paroled into the United States in the 1960s and 1970s as part of the government's willingness to accept refugees from communist countries. Meanwhile, only 100 of approximately 50,000 Black Haitians were granted asylum from 1972 to 1980. Detention of Haitians was an experiment to discourage what INS officials feared would become a "flood of economic refugees from all over the Caribbean."[33]

In 1979, the Haitian Refugee Center filed a lawsuit against the attorney general asserting that Haitian asylum claims were handled in a discriminatory manner based on the petitioner's national origin. In his ruling in favor of the Haitians, Judge King of the Southern District of Florida noted the racism inherent in denying almost all asylum claims from Black Haitians while granting the applications of predominantly white Cubans. Although the judge recognized that prospective entrants do not have the full panoply of due process rights as citizens, he argued that the law demanded that the INS follow its own procedures. The government argued that district courts had no jurisdiction to review deportation cases, but Judge King reasoned that while political asylum itself could not be questioned by the court, "procedural irregularities therein are reviewable in the district court."[34] This case, however, was largely a Pyrrhic victory because it applied only to Florida's southern district. The government could continue to process the Haitians outside of the district and that's exactly what the Carter administration did when it announced it would be processing Haitians at Fort Allen, a US army base in Puerto Rico.[35] In July 1980, just at the moment Judge King issued his decision, tens of thousands of Cubans were landing in Florida. Although the Haitian case seemed to suggest some limits on government discrimination, the issue of exactly what constituted due process was still undefined.

In the early 1980s, district courts throughout the country followed Judge King's lead, repeatedly ruling in favor of Cuban refugees and putting limits on the government's authority to detain them indefinitely. In the case of Pedro Rodriguez Fernandez, who arrived in June 1980 from Cuba, Kansas District Court Judge Rodgers ruled that although Fernandez could be excluded from the country, he could not be detained indefinitely in the Leavenworth Penitentiary. Judge Rogers did not question the excludability of Rodriguez based on his admission that he was convicted several times of theft in Cuba. However, in the words of the judge, "Indeterminate detention of petitioner in a maximum-security prison pending unforeseeable deportation constitutes arbitrary detention." Rogers argued that such detention was an "abuse of customary international law" and an "abuse of discretion" by the attorney general.[36] This district court decision thus questioned the government's right to indefinitely detain immigrants who posed no real security or safety threat to the nation. The 10th Circuit Court of Appeals concurred. The court asserted that indefinite detention was clearly punishment, and as such it was arbitrary since Rodriguez had never been convicted or even charged with a crime in the United States.[37]

In the early 1980s, Judge Shoob of the Northern District of Georgia also ruled against indefinite detention in a class action suit on behalf of Mariel detainees held at the Atlanta Penitentiary. Rather than relying on international law, however, Shoob based his decision on the lack of rationality in the government's detention policy, the fact that it departed from established procedures and its discrimination against a race or group. While

Shoob granted that the government had the right to detain excludable aliens pursuant to their deportation, once it was clear that they were not deportable, he asserted that their "liberty interest" had to be respected. Importantly, Shoob based his decision on constitutional as well as statutory grounds. As he put it, "The Court concludes that petitioners have an interest in their freedom from administrative detention that is protected by the due process clause of the fifth amendment."[38] However, Shoob did not order the release of the detainees but rather directed the attorney general to initiate a Status Review Plan to determine which Cubans should be released.

By the mid-1980s there were several major district court decisions in cases involving both Haitians and Cubans that upheld the idea that excludable aliens held in indefinite detention had some constitutional protections. However, the 11th Circuit Court of Appeals held the opposite view, and reversed Judge Shoob's ruling, arguing that the Cubans "lack a constitutional liberty interest." Since they were not protected by the constitution, they had no rights to due process. While the decision was a setback for the Mariel Cuban detainees, the 11th Circuit Court importantly rejected the government's argument that the decisions of the attorney general were not reviewable by courts.[39] By the time of the Oakdale and Atlanta prison uprisings in 1987, a handful of district judges in Kansas, Georgia, Virginia, and Wyoming had all ruled against indefinite detention. On the other hand, higher level circuit courts were divided over whether excludable aliens had due process protections.[40]

The Supreme Court took issue with the appeals court not on the merits, but based on their jurisdiction. It argued that the appeals court should not have ruled based on the constitutional question because non-discrimination was already prohibited by statute. Therefore, the Supreme Court's refusal to engage the constitutional question left the issue of excludable aliens' equal protection rights unsettled for the next twenty years.[41] Nonetheless, in a legal analysis appended to the congressional inquiry into conditions at the Atlanta Penitentiary in 1986, a lawyer for the Congressional Research Center concluded, "Detainees have no inherent constitutional rights regarding continued detention pending expulsion."[42] In practice, this meant that Mariel Cuban detainees had exhausted their legal appeals by 1986.

Given the competing circuit court decisions and the refusal of the Supreme Court to clarify the issue, confusion reigned at the congressional hearing following the Atlanta prison uprising. Deputy Attorney General Burns cited the 11th Circuit to show that the United States "has the authority indefinitely to detain excludable aliens who cannot practicably be sent elsewhere." Burns argued that as the Supreme Court refused to review the 11th Circuit's decision, it "is the law."[43] Judge Shoob was more circum-spect in his testimony, arguing that the law was still not settled on the issue because the 10th Circuit had ruled that detainees did have consti-tutional rights.[44] The question of whether excludable aliens had constitu-tional rights and under what circumstances depended to a great degree on which part of the country they were in. The issue would remain unsettled until 2005 when the Supreme Court finally ruled on the matter in a case involving Mariel Cubans. However, even today the question of whether in-definite detention is constitutional continues to be revisited by the courts.

If Cubans could not appeal to judicial review, they had to rely on an INS re-view process that was arbitrary and flawed. Detainees regularly complained that their INS records were filled with inaccuracies that they could not get corrected. For instance, Roberto Salabarria Gomez wrote from Atlanta Penitentiary to Senator Paula Hawkins explaining that his INS record er-roneously indicated he had been interned in Cuba at a hospital for alco-holics and the mentally ill when in reality he was at a hospital for a peptic ulcer. Furthermore, he wrote to Senator Mack Mattingly to let him know that he was "sanctioned by the communist Sons of Bitches for bringing two steaks to his children," hardly the rap sheet of a hardened criminal.[45] At a congressional hearing, Sally Sandige, representing the Coalition to Support Cuban Detainees, described some of the problems in the INS hearings. As she put it, the INS file on which judgment was based, was an "inadequate hodge-podge of misinformation and speculation." She pointed to the case of Julia Martinez Leon who was denied release from detention by the INS for a cocaine and marijuana conviction. In truth, Martinez Leon had never had a cocaine conviction and she was only convicted for possessing a small amount of marijuana for which she was sentenced to probation. Both she and her husband were put into detention for five years and separated from their two babies, both of whom were US citizens. The INS records did not even indicate that she had children, and she was given no information about them for many years. These cases proved that the INS hearings were often based on flawed or false information to which detainees might not even have access. Furthermore, the detainees had no proper legal counsel and so they relied on law students, ministers, and concerned citizens to go to their hearings with them; even then, their informal legal assistants were forbidden from speaking until the very end of the hearing.[46]

Many of the original criminal cases that landed the Cubans in prison had also been flawed since their public defenders who pushed them to plead guilty to charges were unaware that a guilty plea would automati-cally result in deportation. One such case was that of Jose Borcella Pozo, who pled guilty to second-degree sexual assault and escape. Since sexual assault is a crime of moral turpitude, Borcello was detained by the INS after serving two and half years in a Colorado prison. The exclusion of those convicted of crimes of "moral turpitude" was first encoded in immigration law in 1891, but the definition of this term has remained vague ever since.[47] In June 1985, the Appeals Court in Colorado found that Borcello had received ineffective counsel and ordered his guilty plea retracted and a new trial ordered.[48] It is unclear if this case was ever reviewed by the Colorado Supreme Court, but by fall 1985, the 11th Circuit had issued a couple of rulings that all but eliminated judicial review for Mariel Cubans.[49] Enrique González Sarasa wrote about his experiences being repeatedly imprisoned for supposedly violating parole by moving to a different city. As he put it, "I was locked up unjustly for eight years. It's enough to drive one crazy."[50] No matter how they got ensnared in the criminal justice system, once they were in its jaws, it was virtually impossible for Mariel Cubans to escape. The most minor criminal offense or even the admission they had been imprisoned in Cuba for stealing food resulted in indefinite detention.

Beyond the flawed criminal trials and the review hearing process, even after the detainees had been approved for parole, many remained in detention for months, if not years, while awaiting a sponsor. In order to be released, detainees either had to have a family sponsor or be accepted by a halfway house that would provide a transition into US society. However, according to the deputy attorney general, as of early 1988, there were still 1,000 Cuban detainees who were approved for release and were still being held in detention pending placement in halfway houses.[51] Given the lack of government funding for halfway houses and that each one could accept or reject particular detainees, it seemed that the Cubans would be imprisoned for a long time even though the government had already decided they did not pose a security risk. As one detainee in Oakdale complained, "All I ever got from the government was pocket freedom."[52] "Pocket freedom" was what the Cubans called the papers they kept in their pockets indicating they had been approved for release. The phrase expressed the detainees' feelings of betrayal by the government's false promise of freedom, like President Carter's false promise to welcome them "with open hearts and open arms."[53]

Although the INS detention policy was not explicitly racist, its sponsorship programs resulted in an advantage for white Cubans over Black ones. As family sponsorship was the quickest way to get released, and Black Cubans were the least likely to have family in the United States, the release policy tended to favor lighter-skinned Cubans. Historian Alexander Stephens discovered that by the end of 1981, 95 percent of the 1,600 Cubans who remained in detention in Fort Chaffee in Arkansas were young

Black men.[54] When the Klansmen protested the arrival of Cuban refugees, it was not just their nationality but their blackness that offended the protesters. Church groups and prison employees who had been eager to sponsor lighter-skinned Cubans were more wary of taking in a Black refugee. For example, Carol Whitlock, who had joined with other families in sponsoring a Vietnamese refugee, was worried that a Black Cuban wouldn't be accepted in her all-white Wisconsin town. As she admitted in a *Miami Herald* article, "Maybe I secretly feel safer with a lighter-skinned man around." Although she and her husband did eventually sponsor a Black Cuban, many others could not overcome their prejudice.[55] Over time, most white Mariel Cubans were released on parole to their families, while the ones who remained locked behind bars were overwhelmingly Black.

RESISTING DETENTION

The proximate cause of the 1987 prison uprising was the imminent deportation of Cubans, but detainees had long-standing complaints about conditions in the prisons, their lack of due process, and their indefinite detention. At a 1988 congressional hearing, Deputy Attorney General Burns asserted that the 1987 prison uprising was a response to the November agreement between the United States and Cuba to deport excludable detainees. However, that narrative ignores the long history of riots and violence at detainee camps and prisons. In fact, from the moment Cubans were locked up in 1980, they regularly attempted to escape, destroyed prison facilities, and engaged in hunger strikes and suicide attempts as desperate acts of resistance. At Fort Chaffee, 200 detainees tried to escape through an unlocked gate at the end of May 1980, and a week later 1,000 detainees burned buildings and stormed the gates. By the end of the confrontation with Arkansas State Troopers, one Cuban was killed, forty were seriously injured, and fifteen state troopers were hurt. Around the same time as the Fort Chaffee escape attempt, sixty detainees at the prison at Fort Walton Beach, Florida, threw rocks at guards while dozens tried to scale a barbed wire fence. These prison rebellions had three effects. First, security at detainee camps was militarized, with thousands of army soldiers acting as guards. Second, the rebellions helped to popularize the myth of Marielitos as hardened and violent criminals. And third, the outbreaks forced the government to speed up the processing of detainees. By October 1980, almost all of the 120,000 Marielitos had been released into the community. The INS, however, identified 1,306 "potentially excludable" Cubans whom they scattered across the country in several minimum-security prisons and eventually paroled. A much smaller group of 350, representing less than half of 1 percent of the total number of Marielitos, were deemed by the INS to have serious criminal backgrounds. This group was sent to a US penitentiary in Talladega, Alabama, for indefinite detention.[56]

The view from inside the prison looked very different depending on who was reporting. Spanish-language newsletters produced at Fort Chaffee by the Cubans and overseen by camp officials provided a heavily censored view of life inside the camp. *La Vida Nueva*, for example, published an editorial from a Cuban detainee that condemned the rioters, declaring "'only a perfect imbecile or a Castro agent could be so impatient' as to participate in the riots."[57] While this official view of the Fort Chaffee uprising was perhaps shared by some of the detainees, others recognized the irony of being placed in a military prison camp surrounded by barbed wire in the land of liberty. As one journalist who described the similarities between the Cuban port of Mariel and Fort Chaffee put it, "There are barricades, loudspeakers, with voices in Cuban accents urging *'adelante'*—'get moving'—and men in uniforms, carrying clubs, posted every few yards."[58] One young detainee, Rosendo Tabio, remarked simply, "I'm in America, but I'm not free."[59] In countless letters sent from the Atlanta Penitentiary, detainees expressed their frustration for being imprisoned in what was supposed to be the land of freedom.

The Mariel detainees considered the most dangerous were sent to the maximum security prison in Atlanta. In May 1986, following a riot at Miami's Krome detention center in which Cubans burned mattresses and threw stones at guards, a group of fifty-five accused of starting the melee was put on a caged bus bound for Atlanta. The Cubans began to rock the bus when they reached northern Florida, forcing the bus driver to pull over on the side of Interstate 75. Forty police officers swarmed the bus, removing the Cubans to a local jail where they were searched, re-handcuffed, and put back on the bus to Atlanta. Although conditions at Krome were far from idyllic, the Cubans were aware that they were being sent to a severely overcrowded prison, where other Mariel refugees were being held eight to a cell in a space designed for four, and locked behind bars twenty-three hours a day. As Monsignor Bryan O. Walsh, head of Catholic Services in Miami, put it, "Cubans at Krome and Atlanta have no human rights whatsoever."[60]

People held at the Atlanta Penitentiary had been complaining about the conditions at the prison even before the Cubans arrived. In late 1979, one inmate, Richard Loe, filed a lawsuit against prison administrators with hundreds of pages of complaints. In 1983, another group of inmates filed their own complaints along with Cuban detainees. Although these consolidated suits resulted in court-ordered consent decrees on March 2 and July 26,

1984, prison administrators continued to abuse prisoners.[61] Just a few months after the consent decree, detainees at Atlanta Penitentiary were protesting their incarceration again.

On October 13, 1984, a group of fifty detainees marched to the yard, unfurling banners on bed sheets that proclaimed "LIBERTY OR DEATH" and "LIBERTAD." The group quickly tripled in size, defying guards' orders and damaging property as they marched back to their cells. Although this was a non-violent act of defiance and expression of frustration for being locked up indefinitely, the warden responded by locking down the entire prison and confining the Cubans to their cells. When prison officials tried to place a leader of the disturbances in administrative detention on November 1, he managed to break free with the help of other detainees and seized one of the cellblocks. The Cubans set fires and rampaged through the cellblock for hours, injuring three or four guards in the melee. Guards eventually retook the cellblock by deploying large quantities of tear gas. Afterward the warden instituted a prison-wide lockdown that remained in place for more than two years.[62] In the face of the harsh response to what began as a non-violent expression of their desire to be free, two of the detainees began a hunger strike to protest their indefinite incarceration, one of whom was force-fed after five days of refusing to eat.[63]

Patrick O'Neil, a peace activist who at the time was at the federal prison camp just outside the penitentiary, described being enlisted to confiscate anything flammable from the Cuban cells, including personal letters and photographs, clothes and mattresses. All of these materials were brought outside the walls of the prison and burned in a massive bonfire. O'Neil rescued some of these items, including one half-singed Bible, and smuggled them out to journalists at the *Atlanta Journal Constitution* so they would know that the detainees' personal belongings were being burned.[64] The 1984 rebellion cost the prison $1 million to $5 million in property destroyed and overtime salaries. Although a few staff suffered minor injuries, no hostages were taken.[65]

The 1984 rebellion demonstrated what the Cubans could accomplish if even a small group of them acted in concert. In retrospect, the 1984 rebellion prepared the way for the much larger, long-lasting, and coordinated prison takeover in 1987. It also alerted the public to conditions inside the prison and the plight of the Cuban detainees. After the rebellion, two of the ostensible ringleaders of the disturbances were criminally charged and faced a jury trial presided over by Judge Shoob. In spite of what Shoob saw as overwhelming evidence of their guilt, the jury found them not guilty. As Judge Shoob put it, the jury was so "incensed that people would be incarcerated for years on end without a hearing" in such dismal conditions that they in essence "pardoned those two ringleaders."[66]

The two-year lockdown may have prevented a full-scale rebellion, but it also resulted in high levels of violence in the prison. When the BOP compared the seventeen months during the lockdown to the same period following the lockdown, they discovered that inmate and staff assaults were almost twice as high under the lockdown. Prison officials attributed the reduction in violence following the lockdown to enhanced educational, vocational, and recreational activities at the prison.[67] However, in spite of the Atlanta prison officials' self-evaluation that the detainees' response to the changes was "more positive than it had been in several years," a February 1986 congressional investigation revealed serious detainee complaints about the condition of the physical plant, healthcare, food, hygiene, violence, and discipline at the prison.[68]

Given the lockdown and the inability to achieve reforms through legal channels, detainees used their bodies as the means to make demands. Sometime in the summer of 1985 hundreds of detainees refused to eat in a mass hunger strike. A small note in the *New York Times* on September 2 indicated that fifty Cuban hunger strikers in the prison were being force-fed, but the article provided no details about the strike.[69] On September 13, detainees smuggled a letter out of the prison that explained why they engaged in a hunger strike and how the strike was continuing despite the prison officials' claim that it had ended. The letter signed by thirty-three Cuban detainees promised to continue the hunger strike "until the end of our lives." They blamed the prison officials for collaborating with the INS in force-feeding the strikers, and they provided a vivid account of the complicity of the prison's medical doctor. According to the detainees, the prison doctor, Bolivar Martineau, had told them, "You better eat or I will make all of you crazy so this way nobody will believe anything you say." The detainees worried that the doctor would carry out his threat because, according to them, he had already made hundreds of Cubans crazy. It was difficult to communicate to the outside world about the strike since they were being held incommunicado in the "hole," were allowed out only once a day for forced feeding, had no access to telephones, and had all their mail intercepted. Nonetheless, they managed to surreptitiously get a letter into the hands of *Atlanta Journal Constitution* reporter Ann Woolner who wrote a story about the strike two days later.[70]

Woolner's article featured two Cuban hunger strikers, Julio Moret and Ernesto Crespo. Julio Moret had not eaten for fifteen days when prison staff "cuffed his arms and legs to a bed, stuck a plastic tube up his nose and down into his throat, and poured something liquid into it." Although the prison had had hunger strikes before, this was the first time the detainees had organized a coordinated mass effort. The prison was force-feeding 50 to 120 detainees each day, and hundreds more refused to eat. The strike was an attempt to draw attention to their purgatory, some having been imprisoned for five years since they arrived in 1980. Moret asked, "If we're not going back to Cuba. Why are we still here?" The twenty-three-year-old Ernesto Crespo, who was able to go to the exercise yard for only an hour every three days, explained why he joined the hunger strike. "I thought it was the only way the government would pay attention to our request."[71] It's not clear when the hunger strike ended, but in their letter the detainees claimed they had refused to eat for fifty-five days.[72]

In addition to the general mistreatment of detainees, guards appeared to target those perceived as leaders. Just a couple of weeks after congressional representatives toured the facility in 1987, prison guards beat Santiago Peralta-Ocana to death. One of the guards commented, "Peralta was a bad ass. The macho of the macho." Fellow detainees looked up to him as a leader, perhaps because he had proven himself to be an invincible prison fighter after withstanding forty knife and club wounds. Even after being confined to his own cell, he managed to kick the three-inch steel door off of its hinges a couple of times. On February 18, 1987, Peralta started shouting at a guard, accusing him of serving cold food. There had been a feud between the Black Peralta and this white guard, which started when the guard said he didn't like coffee "because it was black," a comment that Peralta interpreted as racist. Peralta retaliated against the guard by throwing urine on him when he passed by; the guard in turn withheld Peralta's mail and served him cold food. When the guard ignored Peralta's protest about the food, Peralta started to kick the door off the hinges, at which point the guard called for backup, handcuffed Peralta, and began kicking and choking him. Peralta was choked to death in front of six detainees and seventeen guards.[73]

A guard insisted on handcuffing Peralta's cadaver to a gurney, a final humiliation. Guards claimed Peralta hanged himself, but paramedics could tell from the neck bruises that he had been choked to death. The next day, Warden Petrovsky issued a press release claiming Peralta died of a heart attack. Although Petrovsky initially refused to release the autopsy and took the unusual step of ordering a second one, both autopsies plus eyewitness accounts revealed the truth.[74] Later in the month he received a message from a detainee, Geraldo Mesa-Rodriguez, that read, "We all know it was a brutal crime and we all are witness of that crime. And you know that any crime is neither legal or justifiable. And although Santiago Peralta Ocana has been a bad Cuban detainee, his death will not be justified."[75] In 1997, one of the Cubans who was deported back to Cuba told a filmmaker that he had witnessed the guards smother Peralta Ocana with a pillow.[76] Even with several eyewitness accounts and two autopsies that concluded Peralta Ocana had been choked to death, there were no indictments in the case. Geraldo Mesa-Rodriguez, who was a leader of the 1984 protest and had written to the warden about Peralta Ocana's murder, was also one of the leaders of the uprising that broke out less than a year after the murder.[77]

The killing of Peralta highlighted conditions in the Atlanta Penitentiary not just for the detainees, but for guards as well. Guards were underpaid, suffered violent attacks by prisoners, and were poorly trained. As soon as a guard could quit, he would. The Atlanta Penitentiary had earned a reputation as one of the most violent of all of the federal prisons, along with Fort Leavenworth in Kansas. Although the penitentiary had just 10 percent of the prison population, it accounted for 19 percent of all assaults on inmates or guards.[78]

Even at Oakdale, which was designed as a minimum-security prison and conditions there were supposed to be better than at Atlanta, disciplinary infractions spiked just prior to the revolt, averaging thirty to thirty-five per week. The rate of assaults in Oakdale was almost twice as high as at the Atlanta Penitentiary (60 per 1,000 inmates as opposed to 35 per 1,000) and six times the average rate of assaults in all federal prisons. In the ten months after Cuban detainees were sent to Oakdale (November 1986 to September 1987), there were two escapes, twenty-one inmate-on-inmate assaults, and seventeen inmate-on-staff assaults. In one incident, on September 9, 1987, an inmate who threw his tray on the floor in the dining room was restrained after he attempted to strike a guard. A large group of detainees blocked the entrance to the lieutenant's office where the Cuban was being held, and they refused to leave until they were assured that the Cuban was not being abused. This incident showed the power of the detainees when they banded together to defend one another. Two months later another detainee threw his tray in the cafeteria, sparking the 1987 prison takeover. In addition to the violence, Oakdale detainees were angry at the INS for making false promises to release them.

Therefore, although the conditions in Atlanta and Oakdale were not exactly the same, in many ways these were two branches of the same prison. The detainees at Oakdale had previously been held at Atlanta, and some thirty detainees who misbehaved in Oakdale were returned to Atlanta.[79] The exchange of detainees between the two prisons allowed for a flow of information and the development of personal relationships that help explain why the two prisons exploded almost simultaneously. The announcement of the agreement with Cuba in 1987 was the match, but the fuel had been collecting for some time, and when ignited, detainees at facilities 600 miles apart acted in unison.

"IT WILL BLOW"

On Thursday evening, November 19, 1987, Michael Kozak, principal deputy legal advisor at the State Department, finally wrapped up secret negotiations with his Cuban counterparts in Mexico City.[80] The next morning, the regional director of the Bureau of Prisons telephoned the wardens at the Oakdale Federal Detention Center and at the Atlanta Penitentiary to inform them about the agreement with the Cuban government to take back more than 2,000 Cuban detainees. In reality, the talks in Mexico City merely re-initiated a 1984 agreement that had been suspended when President Ronald Reagan began anti-Castro Radio Martí broadcasts into Cuba. The wardens knew this news could be potentially explosive for the Cubans at the prisons, so they quietly increased staffing and posted guards on the perimeter. As Oakdale was not a maximum-security prison, locking down the institution was deemed impossible. By early afternoon, bilingual staff began to inform the Cuban detainees about the agreement, trying to calm their fears and cautioning that it wasn't clear how many, if any, of those at Oakdale would be deported.[81] In Atlanta, the warden ordered staff to circulate among detainees and tell them that very few of them would be affected and that they should be "cool" until they had more information. INS hearings scheduled in the afternoon were canceled, but otherwise the prison seemed to be running normally.[82]

Detainees' reaction to the news at Oakdale was mixed, with some acting "sullen," and others walking off their jobs and becoming "vocally critical." Aside from a window being broken in the laundry, the afternoon proceeded without incident, but the prison's rapid response team (SORT) remained on standby into the evening. At the evening meal, a drunk detainee overturned his food tray and hurled it at a food service foreman, sparking other detainees to break dishes, throw food, and trash the cafeteria. It would become apparent in the next few days that detainees had access to contraband, including alcohol and handmade weapons. Guards escorted the Cubans to their housing units, but no other measures were taken for fear of provoking a more intense response. The warden, who was on his way to a retirement party at the time of the cafeteria incident, returned to the prison when he learned what had happened. Although the mood in the prison was tense, the day ended without any further disturbances. The warden returned home to sleep.[83]

On Saturday morning, Cuban detainees began telling guards that a major incident was going to happen that evening; rumors circulated that the Cubans would seize the female guards and rape them. The warden believed the threat credible enough that he removed female staff from the prison and brought in INS agents to guard the perimeter; by the afternoon he called in the Border Patrol Tactical team (BORTAC) from El Paso. In addition to the informants' warnings, guards witnessed the detainees gathering food, packing up their personal property, and wearing multiple layers of clothes, all signs that an uprising was imminent. Nonetheless, the warden refused to institute a lockdown or do anything drastic, fearing that would incite the riot they were attempting to prevent. Unit officers were also told that if anything should happen, they were not supposed to play "John Wayne" and should surrender their keys and radios.[84]

Just before 7 P.M., a large group of more than 200 detainees gathered on the grass in the yard brandishing clubs and other weapons, and headed toward the front entrance. The Control Center radioed the alert code, "Lt. Houston, now!" The prison's tactical response team stormed out of the INS building and fired several volleys of tear gas at the detainees, succeeding in repelling them momentarily. The detainees responded by setting fire to buildings and every two or three minutes charging the front entrance. By this point the detainees had managed to find fire axes and picks, and the tactical team had used up its supply of tear gas. The Cubans rushed to take hostages, but in the chaos a couple of dozen staff managed to escape through the security doors before the tactical team retreated.

By 7:30 P.M., the Cubans had control of the prison. The tactical response team watched helplessly as detainees set fires, broke windows, and chased staff. Hoping to escape, detainees banged on windows in the lobby, but the bulletproof glass held. Using hostages as shields, detainees used wire cutters to try to breach the fence but were forced to retreat by officers brandishing shotguns. In the chaos, groups of American prisoners helped some guards to escape and begged to be let out of the prison. Meanwhile, the mood among the Cubans was jubilant. They had succeeded in taking over the prison without anyone being seriously injured. The Cubans even threw one officer into a laundry cart and, in a sort of victory lap, paraded him around the prison while beating on the cart with clubs.[85] In just over half an hour, the Cubans had turned the tables; they were in charge.

By Saturday evening, detainees in Atlanta had heard through news reports, and perhaps also phone calls, about the Oakdale uprising, but prison officials didn't notice any abnormal activity. On Sunday, some detainees told guards that there would be problems on Monday and advised them not to come to work, but these reports never reached the warden.

Gary Leshaw, the detainee legal aid lawyer, also visited the prison on Sunday, and he advised the warden not to lock down the prison, predicting that if he did so "it will blow."[86]

On Monday morning, detainees reported to work with tennis shoes instead of their work shoes, and some reportedly wore extra layers of clothes. The foremen in the Federal Prison Industries (UNICOR), a prison factory, witnessed detainees working slowly and huddled in groups talking about the news, but he tried to calm tension by not citing them for violations such as wearing inappropriate footwear or bringing newspapers. Detainees began to warn guards that female staff should be removed and that they should be careful. It was apparent that something was afoot.

Then, just after 10 A.M., detainees throughout the prison seized hostages, set fires, and took control of the prison by wielding machetes and makeshift weapons. Detainees seized staff members' radios and keys, handcuffed them and forced them into a tool cage. The prison erupted in complete bedlam, alarms sounded from all corners, inmates threatened to kill hostages, and sharpshooters in the towers began firing at the detainees. It was in these first ten minutes that a guard shot and killed a detainee, whom he had observed chasing a staff member with a home-made knife. Five other detainees were shot and sustained minor injuries. Finally, when detainees threatened to kill hostages, the shooting ended. The regional director of the BOP arrived at the prison within a few minutes

Figure 4.2 Atlanta Penitentiary set ablaze by Cuban detainees in 1987.
Source: Calvin Cruce, *Atlanta Journal-Constitution* via AP.

Figure 4.3 Buildings burning in Atlanta Penitentiary takeover in 1987.
Source: Atlanta History Center.

of the uprising and immediately called the director to inform him that the Atlanta Penitentiary was "coming apart."[87]

SANTERÍA

The prison uprising can be understood in terms of the legal and political predicament that faced Cuban detainees, but the spiritual resources the detainees relied upon to survive in prison provides a different perspective on their experience of incarceration. The Cuban detainees had few legal resources with which to fight their incarceration, but many of them relied on religious faith as a way to survive prison and also to give them hope for liberation. Prison guards were unfamiliar with Santería, and so when they discovered detainees constructing elaborate altars in their cells they imagined it was "some kind of voodoo." In 1980, prison guards were in the process of inspecting Cellhouse C in the Atlanta Penitentiary when they detected a putrid smell emanating from the cell of one of the Cuban detainees. Upon entering, they found the smell emanating from rancid butter that was putrefying in a dozen milk cartons beneath his bed. In the corner of the cell, the guards found an altar made from fifty empty cereal boxes, surrounded by cigar butts, coffee, rotting oranges, and rock candy. There were pigeon feathers and holy cards of Catholic saints along with candles on the altar.[88]

Sally Sandidge, Carla Dudeck, Mora O'Neill
Patric O'Neill

Figure 4.4 Photograph of Sally Sandige, Carla Dudeck, Patrick O'Neil, and his daughter, Mora, organizers of the Coalition to Support Cuban Detainees.
Source: Courtesy of Sally Sandige.

Mark Hamm, a criminologist who would later write an account of the 1987 prison uprisings, did an eight-month study of Santería among Mariel detainees in the prison at Terra Haute, Indiana. He published his findings in the *Federal Prisons Journal* as an "informational" guide to Santería to help guards better understand the psychological and spiritual resources of their charges. His student, who was also a guard, acted as his research assistant on this project, using the time he spent in prison to observe Santería rituals and altars. The two researchers also interviewed twenty-three Santería devotees among the Mariel detainees. While Hamm appeared to sympathize with the plight of the Cuban detainees, his article was intended to show guards how Santería could help to manage the experience of incarceration. Hamm argued that just as Santería was developed as a coping mechanism to "survive the savage conditions of slavery with increased hope, dignity and human betterment," he believed it could help Cubans to "withstand their experience of confinement."[89] The importance of religious faith in motivating and sustaining Mariel detainees remains shrouded in mystery, but it is clear that spirituality was a crucial resource for them in undertaking the biggest prison uprising in US history.

If Santería was a spiritual resource, Cuban detainees also relied on allies outside the prison. Over the years, Gary Leshaw had built trust with the Cubans, and he was at the prison the day before the uprising. When they finally rebelled, Leshaw offered himself as a mediator. Prison officials and the FBI were reluctant to involve outsiders as negotiators, but they recognized that Leshaw could help them gain the trust of the Cubans. The first night of the uprising, Leshaw was brought into the prison at the request of the Cubans for an hour-long discussion with two US officials and a hostage negotiator. As Carla Dudeck, coordinator of the Coalition to Support Cuban Detainees, put it, "a lot of the guys know Gary, and a lot of them obviously trust his judgment."[90] Detainees wrote Gary Leshaw's name on the signs they painted as well as the graffiti on prison walls. He, along with Sally Sandige and Carla Dudeck of the Coalition, were trusted allies.

By the early afternoon, talks between a detainee representative and FBI negotiators had begun. Detainees provided Polaroid photographs of hostages to prove they were safe and even released ten who had been injured or were ill. Meanwhile, firemen had a difficult time putting out the blaze in the factory building from outside the walls of the prison. The National Guard would later fly helicopters with forest fire buckets and dump water on the burning building from the air.[91] Sally Sandige, one of the main organizers of the Coalition to Support Cuban Detainees, remembers seeing the huge plume of smoke rising from the prison all the way from

Figure 4.5 Cuban detainees holding homemade sword with FBI SWAT agent.
Source: Atlanta History Center.

Decatur, five miles away.[92] Detainees became especially agitated when the National Guard buzzed the prison with helicopters, a tactic that was designed to keep the detainees on edge. Government officials finally called off the helicopters when they overheard detainees on the prison radio channel threatening to throw hostages from the windows if the government attempted an armed takeover or if the helicopters flew over again.[93]

HOSTAGES AND NEGOTIATIONS

The takeover of two prisons by more than 2,000 detainees and the seizing of well over 100 hostages occurred with surprisingly little violence and injury. Except for one detainee who was killed at the Atlanta Penitentiary in the first few hours of the uprising, almost nobody else was injured during the eleven-day standoff. However, in the first few days of the takeover, it was not clear that it would end so peacefully. The 1971 Attica prison uprising in which 1,000 inmates seized more than 40 hostages ended with the bloody deaths of 33 inmates and 10 guards when New York State troopers stormed the prison.[94] As one Atlanta official said, "We didn't want another Attica on our hands."[95]

In Oakdale, there were several tense moments when it looked like detainees would try to blow up the front gate or burn hostages alive, but both sides backed down and tensions eased. On Sunday, detainees began moving wood and other flammable material in laundry carts against the front entrance in an apparent attempt to light the roof of the prison on fire. A SWAT team was deployed to the roof, and detainees were given an ultimatum: move the laundry carts or face an armed attack. Detainees withdrew the laundry carts. By Monday night tensions flared again as helicopters buzzed the prison every couple of hours, "creating havoc among the detainees." Detainees demanded the flights be stopped or hostages would be harmed; they cut the line that had served as their only means of communication and negotiations ceased. At around 3 A.M., Cubans began to construct a makeshift platform surrounded by mattresses and rags doused in fuel, and placed a chair on top of it. The implication was clear to prison authorities. If the helicopter flights didn't stop, a hostage would be set aflame on the execution chair. The helicopter flights were ended. On Wednesday night, the detainees broadcast a radio transmission from one of the hostages: "They have us handcuffed and have machetes at our throats and would behead us if you try to come in with force."[96] Given all the moments when a sniper's twitchy finger or a nervous detainee might have started an all-out bloodbath, it is remarkable that nobody was harmed.

On Sunday night, one day after the Oakdale uprising, Attorney General Meese laid out his offer, including a moratorium of repatriations to Cuba and a "full, fair and equitable review" of each case. The detainees flatly rejected the proposal. As one detainee would later put it, "We didn't trust Meese. He's a liar."[97] As the crisis dragged on, the government became more willing to accept the intervention of certain outsiders. The government brought into Atlanta's prison three well-known Cuban Americans from Miami on Thanksgiving to help with negotiations: Jorge Mas Canosa, chairman of the anti-Castro Cuban American National Foundation; Robert Martinez Perez Rodriguez, a former Cuban political prisoner; and Armando Valladares, a writer who had spent twenty-two years in Cuban prisons and was then appointed US ambassador to the United Nations Commission on Human Rights. The detainees booed Valladares when he entered the prison, and they eventually rejected an agreement negotiated with the three Cuban Americans from Miami. Leshaw explained that the detainees wondered "what the hell . . . these three guys were doing here. They had nothing to do [with the riot or the deportations]. They had never been sympathetic to [Atlanta] Cubans. Why are they [Meese and Quinlan] trying to use them to negotiate?"[98] Since the government had rejected the detainees' picks as intermediaries, Leshaw and Pickard, detainees were not convinced that these Cuban Americans represented their interests. Not only had they not been sympathetic to the plight of detainees previously, Mas Canosa had even praised the immigration agreement with Cuba as a great achievement of the Reagan administration.[99] In his memoir, one of the detainees, Enrique González Sarasa, explained they were not interested in joining with the Miami counterrevolutionaries. "We did not accept them and we told them to go to hell" (No lo aceptamos y lo mandamos pa'l coño de su madre).[100]

Even when hostage releases had been negotiated, the government reneged on its promises. At one point the detainees had agreed to release fifty hostages in exchange for a televised press conference, but when the detainees only produced three Black hostages, the government negotiators refused to accept them. The detainees interpreted this refusal as a sign of racism. The inability of Miami Cuban Americans to negotiate a settlement illustrated the ways class and race tensions fractured political alliances of Cubans in the United States. The Cuban American advisors remained in Atlanta until Monday evening, serving as advisors to government negotiators and meeting with detainees for a second time on Sunday evening.[101] The older generation of whiter, wealthier, and more conservative Miami Cubans had distanced themselves from the poorer and blacker Mariel refugees. Both sets of Cubans may have hated Castro, but that hatred was not enough to unite them.

Other Miami Cubans tried to use the Atlanta prison uprising as a moment to score political points. At one point, a Dade County commissioner flew up to Atlanta and in front of a Miami TV news camera offered to exchange himself for a hostage, knowing full well that his offer would be rejected.[102] On Friday, November 27, the mayor of Miami and another representative briefly met with the Cuban detainees, held a press conference, and then departed.[103] Cuban detainees in Atlanta trusted only their legal aid lawyer, the Coalition to Support Cuban Detainees, one local TV journalist, and Miami's Auxiliary Bishop Agustin Román.

Bishop Román had been a strong defender of the rights of Mariel detainees since their arrival in 1980. In his widely publicized *Importancia de la Misericordia*, Román argued that because the Mariel refugees had established families and put down roots in the United States, the attempt to deport them was "never a solution."[104] Four days before the outbreak of the prison uprising in Oakdale, Román's final act as chair of the Catholic Conference in Washington, DC, was to compile a list of more than 700 Mariel detainees who had long since completed their sentences but who remained under INS custody. The bishop sent this list to Attorney General Meese, the man who would oversee the hostage negotiations in the coming weeks. On several occasions Meese attempted to sideline the bishop's offer of assistance to resolve the prison takeovers. First, on Monday morning, November 23, Román was about to leave for Oakdale at the request of the director of the BOP, Michael Quinlan. Suddenly word came from Quinlan, apparently under pressure from Meese, to abort the flight. Román also traveled to Washington, DC, on the fifth day of the uprising to offer his assistance directly to Meese, who rebuffed him.[105] Throughout the prison takeover, Meese tried to keep Román out of the negotiations or to minimize his role.

By Saturday, November 28, negotiations at Oakdale had broken down, with detainees displaying banners blaming the government for the stalemate and demanding that Bishop Román be allowed into negotiations. Quinlan still refused, but he had Román flown to a nearby airbase in case he could be useful. Quinlan finally agreed to permit Román to videotape a message to the detainees. On Sunday morning, prison officials projected a three-minute video on large screens around the perimeter of the prison in which Román urged the detainees to accept the attorney general's promises and release all of the hostages. Afterward, detainees brought a large sign to the front gate: "We Want the Bishop, or Legal Representatives, and National Press Inside Before We Sign or There Will Be No Agreement." A few hours later, Quinlan ordered the National Guard to fly Bishop Román to the prison. Román was driven around the perimeter in the back of a pickup truck, making the sign of the cross as he proceeded. Detainees clapped, cried, and hugged one another when they saw the bishop. He then proceeded to address the Cubans directly, telling them that the attorney general's promised moratorium on deportations was a good one and that they should immediately release all hostages. Fifteen minutes later, more than 900 detainees laid down their weapons, set free their hostages, and surrendered. Bishop Román performed a mass for the detainees and hostages.[106] The Oakdale prison takeover, which had lasted eight days, was finally over, with the detainees accepting the attorney general's offer of an immediate halt to deportations and individual reviews.

Meanwhile, in Atlanta, the takeover dragged on even after prisoners received news that Oakdale Cubans had surrendered. The Legal Aid lawyer Gary Leshaw came up with an idea to ask the Cubans to release a hostage as a show of good faith on Carla Dudeck's birthday. Dudeck had been one of the principal organizers of the Coalition to Support Cuban Detainees. Leshaw got the go-ahead from Washington, and so he went on Ernesto Perez's radio show on Tuesday and did his "shtick about Carla's birthday." That night, more than a week after the uprising began, the government finally allowed Gary Leshaw into the prison to speak with the detainees. In exchange, detainees released a guard. Leshaw became actively involved in mediating a solution at this point, but the detainees insisted on a definitive promise not to deport anyone to Cuba, a point that was unacceptable to the government.[107]

At that first negotiating session, Leshaw did most of the talking. Emotions were running very high, especially when the Cubans mentioned the killing of the thirty-two-year-old José Peña Pérez. The Cubans told Leshaw, "My God, they even killed one of our own." The Cubans brought the body of their slain fellow detainee down to the negotiating room, and four of them "cried over the body." After the body was photographed and removed from the prison, the issue of the killing never came up again. The name José Peña Pérez does not appear in any of the newspaper reports at the time, nor does it appear in the congressional report and detailed analysis by the BOP. Although the killing is mentioned in these reports, the name of the only person killed in the prison takeover was systematically erased.[108]

On Wednesday, Bishop Román reiterated his willingness to help negotiate a resolution, and he recorded a three-minute audiotape that was broadcast to the detainees on a public address system. On Thursday, negotiators sat down and went through the final agreement, but at the last moment a "young Turk" demanded more revisions. At that point, one of the FBI negotiators, Pedro Toledo, launched into an impassioned ten-minute monologue in Spanish: "The United States of America is the most

Figure 4.6 Cubans on roof of Atlanta Penitentiary during takeover in 1987 with US and Cuban flags.
Source: Scott Robinson, *Atlanta Journal-Constitution* via AP.

benevolent and the most democratic nation on the face of the earth today, but don't kid yourselves in thinking that that benevolence is everlasting. For I tell you right now, gentlemen, you cannot and you will not bring the United States to its knees. For by demanding upon demands is a direct insult to the people of the United States." Apparently, this plea swayed the eight members of the Cuban detainee commission. They all initialed the agreement and took it back inside the prison for ratification.[109]

The Cuban detainees voted in favor of the eight-point proposal that excluded the no deportation clause: 1,100 voted in favor and 270 voted against. The potential problem was that the 270 against the agreement were the ones guarding the hostages, and therefore they could have insisted on rejecting the agreement. However, once the vote was concluded, these holdouts acceded to the majority.[110] Years later in Havana, Enrique González Sarasa reflected on the negotiations as a sham, arguing that they were misled by Bishop Román and fellow Cuban detainees who were clandestinely working for the US government, leading them believe that none of them would be deported.[111] Leshaw was called back inside to review the agreement once more with the detainees. He brought FBI agent Rosario as his translator because the two men had grown to trust each other. At that point, a small, frail man in a double-breasted black raincoat entered the negotiating room. It was Bishop Román, who at long last was allowed to enter the prison. The Cubans became very emotional when the bishop arrived, and he proceeded to make a speech in Spanish imploring them to accept the agreement and end the takeover peacefully. The last point holding up the negotiations was the person who would sign for the government. The detainees didn't trust Gary McCune, regional BOP director, since he had lied to them in the past. In the end, Bishop Román called Associate Attorney General Trott on the phone, and Trott pledged to the detainees, "You have my word, the attorney general and the government will stand behind the package."[112] Some of the Cuban negotiators wanted to wait until morning, but Leshaw was anxious to sign the agreement, telling

Figure 4.7 Juanita Diaz with children of Cuban detainees in Atlanta Penitentiary.
Source: William Berry, *Atlanta Journal-Constitution* via AP.

them, "Look, the media's outside. Everybody's ready. Momentum is in your favor. Let's do it." Leshaw also credited the bishop's presence for convincing the Cubans to take the deal. "I don't know that I would have been able to do it without the bishop that night," Leshaw later recalled.

And then, just as the Cubans were about to sign, they said they wanted to go back into the prison one more time. The government negotiators were livid. They had been negotiating for eleven days, and now that they had finally come to terms, they were afraid the whole agreement would unravel. The Cubans left the negotiating table. When they returned twenty minutes later, a detainee had a Cuban flag draped over one shoulder, wore a US flag over the other one, and carried a crucifix. The Cubans had retreated to the prison in order to dress for the theatrics of the signing ritual. Carlos Marrero Gonzalez dramatically stood up and asked a contingent of fellow detainees whether they should sign. They responded with a resounding yes and broke into applause. On Friday at 1 A.M. with Bishop Román, Gary Leshaw, and the media present, the detainees signed the agreement with the BOP regional director.[113]

The Cubans in Atlanta ultimately surrendered on December 4, the day of the patron saint of Cuba, Santa Barbara. Pedro Toledo, one of the FBI negotiators, knew about the importance of the day in Cuba, and he pressed the detainees to end their takeover on that day to honor Santa Barbara. Thus, it is not a mere coincidence that the two-week standoff ended when it did. Ultimately, the detainees accepted the terms laid out by attorney general Meese at the outset of the takeover, so their assent cannot be explained by the government's willingness to bend. When the two sides finally came to an agreement, FBI negotiators passed out candles and beads for the detainee altars; this suggests that that the negotiators recognized the importance of the Afro-Cuban religion Santería to the detainees, many of whom were Black Cubans who practiced the religion.[114] Santa Barbara is the patron saint of artillery and is linked to militarism. In Santería, a blend of West African Yoruban religion and Catholicism, the *orisha* (deity) Changó, is the Yoruban analog to Santa Barbara. Associated with anger and power, Changó is seen as a warrior.

The terms of the agreement included a delay in deportation of the Cubans until individual reviews of each case could be completed. They also included a promise not to prosecute those who participated in the takeover unless there was specific evidence of violent acts. According to one of the principal Cuban negotiators, Carlos Marrero González, it "took all of our efforts and all of our force" to persuade the other inmates to accept the deal. Still, about 200 "hardliners" held out, refusing to ratify it. The takeover ended with loud joyous cheers as the hostages streamed out of the prison into the embrace of their family members as salsa music blared from

Figure 4.8 Cuban detainees at Atlanta Penitentiary leaving prison after negotiated end to takeover, 4 December 1987.
Source: Diane Laakso, *Atlanta Journal-Constitution* via AP.

speakers the detainees had set up.[115] The signing and release of hostages was broadcast live on CNN.[116] The longest-lasting prison takeover in the nation's history was finally over.

AFTERMATH

After their surrender, the Cuban detainees from Oakdale and Atlanta were dispatched to federal prisons throughout the country. The INS conducted its reviews of the detainees, releasing those eligible for parole and deporting those who were found to pose a danger to society. By early February 1988,

1,300 of the 2,400 Mariel detainees had been approved for release, and yet only 280 of them had actually been set free. The lack of halfway houses had become the main obstacle for release. Meanwhile, detainees complained that they were being retaliated against by being subjected to lockdowns in which they were confined to their cells for twenty-four hours a day. Gary Leshaw noted that the lack of outrage from the general public was due to racism. "If these were light-skinned or blond Nordic types, there would be so much outrage you couldn't contain it." The detainees found themselves facing the same problems as before the uprising: insufficient due process and being imprisoned long after they had been determined to be releasable. As Ronaldo Suarez, a detainee in the federal prison at Terra Haute, Indiana, wrote plaintively to his supporters, "If they try [to] send [me] to Cuba I'm going to hung myself."[117]

In a series of letters written by detainees immediately following the end of the Atlanta uprising, Cubans expressed their desperation and graphically described the brutal treatment they were receiving from guards. Juan Sarria Miranda wrote to Gary Leshaw on 18 December to complain that they were sleeping on the floors in Fort Leavenworth, locked in their cells twenty-four hours a day, and were put in "torture" cells where they were "shackled by their hands and feet." A guard had banged Sarria's head against a gate and he worried that at any moment they would begin to kill detainees as they had done in Atlanta. In short, Sarria Miranda wrote, "This is worse than Atlanta."[118] Jose Narbona Sanchez wrote from Fort Leavenworth to explain that some detainees were so frustrated by the conditions that they threw trash and water at guards. One detainee was punished by being chained to his bunk for eight hours.[119]

Nine months later, conditions had not improved. Gustavo Pique Perez wrote to Leshaw on September 15, 1987, that Atlanta was a "palace compared to the roughness" of Fort Leavenworth. Perhaps the authorities had created such a "hell," he surmised, so the detainees would scream, "Please get me out of here, send me to Cuba, but get me out of here." Pique Perez described having to sleep with no space between mattresses and being forced to walk naked and strip-searched upon arrival. Finally, he accused guards of retaliating for minor infractions like throwing paper in a hallway by chaining naked detainees to their cold beds for eight hours at a time.[120] In April 1990, Manuel Diaz Bandera wrote to Carla Dudeck about the terrible conditions in Tangipahoa parish jail in Louisiana, including lack of medical assistance, sub-standard meals, extremely limited access to the legal library, no towels or underwear, being able to shave only once a week, and having no heat in the winter. One detainee who was supposed to be in a hospital was locked down for eleven months without a mattress, the air conditioning constantly on, with only a sheet and blanket with which to cover himself.[121] Although the agreement with the government indicated that they would not be punished for having participated in the prison uprising, what the Cubans were experiencing felt like retaliation.

Although the individual reviews that were agreed to by the government took time to implement, the pace of reviews began to pick up as a two-person team traveled to the seventy-two prisons that held Cuban detainees to conduct interviews. By the end of April 1988 they had recommended the release of 2,224, about half of whom had actually left prison. The panel denied release to 1,193 and ordered deportation for fourteen individuals. Although the process had been accelerated and liberalized, Leshaw pointed out that the INS hearing officers still acted as "judge, jury and prosecutor," and that detainees could not bring witnesses or cross-examine those making allegations. Many of the volunteers who advised Cubans during their hearing were horrified by the lack of due process, the unprofessionalism of the INS officers, and the disparate criteria for release in different venues.[122] By the middle of November, the first fifteen detainees who had been through the review process and been denied by the appeal board were being readied for deportation back to Cuba. The government asserted that these individuals had committed murder, attempted murder, and rape, and were likely to commit violent crimes again.[123]

The fifteen detainees who had final orders of deportations appealed to a federal court in Birmingham, Alabama, and then to the 11th Circuit Court of Appeals, arguing that the review procedures had been violated. They lost in both of those courts. However, unlike the government's depiction of all of these people as rapists and murderers, some were just convicted of theft, battery, and burglary.[124] Over the next few years, the United States regularly deported small groups of Mariel detainees on US marshal flights to Havana.

The frustrations of the Mariel detainees and their resistance to deportation did not end with the 1987 uprising. In August 1991, a group of 121 Cuban Mariel detainees being held at Talladega federal prison in Alabama had gone through the review process and exhausted all of their appeals. All told, there were 175 people at that point whose cases had been reviewed and who had final orders of deportation. Fearing their deportation was imminent, the Talladega group rebelled on August 21, seizing ten hostages in Alpha cellblock unit. As one of their lawyers put it, "They are like a cornered and wounded animal. They have no hope and they are that much more dangerous." As in 1987, Bishop Román served as an intermediary, talking by phone with the detainees.[125]

Working at Talladega, a docket clerk for the INS, Linda Calhoun, ended up as one of the hostages in the takeover. Although she was scared for her life, she also sympathized with the Cuban detainees and was not surprised that they had revolted. Calhoun described speaking to one of the detainees, Lazo Hernandez, who used to cut himself. Rather than fearing the detainees, she tried to help them. However, the deportation officer was not as nice, and the detainees responded by throwing feces on him. "Did he learn? No. So he was still an ass to them and he still antagonized them." Calhoun said that she and the language specialists knew what was going to happen "just by looking at the Cubans through the bars."[126]

Tougher drug and crime laws had an immediate impact on Cuban detainees who were suddenly being deported for offenses that they had committed years earlier. Gary Leshaw noted that in 1990 Congress made any Mariel Cuban serving a sentence of five years or more or convicted of "any illicit trafficking in a controlled substance ineligible for citizenship and liable for deportations." Three of Leshaw's clients who had been approved for release were back on the deportation list after passage of the bill. The same people who would have been free were now going to be deported to Cuba.[127] Negotiations in Talladega dragged on for ten days, but unlike in Oakdale and Atlanta, the takeover ended when 200 specially trained BOP and FBI agents stormed the prison in a pre-dawn raid. None of the hostages were injured and only one Cuban sustained minor injuries. The next day, thirty-one Cuban detainees were shackled and transported to Birmingham's airport and flown to Havana on a Justice Department airplane.[128]

In the 1990s, filmmaker Estela Bravo documented the return to Havana of Mariel detainees from Talladega federal prison. Thirty men are shown handcuffed and shackled as their feet descend from a US Justice Department airplane in Havana; some are so old and infirm they can barely walk. Bravo interviewed the deportees on a bus as it idled on the tarmac. Some of them expressed regret for having to return while others said they should never have left in the first place. One man who was eighteen years old when he left Cuba explains that in Cuba he never took drugs, but that he got involved with drugs in the United States, and for that he was sent to prison. Another man says he was sentenced to six months in prison for a DUI (driving under the influence) charge, but spent ten years in prison waiting to be deported. The men described their experiences of being beaten and humiliated in United States prisons, emphasizing the racism they suffered. Most of the detainees would be considered Black in the United States. The men described having to eat, defecate, and sleep while shackled for up to seventeen days. They had three minutes to eat with their hands chained to their waists, so cellmates would have to feed each other. One man removed his shirt to display a big purple bruise that he said was caused by a guard beating him with a baton. Other detainees told stories of having spent up to ten years in prison for bouncing a check or stealing $43. It was less the physical than the psychological abuse, one detainee said: "They destroyed us mentally." One Cuban described how guards killed another detainee, Peralta, by suffocating him with a pillow. The detainees were transferred directly to a Cuban prison where they spent forty days while their cases were reviewed. At that point, more than 900 Marielitos had been returned to Cuba.[129]

One of the most vivid memories of the deportees was of the chief medical doctor in the prison, Puerto Rican Dr. Bolivar Martineau, whom they accused of using drugs and pills to turn the detainees into "total vegetables." Others complained about being force-fed sedatives like Thorazine and Haldol. If patients refused the pills, they claimed that the doctor would have nurses sneak the medication into their food. As one man put it, "They drove people crazy, then said the government had sent lunatics." A detainee, with his downcast eyes, barely able to talk, said he was in the prison hospital for eleven years and was continuously injected with drugs. Martineau would tell detainees that if one of the "locos" gave them trouble, he would "triple the dosage and invent something new for them." In an interview with the filmmaker, Dr. Martineau denied experimenting on the detainees and claimed that only forty-eight of more than 1,000 detainees in Atlanta could be considered "normal." "The whole prison, as far as I was concerned," said Martineau, "was a psychiatric social laboratory. It was just fabulous." Years later one of the guards described Martineau as a "snake in the grass" who would have worked well "under Hitler."[130]

The documentary ends with Judge Shoob reflecting on the inhumane conditions of the prisons, with detainees separated from their families and locked up for years without trial. As Judge Shoob put it, "History is not going to record with any great approval of our activities during this period. I never thought this could happen in America, but it can." At the end of the 1990s, there were still Mariel Cubans in prison. The filmmaker interviewed three Mariel detainees in the Terra Haute, Indiana, federal prison, who told her stories of being assaulted by other inmates and of young detainees hanging themselves. Humberto Macias reflected that they were being used as pawns in a geopolitical war between communism and capitalism. "Meanwhile we're trapped in the political impasse between two countries. We've nothing to do with politics, we're human beings, but we have no rights at all." This feeling of having no rights and of being stuck at a political impasse is at the center of what it means to be excludable and stateless. The Cuban Marielitos, like so many other migrants, have come to the United States in search of a better life and freedom, but their dreams remained elusive. One of the Terra Haute detainees, Segundo Rivera, summed it up: "I just want to be free."

NORMALIZATION OF RELATIONS WITH CUBA AND
NEW DEPORTATIONS

The Mariel detentions and deportations continued into the last years of Obama's presidency. By June of 2016, only 478 of the original 2,746 who were on the list of deportees remained in the United States, 250 had died, and about 2,000 had been deported to Cuba. In January 2017, just before leaving office, President Obama ended the so-called wet-foot-dry-foot policy that granted asylum to any Cuban who reached US shores and in exchange the Cubans agreed to repatriate up to 500 Mariel Cubans who were not on the original 1984 list of deportees but had committed crimes since the list was established.[131] By 2016, the original list of people who faced deportation to Cuba ballooned from under 3,000 to over 36,000, but most of these people were allowed to live freely in the country. ICE, however, still held 600 in custody.[132] Although the US-Cuba normalization agreement did not mention Cuban felon deportation, one section mentions those who remain in the United States in "violation of US law." Of the tens of thousands of deportable Cubans, 2,000 have murder convictions while more than 6,000 are deportable due to non-criminal immigration violations.[133] Under the Trump administration, Mariel Cubans who have minor drug violations dating back two decades are being arrested and facing deportation to Cuba.[134] Meanwhile, after Obama's announcement, the number of Cubans being held in ICE custody pending immigration hearings shot up to over 1,300 in just six months.[135] As many as 1,200 Cubans were deported in 2019, including some who had been living in the United States for more than fifty years.[136] In the never-ending saga of incarceration, thousands more Mariel Cubans may be put in indefinite immigration detention, awaiting a deportation that may never come.

The linking of criminal and immigration law resulted in thousands of Cuban refugees being held indefinitely in some of the country's worst prisons. In the 1990s and 2000s, legislation would expand the number of crimes that would render immigrants deportable and even allow minor crimes committed decades earlier to be used as deportable offenses. The Mariel Cubans set the stage for the most recent moment of mass immigrant incarceration.

CHAPTER 5

"A Particularly Serious Crime"

Mayra Machado in an Age of Crimmigration

In April 2019, I received a call with an automated message from the La Salle Detention Center in Jena, Louisiana. The recorded message said, "A detainee is attempting to call you. Will you accept the call?" The woman on the other end of the line introduced herself as Mayra Machado. I had provided expert witness testimony for her three years prior and had forgotten about her case. She had been deported to El Salvador in early 2017 and was separated from her three US citizen children, but she had returned to the country and was again in deportation proceedings. Machado was representing herself because she couldn't find a pro bono lawyer willing to take her case in a remote part of Louisiana. She asked whether I would be willing to testify on country conditions for her case. I immediately agreed, and I also told her that I would try to find her legal representation. Given the complexity of immigration law, trying to represent herself in what was a complex case with felony convictions on her record was going to be an uphill battle.

In some ways this story seems mundane. An undocumented immigrant being picked up and deported is not the stuff of news since it happens so often. However, the details of Machado's story reveal a radical shift that had been happening since the mid-1990s, and was accelerated under President Obama. Unprecedented numbers of immigrants were being caught in a system that penalized people by mandatory deportations for relatively low-level crimes. Machado's story did become news, not because it was out of the ordinary but because it seemed to be happening everywhere. Machado hardly seemed to fit the profile of scary felons that Obama had invoked when he made his landmark immigration speech in 2014 that announced the Deferred Action for Childhood Arrivals (DACA) program and reinforced a distinction between "felons" on the one hand and "families" on the other. Machado, like so many others, is both.

Machado was just five years old in 1990 when she was brought to the United States by her mother, who was desperate to escape the civil war raging in their home country of El Salvador; she wanted a better life for her two young daughters. Machado grew up with her grandmother in southern California as an American kid, unaware of her status as an undocumented alien. She spoke English with a southern California accent and embraced free expression, women's empowerment, and a can-do attitude. Although Machado was considered an illegal alien by the US government, in her heart she was very much an American who had only dim memories of El Salvador and who spoke stilted Spanish. Her three children who were in the car on the day she was arrested in 2015 were all born in this country and were US citizens.

Machado's felony convictions stemmed from three fraudulent checks that she had written in 2004 when she was eighteen years old as well as being in the possession of a friend's debit card. In that case, the judge took her lack of a prior criminal record and her age into consideration and gave Machado a suspended sentence and probation for six years in exchange for a guilty plea. Probation meant that even though Machado was not in prison, any tiny infraction would result in severe charges. The court also imposed over $7,000 in fines and restitution fees, as well as ongoing charges of $30 a month in probation fees. For an eighteen-year-old from a poor immigrant family, these fees amounted to an insurmountable debt. The court also warned that any violations of probation could result in a prison sentence of twenty years. Nonetheless, the judge allowed Machado to enter her plea under an Arkansas law for qualifying first time offenders (Act 346), which meant that her record could be expunged if she completed her probation successfully.[1] Although Machado was represented by an attorney, he did not inform her of the potential legal immigration implications of a guilty plea to a felony charge.

It's not clear exactly what happened because Machado had already pled guilty in September 2004, but she was re-arrested in spring 2005 for failing to appear in court in January. It may be that she was required to check in periodically to the court and failed to appear, or that her attorney failed to inform her that she had a court date even though she had already pled guilty. The official judicial record is unclear and contradictory on this issue. Neither Machado nor her current attorney can explain the inconsistent record, which raises serious questions about shoddy record keeping that

can have such important ramifications. As a result of the alleged probation violations, the court sentenced her to the full amount of ten years for
each of five separate charges. The judge's sentence was harsh, yet, seeing
that she was pregnant, he offered her the chance to complete an alterna-
tive boot camp for several months, after which she would be on probation
for ten years.[2] The judges in her case have both shown a propensity toward
egregious overcharging and mercy, but the serious criminal record was the
long-lasting legacy of her involvement with the criminal justice system.

Machado successfully completed the boot camp and her ten-year proba-
tionary period without having further interactions with the criminal justice
system. In none of these complicated interactions with the courts in 2004
and 2005 was her immigration status ever discussed. By the time of her traffic
stop in 2015, she had paid her debt to society for bad choices she had made
as a teenager, and she was a mother of three young children with a good job.

The traffic stop in 2015, however, set in motion a cascade that would ultimately lead to her deportation in January 2017. Although the 287(g) program had been in existence since the 1996 Illegal Immigration Reform and
Immigrant Responsibility Act (IIRAIRA), the program was greatly expanded
as federal funding skyrocketed under Obama from $5 million in 2006 to
$68 million in 2010.[3] Machado was handed over to ICE based on her undo-
cumented status and her record of felony convictions dating back a decade.
Enlisting an immigration lawyer in New Orleans and reaching out to media
to explain her plight, Machado fought her deportation. A sympathetic *Los
Angeles Times* article quoted Machado's plea from detention. "I was an everyday soccer mom. . . . I'm not a bad person. I shouldn't be here. . . . I'm not
a threat to society and I'm not going to hurt anybody. I should be taking
care of my children."[4] In addition to the media attention, Machado's family
enlisted the support of the National Day Laborer's Organizing Network
(NDLON), which started a petition on her behalf. As a photogenic young
mother, Mayra Machado briefly became the face for millions of other
immigrants caught up in the nexus between harsh criminal sentences and
draconian deportation policies. I received a request from Machado's lawyer
the day after Donald Trump was elected asking if I would serve as an expert
witness on country conditions in her case. Due to her felony convictions,
she was denied bail. She had already lost her asylum claims in immigration
court and had an appeal pending in the Board of Immigration Appeals. Her
lawyer was trying to reopen the case on the grounds that she was eligible
for relief based on the Convention against Torture. I accepted the case and
wrote a declaration, but she was denied again by the courts. Even before
her appeal was decided, ICE shackled Machado and placed her on a flight
from Alexandria, Louisiana, to El Salvador, a country she had left as a child

twenty-seven years earlier. Barack Obama was still president on the day she was deported.

Machado's deportation to El Salvador was traumatic from the beginning. She had three US citizen children whom she left in the care of her mother in Arkansas. Her mother had been able to legalize her status, but Mayra Machado was barred from doing so due to her criminal convictions. Machado did not want to bring her children with her to El Salvador and subject them to living in a country where teenage boys face recruitment by gangs and young girls are forced to be the girlfriends of gang members. Her oldest child, twelve-year-old Dominic, suffered not only from being separated from his mother but because he blamed himself for her arrest. She had returned to a Hobby Lobby where she was shopping for Christmas decorations to find his eyeglasses, when she was stopped by police for failure to yield. In the course of this stop, the police officer discovered an unpaid traffic ticket, leading to her arrest and subsequent detention on an immigration hold. Once his mom was deported, Dominic began lashing out at his younger sister and his grades in school began to slip. In the videocalls with her three children, Machado hid the fact that the small town where she was living in El Salvador was overrun with gangs who had threatened her. Instead, she just told them she was fine, and promised to be home soon.[5]

Figure 5.1 Photograph of Mayra Machado and her three US citizen children, Dominic, Dayara, Dorian. Courtesy of Mayra Machado.

Machado's asylum case is complicated by the egregious sentencing she eventually received for her original offense of forging checks. What began as an offense of forging someone's signature on three checks for $1,500 became five felonies, each carrying a ten-year sentence. Even though these sentences were to be served concurrently, this was an extreme sentence given the crimes she had committed. The ten-year sentence, equivalent to what the Arkansas sentencing guideline suggests for a first-time-offender intentional murder conviction, was harsh for what amounted to a minor infraction by an eighteen-year-old who forged a check to make a car payment.[6] The definition of an "aggravated felony" in the immigration act lists twenty-one subsections which include everything from "murder rape or sexual abuse of a minor" to "receipt of stolen property," "supervising of a prostitution business," and "failure to appear if the underlying offense is punishable by imprisonment for a term of 5 years or more."[7] Since Machado pled guilty in 2005 to receiving stolen property (possessing her friend's debit card) and since she had a failure to appear sentence of ten years, according to immigration law, she was guilty of an "aggravated felony" and not eligible for most kinds of asylum relief.

Most people tend to think of felonies and aggravated felonies as very serious crimes, involving violence or large-scale theft, but as a result of "tough-on-crime" politics in the 1990s, combined with stricter enforcement of immigration laws, people with minor infractions were suddenly categorized as having committed serious crimes. The fact that the "aggravated felony" language was invented in an anti-drug law illustrates how criminal and immigration law worked together to trap immigrants in a carceral web.

Illegal entry was punished as a crime from the mid-1880s through 1896 when the Supreme Court ruled that a criminal sentence could not be imposed without a judicial trial. For the next thirty-three years, illegal entry was not a crime per se, but those found to be unlawfully in the country could still be deported. In 1929, illegal entry became a misdemeanor for the first offense and a felony for illegal reentry with a maximum sentence of two years in prison.[8] Even by 1952, the maximum penalty for illegal reentry was two years in prison. However, in 1988, Congress expanded the range of crimes that would lead to deportation by adding the "aggravated felony" category in the Anti-Drug Abuse Act.[9] However, in 1988, "aggravated felony" only referred to murder, federal drug trafficking, and illicit trafficking of certain arms and destructive devices. The list expanded over the years to include thirty types of offenses.[10] Beefing up immigration enforcement and tough-on-crime bills during the Clinton presidency helped to further criminalize immigrants and impose harsher sentences on those who violated the law. The 1996 Antiterrorism and Effective Death Penalty Act (AEDPA) and the IIRAIRA led to a sharp increase in the numbers of immigrant detentions and deportations. In addition to allowing for mandatory detention of non-citizens without bond, these two acts expanded the category of crimes for which even lawful permanent residents could be deported by enlarging the definition of "aggravated felony" and then applying such measures retroactively.[11] Legal permanent residents were thus caught up in the rush to criminalize all immigrants, although it is not clear how many of the millions of deportees were legal residents.[12] For Machado, who was not a legal immigrant, a 2005 conviction from a crime committed when she was eighteen triggered a deportation order more than a decade after the offense.

In addition to changing the laws, the immigration enforcement bureaucracy exploded, and existing laws criminalizing immigration began to be enforced more rigorously throughout the 1990s and 2000s. The immigration enforcement budget doubled approximately every five years from 1975 to 2000, tripled between 2000 and 2005, and has doubled again in the last fifteen years. In 1988, the Immigration and Naturalization Service (INS) budget topped $1 billion for the first time; in 2019, the DHS budget had grown to over $23 billion.[13] Whereas in 1986 immigration enforcement was about one-quarter of spending of all other types of law enforcement, by 2012, more money was spent on immigration enforcement than on all other types of federal law enforcement combined.[14] Presidents Clinton

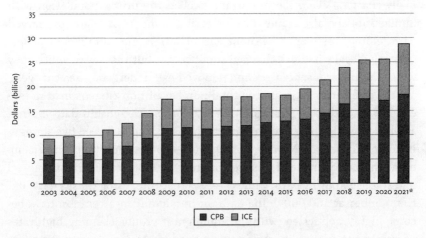

Figure 5.2 Immigration enforcement spending, 2003–2021.
Source: Department of Homeland Security, *Budget in Brief*, 2003–2021.

(1992–2000) and Bush (2000–2008) each doubled the number of Border Patrol agents, and under Obama the number of agents swelled to over 21,000 in 2011.[15] More money meant more enforcement, more detentions, and more deportations. Under Clinton, deportations, including formal removals and "voluntary" returns, hit all-time highs, reaching almost 2 million at the end of Clinton's second term.[16]

Although migrant apprehensions were trending upward under Clinton, following the September 11, 2001, attacks, George W. Bush ramped up prosecutions of immigrants. Whereas Clinton removed more people from the country than any other president before or since, Bush began to send increasing numbers of migrants through criminal proceedings, a trend accelerated under the Obama administration. For example, while illegal entry had long been a federal misdemeanor and reentry a felony, in 2005 the government established Operation Streamline in Texas which began enforcing the law on all illegal entrants. Instead of "catch-and-return," which had long been the practice, it became "catch and keep." Migrants caught entering the country were hauled before judges, up to 80 or 100 at a time, and encouraged to plead guilty to misdemeanor illegal entry punishable by up to six months in prison. Most of the time, migrants were sentenced to time served and deported, but the ones who were charged with reentry received sentences from two to twenty years in prison.[17] Operation Streamline led to a quadrupling of criminal prosecutions of first-time illegal entry border crossers or reentry from 4,000 in 2003 to 16,500 in 2005. As Operation Streamline expanded from Texas to all border states except California, criminal prosecutions grew to 44,000 in 2010 and peaked at 97,000 in 2013.[18] This dramatic shift from allowing voluntary departure to criminally charging every illegal entrant swelled the prison population with immigrants and also resulted in increasing numbers of migrants charged with felonies for reentry without authorization. The numbers of people crossing illegally had not changed significantly, but the way in which they were criminalized, sentenced, and removed had undergone a sea change.

It is difficult to estimate the total number of non-citizens held in federal, state, and local prisons and jails, because citizenship data are not available for all people held in state prisons and local jails, and five states— including California, Nevada, and Oregon—do not report any citizenship data. The Department of Justice counted 83,000 non-citizens in federal and state custody in 2016, while the Cato Institute, using census data, put the number at 160,000.[19] The data on immigrant incarceration have become highly politicized, with anti-immigrant groups claiming high rates of immigrant criminality and immigrant advocates pointing to the opposite. The anti-immigrant Center for Immigration Studies, for example, uses data from the US Sentencing Commission to show that between 2011 and 2016, non-citizens comprised more than 44 percent of all federal criminal convictions, over 21 percent if immigration offenses are removed. Reading beneath the headline, however, the author acknowledges that the vast majority are crimes are at the state-level and that extrapolating from federal data is "not reasonable."[20] The Cato Institute report, which is the most robust analysis to date and corroborates the findings of many other studies, clearly shows that immigrants are incarcerated at much lower rates than native-born people. Undocumented immigrants are incarcerated at about half the rate of native-born people, and legal immigrants at about one-fifth the rate of native-born people. Even accounting for race, immigrants are far less likely than their native-born counterparts to be found in prisons.[21] The Marshall Project correlated changes in immigrant populations, both documented and undocumented, to crime rates, and it concluded that immigration has either no effect on crime or marginally decreases the rate of property crimes.[22]

Although the overall incarceration rate of immigrants is lower than for native-born people, increasing numbers of immigrants have been put into federal prisons for immigration and drug charges. The federal Bureau of Prisons keeps track of the citizenship of its prisoners. However, given that federal prisons account for less than 10 percent of those in state prisons and local jails, it would be misleading to extrapolate immigrant incarceration levels based on these figures.[23] Nonetheless, because immigration violations are prosecuted at the federal level, it is an important arena of immigrant incarceration. The federal prison population has grown more than sevenfold from 1980 until 2019, peaking in 2013 at almost 220,000, and declining to about 175,000 in 2020.[24] In 2017, Trump directed the Department of Justice to publish quarterly data on aliens in federal custody, and these reports have determined that non-citizens make up one-fifth of the Bureau of Prisons population. For the second quarter of fiscal year 2018 (the last published report), almost half of the non-citizens in custody were held on drug-related charges, more than a quarter had committed immigration offenses, and about one-tenth were awaiting trial on drug or immigration-related charges. The number of non-citizens being held for violent crimes was so low that the report lumped them together in an "other category" that included kidnapping, murder, larceny, terrorism, escape, bribery and extortion, rape, and other offenses. The US Marshal Service detained more than 21,000 non-citizens, with almost 80 percent of them held for immigration (56%) and drug-related (23%) charges.[25] What this means is that more than 80 percent of non-citizens in federal custody are being held on drug or immigration charges, and given the overall growth of the federal inmate population since the 1980s, more non-citizens are being held in these prisons than at any other time in US history. A General Accountability Office study for 2011–16 estimated that an even higher percentage 92%—of criminal aliens incarcerated in federal prisons were convicted of either immigration (63 percent) or drug (29 percent) charges.[26]

Zero tolerance policies practiced by both Obama and Trump have led to a dramatic rise in federal criminal prosecutions for immigration violations, meaning that more immigrants are being criminalized for the simple act of crossing the border without authorization and spending longer periods of time behind bars. Criminal prosecutions jumped fourfold under Bush and have maintained a high level ever since.[27] The latest push to criminalize immigrants has seen a doubling of federal immigration prosecutions from January 2008 to January 2020.[28] Not only have immigration cases overtaken all federal prosecutions, accounting for more than 60 percent in 2018, but almost all of those cases are for first-time entry violations.[29] In 2013, when federal immigration prosecutions reached their peak, 95 percent were for illegal entry, almost three-quarters for first-time entry, and another fifth for reentry.[30] The entire federal criminal justice bureaucracy has essentially been turned into a giant machine to incarcerate immigrants.

By the time Mayra Machado was arrested at a routine traffic stop in December 2015 in Springdale, Arkansas, it had been a decade since she had served her sentence for the felony convictions related to the forged checks.

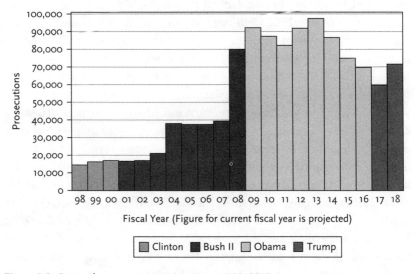

Figure 5.3 Criminal immigration prosecutions, 1998–2018.
Source: Transactional Records Access Clearinghouse, https://trac.syr.edu/immigration/reports/510/.

What could have been a minor inconvenience of settling the unpaid traffic ticket instead became a nightmare that led to her being imprisoned for more than a year and then deported to El Salvador. It was the increasing cooperation between ICE and local law enforcement that allowed the police to identify her as a potentially deportable undocumented immigrant. An officer who was deputized to act as an immigration agent discovered Machado's prior felony convictions after running her name through a database.[31] A decade earlier, neither traffic stops nor five felony convictions triggered deportation because nobody at the local or state level inquired about immigration status, but by 2015 the landscape had changed. Since 2007, northwest Arkansas has become a hot bed of cooperation between local law enforcement and ICE; just two counties, Benton and Washington, accounted for almost half of the deportations from Arkansas from 2010 to 2013.[32] While most immigrants were apprehended while trying to cross the border, under Obama and Trump there was a concerted effort to expand enforcement into interior parts of the country, especially through cooperative agreements with local law enforcement. Interior arrests skyrocketed under Obama, reaching a historic high of over 322,000 in 2011, and subsequently declining to just over 100,000 by the time Machado was arrested in 2015.[33]

Three programs sought to integrate local jails and state officers and institutions into the enforcement of federal immigration laws, much in the same way that fugitive slave laws in the mid-nineteenth century enlisted local authorities in the pursuit and capture of escaped slaves.[34] Provision 287(g) of the 1996 immigration act (IIRAIRA) allowed local and state police officers to be deputized as enforcers of federal immigration law. By 2011, sixty-eight state and local law enforcement agencies had signed 287(g) agreements. The Criminal Alien Program (CAP) in 2007 provided ICE agents direct access to local jails. Local law enforcement officers call ICE to let them know when they arrested someone they suspect of being deportable. ICE agents routinely place "immigration holds" or "detainers" on people held in local jails. These "detainers" are essentially requests to hold people beyond the time they would have been released until an ICE agent can arrest the person at the jail. Although ICE issued administrative warrants together with detainers in many cases, these were not judicial warrants and thus had no legal validity. Since 2014, many cities have refused to honor these detainers since they have been ruled unconstitutional by federal courts across the country.[35] The Secure Communities program (2008) gave ICE access to biometric data of people booked into local jails, essentially linking local law enforcement to ICE through an FBI database. Although the government claimed these programs targeted serious criminals, the majority of people being swept up had no criminal convictions. For instance, in the first four years of Secure Communities (FY 2009–12), more than half (54%) of those deported had either never been convicted of a crime or had only one or two low-level misdemeanor convictions. Obama responded to the criticism of Secure Communities by transforming it into a new Priority Enforcement Program in 2014 that purported to target criminals for deportation. However, the infrastructure for information sharing had already been built. Even though "sanctuary" cities and states refused to cooperate with ICE detainer requests or to enter into agreements with ICE, data sharing continued, allowing ICE to access information about every person who was arrested and booked into a local jail.[36] The deportation juggernaut built over three decades would not be easy to dismantle, especially with a president at the helm eager to detain and deport millions of immigrants.

LIFE AS A DEPORTEE

On December 5, 2016, Machado attempted to make a phone call, but her account was not working. She discovered that her account was closed because she would be deported that same day. At that point nobody had informed her that she was being deported in spite of the fact that her appeal had still not been decided. David Rivera, the ICE agent in charge at LaSalle, told her that the tactical team was on hand to forcibly remove her if she resisted. He said that since she had been publicizing her plight, they expected her to put up a fight. That same night, she was shackled and taken to an airport hangar about an hour's drive from Jena. She and 300 other Salvadoran deportees spent the night in the airport waiting for their deportation flight. In the morning, Rivera demanded that she sign a document before being put on the flight. She refused, explaining that her appeal was still pending. The deportees were shackled at the feet and hands in such a way that made walking almost impossible. Machado was wearing the clothes in which she had been arrested a year earlier, black sweat pants and a top. She had no identification, only her telephone and the legal papers she had kept. After the plane left US airspace, guards removed the shackles from Machado and the other deportees, explaining that they were no longer in US custody.[37]

Mayra Machado landed in San Salvador on January 6, 2017, a country she had left when she was five years old. Although it was her birthplace, she didn't know this country at all and only spoke rudimentary Spanish. Most deportees are put aboard a bus and taken to "La Chacra" (the Farm or Grange), a processing center which is located in one of the most dangerous neighborhoods in San Salvador, straddling Barrio 18 and MS-13 gang territories. Up to three deportation flights arrive each week, with up to 135 people on each. Most of the deportees are men between twenty and thirty years old.[38] Machado, however, was processed at a deportee building in the airport. As a young woman, she would have stood out anyway, but the fact that her case was covered extensively in the US and Salvadoran press prior to her deportation made her instantly recognizable upon her return.[39] Machado told me about her ordeal in April and August 2019 on telephone calls from behind bars. She explained how almost immediately she faced threats and intimidation by Salvadoran government officials who pointed to her, muttering that she had talked badly about their country. "I would love to teach you things," said one of the men in uniform. The Salvadoran government officials laughed at her and goaded her to repeat statements she had made in the press about dangerous conditions in El Salvador. She was the only woman in a room full of men. "I can have fun with her tonight," said another. "Oh the things I can do to her." "What does that mouth do?" An official asked the men, including other detainees, if any of them wanted to take her home that evening. One government official demanded that she show him her naked body, including stomach, arms, and back, to check for gang tattoos. When he saw the Juicy Couture logo on her right shoulder blade, the government officer said she was a gang member and that he would "fix" her.[40]

Once she was released from the intake center, Machado was met at the airport by her grandmother's friend who worked as an airport employee. He was supposed to accompany Machado to her birthplace in Usulután, but noticing that they were being followed as they left the deportee building, and fearing for his own safety, he made her wait several hours so they could leave the airport without being seen. Even before leaving the airport, Machado had already been harassed by government officials and followed by unknown people.

Mayra Machado joined hundreds of thousands of others from El Salvador, as well as Honduras and Guatemala, who have been deported in the last decade. In the 2010s, for the first time, more Central Americans than Mexicans were apprehended on the US-Mexico border. Whereas in 2000, 98 percent of all apprehensions were of Mexicans, by 2018, more than half of the people apprehended (52%) came from the Northern Triangle countries of Central America (Guatemala, Honduras, and El Salvador), and almost all of the family apprehensions were from these countries.[41] However, the increase in Central American migration was within the context of overall declines in migration and border apprehensions. In fact, border apprehensions fell dramatically from over 1.6 million in 2000 to just under 400,000 in 2018.[42] Although apprehensions were increasing in 2019, the rates were still far below historic highs. On February 5, 2019, President Trump declared a national emergency in a Rose Garden speech in which he mentioned "invasion" eight times in reference to undocumented migration across the southern border. "We have an invasion of drugs, invasion of gangs, invasion of people, and it's unacceptable," Trump said. Even as the president was talking about the "monstrous caravans" coming from Central America, the number of apprehensions on the southern border was a quarter of what it had been in 2000. Not since the early 1970s were southern apprehensions at such a low level.[43] The crisis on the border Trump alluded to was his creation by demanding that every person claiming asylum or caught entering illegally be detained until the cases could be settled.

Machado was born at Hacienda La Carrera, an agricultural cooperative two hours' drive southeast from San Salvador. In recent years, La Hacienda has been overrun by gangs. When Machado arrived there, she was questioned by two officials who guarded the entry gate to the community about where she would be staying, for how long, and if she had money. Machado refused to answer their questions. "Who are you to be asking me questions about my life?" she said. "I do not owe you or anyone an explanation."[44] She was eventually allowed into the community. On her way in, she noticed young men throwing up gang signs she didn't understand. Being nervous, she laughed. This only enraged the gang members, who began calling her names and following her. She was taken to a house that had been her grandparents' but was now owned by a man named Rubén. In addition to the gang members who trailed Machado to Rubén's home, a young man stood outside menacingly wielding a machete. The young man with the machete commented, "Pablo needs you," a reference to her cousin who was an MS-13 gang leader in the town, who Machado believes was involved in the disappearance of another cousin of hers. "Daughter of a whore, come outside," yelled the machete man just outside the door.

Fearing for his own safety, Rubén told Machado that she would have to leave. Late at night while the teenager with the machete man had grown tired, they jumped a fence and ran to a neighbor's house, where a waiting car whisked Machado to an older woman's house. The older woman had heard that the gang wanted to rape and kill her, and she told Machado to come up with a plan to flee because she was putting her own children at risk by harboring Machado. The woman's son asked about Machado's tattoo and said that the gang had a bounty on her. Machado feared for her life and was worried that the woman's son might turn her over to the gang for money.

Gunshots rang out in the middle of the night. It seemed like the gang realized that she was no longer at Rubén's home, and they were out looking for her. Mayra did not sleep that night. The next morning, she went to a watering hole a few feet from the front door of the house to wash her face since the house had no running water. A young man on a motorcycle kept riding back and forth in front of her. When he realized who she was, he pulled out a gun and began barreling toward her. She ran inside the house and shut the door. For the next few days, she only snuck out in the dark to use the bathroom. "I lived in terror of being found," Mayra said. "My depression and anxiety started to get worse. I was terrified to be found killed and raped. My insomnia became unbearable." Throughout her time in this community, she was repeatedly told that her cousin Pablo was looking for her and wanted naked pictures of her. Once she was discovered at this new home, Pablo sent two young boys with machetes to stand outside and watch her movements.

A teenage woman appeared at the house one day, claiming to be Mayra's cousin, and demanded to take full-body pictures of Mayra to show to Pablo. When Mayra declined, the young woman snapped some photographs of Mayra anyway, grabbed her hand, and said "Orders from Pablo do not go unanswered." She also indicated that Pablo had put a price on her head and that he would make an "example out of me just like Carmen," a reference to Mayra's aunt who had been killed by gang members years earlier.

The next day Mayra sneaked out of La Hacienda and headed for Usulután to obtain a birth certificate and to file a police report about the threats and harassment. It became clear that the police already knew who she was when she arrived at the station because of Facebook posts that had been circulating. A police officer refused to take her complaint, saying that he could not file a report against a local gang leader because this would put his own life in danger, and he "was not going to die over some 'American.'" Her efforts to obtain a formal identification document were also frustrated when the same police official followed her and stared menacingly as she applied for a birth certificate. That police officer reached out to Machado's sister on Facebook, thinking the sister was her. At this point, she not only feared the gangs but also the threatening behavior of the police. She decided to live with a distant aunt and uncle at La Hacienda and try to remain hidden.

Machado agreed to meet Kate Linthicum, a *Los Angeles Times* reporter who had already written several stories about her, and Pablo Alvarado, the co-executive director of the National Day Laborer Organizing Network, who supported Mayra during her yearlong detention. Even though she was trying to keep a low profile, she felt the need to publicize her case. As she put it, "Freedom of speech is a right that I have grown up with and one I am passionate about." The consequence of these outsiders visiting Machado in La Hacienda, showing up in a "shiny 4-door truck" and driving around town taking pictures was that the gang immediately knew exactly where she was staying.[45] The gang again posted young boys to watch her home. Machado's mother in Arkansas also began receiving Facebook messages demanding money and nude pictures of Mayra. On February 25, 2017, Mayra received word from the reporter that the next day the story about her would be published in the *Los Angeles Times*. The very next morning at 5 A.M., Mayra escaped from La Hacienda, while the guards were too groggy to inspect vehicles. She made her way through sugarcane fields to a small road where she boarded a bus to Guatemala. She was headed back to the United States to reunite with her three children. Machado was in El Salvador for less than two months, but in that time she "developed chronic depression, chronic anxiety and insomnia." The journey through Guatemala and Mexico was dangerous and crossing the border illegally was also a risk, but staying in El Salvador was not an option.

Machado spent several weeks hiding in taxi trunks and tractor trailers, forgoing food and showers for days at a time. She had paid a smuggler her remaining savings, $8,000, to reach the United States, but as she was nearing the US border the smuggler put a gun to her head and cocked the trigger. "I'm in the hands of the Gulf cartel," she thought. The first thing that flashed in her mind was how her death would impact her children. "I might die, and my children will never see their mother again."[46] The northeastern Mexican state of Tamaulipas is notoriously dangerous for Central American migrants because some of the most violent drug cartels control the human trafficking through that corridor. In 2010, seventy-two migrants from Central America were massacred at a Tamaulipas ranch when hostages refused to pay a ransom or work for the Zetas cartel as assassins.[47] Machado was forced to cook and clean in a squalid cartel safe house, suffering abuse from her captors who called her "fat and lazy," beat her, and attempted to rape her several times. Finally, the smugglers helped Machado to cross the border on the Fourth of July 2017. She was picked up by family members and drove all night to Arkansas. Her children woke up to the surprise of their lives: their mom was home. "I'm dreaming," said one of her kids as he opened his eyes.[48]

Mayra was happy to be able to be with her children again after being separated from them for more than a year. She finally decided to tell Dominic, her oldest son, the truth. She was not a US citizen and had forged checks when she was young. "It was the worst mistake of my life," Mayra told him. It took a while for Dominic to believe that his mother would not disappear again. Within a month Mayra moved her children in with her fiancé, Tony. The family was reunited, but Mayra had no identification and no job; she rarely ventured outside, fearing being picked up by the police.[49] She was with her family in America, but she was not free.

Since Mayra was deported in early January 2017 and she returned in July, Trump had become president. As one of his first acts in office, Trump restored the Secure Communities program that Obama had discontinued in 2014, and ICE arrests under this program had begun to creep up.[50] On May 22, 2018, Mayra ventured out to pick up her daughter from her final day of fifth grade. On her way, a car stopped short in a roundabout, and Mayra's car hit the car in front, grazing the fender. The woman's Mercedes was not badly damaged but Mayra offered to pay her for repairs on the spot. The woman refused, and Mayra agreed to call the police. Mayra called a friend who suggested she flee. Mayra knew that was the wrong thing to do and instead came up with a plan to pretend she was her friend. Mayra

Figure 5.4 Mayra Machado and her children in hearing in Arkansas on January 18, 2019.
Source: Photograph by Magaly Marvel. Courtesy of Mayra Machado.

gave her friend's name to the officer, but he became suspicious when the photograph on his computer didn't match Machado's face. After threatening to call a fingerprint expert, Machado broke down and admitted who she was. "My name is Mayra." She was charged with a felony for obstruction of government operations, a charge that was subsequently dropped, but Myra's name had been flagged by ICE so she was taken into custody and faced a felony reentry charge, punishable by up to two years in prison. The judge in her case seemed sympathetic to her plight and after seven months sentenced her to time served, but she still had a removal order from DHS. She was interviewed by an asylum officer and found to have credible fear and was then transferred to the LaSalle Detention center in Jena, Louisiana. The prison term scared her less than the prospect of being deported to El Salvador. "At least I'll be safe in prison," she said.[51]

When I received Mayra's phone call in April, she had a little more than a month to prepare her own asylum petition. I called every lawyer I knew in Louisiana and contacted the Southern Poverty Law Center (SPLC), and finally managed to find her a pro bono attorney. Isabel Medina, a law professor at Loyola University in New Orleans, herself a Cuban immigrant, took the case. Benjamin Osorio, an immigration attorney based in Atlanta, also joined the team at the request of SPLC. Pablo Alvarado from NDLON, her family from Arkansas, and I made plans to testify at her hearing at the end of May. Given the legal impediments to asylum with an "aggravated felony" on the record, it was going to be a hard case to win, but Mayra had people all over the country working on her behalf.

LASALLE DETENTION CENTER AT JENA, LOUISIANA

The place where Mayra Machado was detained is located in a sparsely populated agricultural region covered in pine forests and Confederate flags. Jena, the parish seat, is best known for a 2006 incident at the local high school in which six Black students were charged with attempted murder for the beating of a white student. Nooses found hanging from a campus tree prior to the schoolyard fight were dismissed as a "prank" by the principal and revealed the deep-seated racism in this segregated town of 3,000. Even though some of the Black students were innocent, they all pled guilty to reduced charges of simple battery to avoid facing a trial for attempted murder, and one served eighteen months for second-degree battery. The incident revealed the corruption and racism woven into the criminal justice system in rural Louisiana.[52] That year, 2006, was also the year that Geo, a global prison corporation, opened its detention center in Jena.

The LaSalle Processing Center, as it is called, is one of the largest immigrant prisons in the country, holding close to 1,200 men and women in a sprawling complex of buildings in this remote hamlet in northwestern Louisiana, a three-hour drive from Baton Rouge and four hours from New Orleans. LaSalle was originally built as a juvenile detention center in 1998 and run by Wackenhut, a private prison corporation, but it was forced to close down in 2001 after a federal investigation found that teenage boys were being brutalized by guards, kept in solitary confinement for months, and deprived of clothes and medical care.[53] The facility held prison evacuees from New Orleans during Hurricane Katrina before being converted in 2006 into an immigrant detention center. Geo (formerly Wackenhut) operates the detention center in ways that skirt federal law and limit detainees' access to lawyers and the public. In 2018, the SPLC sued the Department of Homeland Security (DHS) over the lack of access to their clients and arbitrary rules that made it impossible for lawyers to represent immigrants facing deportation.[54]

The detention center is a major driver of the local economy, providing more than $1 million in taxes to LaSalle parish and employing 268 mostly local residents in Jena. The detention center population is roughly one-third that of Jena.[55] At the end of his presidency, Obama announced that the federal government would phase out the use of private prison contractors because of their failure to adhere to federal standards. Once Trump was elected, private prison contractors were back in business, and Geo's stock price more than doubled in a matter of months. By the end of 2019, more than three-quarters of immigrant detainees were held in private prisons, and Geo's revenues approached $2.5 billion.[56] Geo oversees almost 75,000 prison and detention beds at 69 facilities around the country. With the promise of billions more in DHS spending on detention, Geo went on a building spree, constructing a 661-bed facility in Eagle Pass, Texas; erecting a 1,000-bed facility in Conroe, Texas; and adding 700 beds to facilities in Georgia and Colorado. Geo's international operations in Australia, South Africa, and the United Kingdom made it a global prison empire, with total real estate assets valued at over $2.6 billion.[57] Machado was trapped within a rapidly expanding prison industry that had spread its tentacles far beyond US borders.

A National Public Radio study found that ICE now holds more than half of its immigrant detainees in remote rural locations. Access to lawyers and family support is almost impossible in these remote prisons, and the immigration judges in rural areas deny asylum in 87 percent of cases, compared to 54 percent for judges in urban areas.[58] Denial rates by immigration judges across the country reveal huge discrepancies among judges and courts. Someone whose asylum case is heard in Boston, New York, or San Francisco is much more likely to receive asylum than anywhere in Louisiana; one judge in Oakdale, Louisiana, denied asylum in every single one of the 144 cases heard between 2013 and 2018.[59] There are currently eight ICE detention centers in Louisiana, seven of which were recently opened; all of them are located in rural areas.[60] In addition to ICE detention centers, ICE pays local sheriffs in Louisiana five times the rate of state compensation to hold someone convicted of a crime, thus creating a profit motive for local jails to detain immigrants.[61]

The LaSalle "processing center" is a series of single-story buildings that look as mundane as a suburban office park except for layered rows of razor wire on the ground and the top of the double gates surrounding the facility that make it clear this is a prison. When I visited, we entered through a security gate and arrived at a small gray room that serves as the lobby for the courts that are adjacent to the prison. Mayra's two older children, aged thirteen and nine, had driven seven hours from Arkansas with their grandmother to visit their mother. It was the same car that Mayra had driven when she got in the accident that ended in her arrest and detention; the front fender was still smashed up from the collision. Isabel Medina, Machado's attorney, had arranged for her students to attend the hearing along with Mayra's children. When Machado's children were prevented from entering the hearing, Medina protested to the ICE supervisor who threatened to call the sheriff and have her arrested.

Medina was indignant that they would dare to arrest a law school professor for what was a perfectly legal request. Meanwhile the Geo worker kept saying, "Ma'am, I'm just doing my job." "I don't decide anything around here. That man in there is the one who decides everything." The worker was originally from Baton Rouge but she had lived six miles from the detention center for so many years, she said, she might as well be from here. Medina asked who he was. "He's the head of Homeland Security." Medina's co-counsel, Benjamin Osorio, and I looked at each other, and Osorio said, "I'm pretty sure he's not the Interim head of DHS." The Geo employee had worked at the facility for seven years, both inside the prison and in the court facility. When I asked why children were not allowed in, she said, "This is a prison, and there are dangerous people in there. It's to protect the children." The law school students were quick to point out that this was not, in fact, a prison and that none of the people there were serving sentences for crimes. In a way, the Geo worker had it right, even though the law school students were correct. This was a prison. I asked whether there were any violent incidents inside the detention center, and she looked at me and said enigmatically, "We've had all kinds of things go on in there."

The stand-off continued, and after about twenty minutes, Medina was called back to talk to the ICE supervisor again, and this time he apologized to her and allowed the children in.

Since Pablo Alvarado, Mayra's mom, sister, and I were all witnesses, we were told to remain in the lobby until we were called. We began talking about the dangers in El Salvador, the car accident that landed Mayra in prison, and the difficulty Mayra's mom was having in supporting the three kids on her salary of $350 a week from a chicken processing plant. She had recently had some medical bills due to a heart condition, and since she couldn't afford to pay the bills, the hospital had begun garnishing her wages. One week she took home just $90. Feeding and clothing the kids on her paltry salary was difficult, and she had no money left over to help Mayra, who needed money deposited into her account so she could continue to make calls from the detention center at 50 cents a minute. Mayra's mom had to choose between providing money for her daughter to make calls from detention or feeding her grandchildren.

Going into the courtroom requires passing through a metal detector and being buzzed through three heavy steel doors. The courtroom is a small, gray, cinderblock rectangle inside a beige building surrounded by concertina wire. It does not suggest the majesty of justice as much as a supply room. There is no dark wood paneling or windows with light streaming in, no jury box. When I was called in after about two hours of waiting, I saw Mayra for the first time. She was wearing a gray sweatshirt, the color was drained from her face, and she looked much younger than her thirty-five years. She smiled at me as I came in, and I put my hand to my heart and tried to express solidarity. I was told to sit right in front of the table where Mayra and her two lawyers were seated. The youngish looking red-headed judge, Cassie Thogersen, sat at the front of the room, elevated on the dais. She had been an ICE attorney for a decade in Oakdale, Louisiana, when Jeff Sessions appointed her as an immigration judge in September 2018. Before the appointment of four immigration judges to LaSalle, judges were flown in periodically or teleconferenced in from Miami. All of the new immigration judges assigned to LaSalle had worked previously for ICE or the US military; one new judge had been an attorney for the Air Force in Afghanistan, Iraq, and Guantanamo.[62] The DHS lawyer sat alone, not appearing menacing but rather looking resigned to a job he had to do. Like the Geo worker in front who was just doing her job, the DHS lawyer also seemed to be collecting a paycheck but his heart didn't really seem to be in his work.

During my testimony, the judge asked some clarifying questions about statistics I cited on violence against women in El Salvador and then kept asking whether the Salvadoran government had labeled MS-13 a terrorist organization. I said that the US government had done that, but I wasn't sure about the Salvadoran government. And then the questioning ended. The judge thanked me for coming all the way down from beautiful Portland, Oregon. It wasn't clear if this was meant sarcastically. Mayra looked at me, and mouthed "thank you." I left the room and headed for the lobby. Fifteen minutes later the people filed out of the court into the lobby. The case had been continued for two weeks to collect more evidence and to allow the other three witnesses, plus Mayra, to testify. We all gathered in front of the facility to take a picture of the family with the kids. While they were posing, a Geo worker threatened to arrest us for taking pictures on Geo property.

Figure 5.5 Mayra Machado's mother and sister, and two of her children, Dominic and Dayanara, outside the Geo-run La Salle Processing Center, Jena, Louisiana, 21 May 2019. *Source*: Author's photograph.

FELONS, NOT FAMILIES

Mayra Machado's experience is part of a broader trend in the bipartisan criminalization of immigrants that dates back to the late nineteenth century. Since the 1980s, the United States has been locking up and deporting immigrants at alarming rates, but the most extreme efforts to criminalize immigration have occurred under Clinton, Bush, Obama, and Trump, two Democratic and two Republican presidents. Although "voluntary" border returns are clearly marked by violence and brief periods of captivity, formal removals involve a hearing before an immigration judge and can lead to lengthy periods of incarceration while people fight deportation or are serving sentences for immigration-related crimes. Furthermore, formal removals go on offenders' records, and thus reentering would be subject to even more serious felony charges. Therefore, formal removals criminalize immigrants in a way that informal returns do not. Thus, while Clinton removed more immigrants than any president in US history, these were almost entirely accomplished through "voluntary removal" at the border. Obama, however, removed more immigrants than any president through formal deportation proceedings. Obama's first term (2008–12) saw a dramatic growth in formal removals compared to "catch and return." Throughout the 1990s, formal removals were at most a tenth of total removals, and often much less than that. In 2011, formal removals overtook voluntary returns for the first time in seventy years. Although total removals have declined steadily since their high in 2000 at over 1.8 million, Obama's formal removals reached a high of over 432,000 in 2013. Comparing the last three presidencies, during whose presidencies formal removals dramatically increased, reveals a steady upward trend: Clinton deported about 900,000, George W. Bush 2 million, and Obama 3 million. One analysis of deportation since 1990 shows that

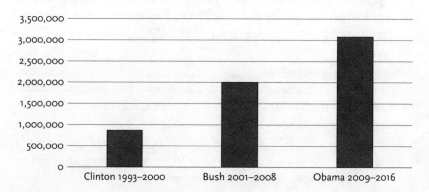

Figure 5.6 Deported by president, 1993–2016.
Source: Department of Homeland Security, *Yearbook of Immigration Statistics: 2017*, Table 39.

Democratic presidents removed far more immigrants than Republican presidents, and even though Trump is ramping up deportations, he will not surpass Obama's record in his first term.[63]

Obama conducted his most aggressive immigration enforcement in his first term, hoping that by showing himself to be tough on illegal immigration, he could convince Republicans to support immigration reform measures. He miscalculated and failed to pass immigration reform through Congress. In his second term, Obama softened his immigration enforcement and announced a new direction that would target enforcement on "criminals" and not on hard-working immigrant families. In November 2014, he announced his Deferred Action for Childhood Arrivals (DACA) program, which provided temporary respite from deportation for certain categories of young people who had lived for long periods of time in the country and had no criminal records. In the same speech Obama proclaimed: "We're going to keep focusing enforcement resources on actual threats to our security. Felons, not families. Criminals, not children. Gang members, not a mom who's working hard to provide for her kids. We'll prioritize, just like law enforcement does every day."[64] The rhetorical flourish, "felons not families" played into the "tough-on-crime" politics that had become so popular during the 1990s among both Democrats and Republicans. The idea was that the "good" immigrants, those brought to the United States as children and those without criminal records, would be accepted and enforcement would be directed at dangerous criminals.

There are several problems with this narrative. First, it was never true during any part of Obama's presidency that immigration enforcement targeted only dangerous criminals, and second, the definitions of felon had been so expanded by 2014 that many non-violent people were caught up in the dragnet that followed.[65] In Obama's first term in office, two-thirds of those deported had only committed minor infractions such as a traffic violation or had no criminal record at all.[66] The Transactional Records Access Clearinghouse (TRAC) found that in 2013 only 12 percent of deportees had committed a serious or "Level 1" offense such as homicide, rape, kidnapping, and smuggling.[67]

By the end of Obama's presidency, a consensus had developed among the mainstream media that Obama had perhaps indiscriminately deported people during his first term but by his second term, he had begun to focus enforcement on criminals. The *New York Times*, which had published articles revealing the opposite, had begun to rewrite history after Trump was elected to show that immigration enforcement had shifted.[68] As one article in the *Times* put it, "Gone are the Obama-era rules that required them to focus only on serious criminals."[69] The data show otherwise. Even in Obama's second term after he announced that he would focus enforcement on "felons not families," more than 60 percent of deportees had no criminal conviction or had immigration charges related to entry or reentry. Only 20 percent of deportees had potentially violent convictions such as assault, DUI, or weapons offenses.[70] In 2016, the last year of Obama's presidency, only 8 percent of deportees were felons or had been accused of being in a street gang.[71] Given how easy it is to end up with a felony or be labeled a street gang member, many of those people who are claimed to be the "worst of the worst" are simply moms like Mayra Machado.

It is clear that the vast majority of people deported by Obama were not felons, but even the 8 percent who were so labeled need to be examined in light of the expansion of the felon category since the mid-1990s. Mayra Machado, who was deported in the last weeks of Obama's presidency was a felon, but she was also a hardworking mother. The "felons not families" slogan tried to juxtapose these two as polar opposites, but Mayra Machado and many others were both. Criminal justice reformers have engaged in a similar sleight of hand, focusing on the non-violent, non-serious, and non-sexual offenders (the so-called non, non, nons), and how to keep them out of prison. However, as legal scholar John Pfaff points out, more than half of state prisoners are violent offenders, and simply freeing people who have committed drug crimes or other non-violent offenses will not end mass incarceration. In fact, only 16 percent of people in state prisons are there for drug crimes, and a portion of these had previous convictions for violent crimes.[72] As Marie Gottschalk notes in *Caught*, "Maintain[ing] and reinforcing the distinction between the non, non, nons and other offenders perpetuates the idea that there is a 'dangerous class' of people who must be contained at all costs."[73] Ending mass incarceration thus requires reducing the numbers of violent criminals locked behind bars and unpacking what it means to be violent. It also means reducing the number of immigrants in detention, whether they have been criminalized or not.

Although more than 90 percent of immigrants being deported have not been convicted of a violent crime, any infraction by this vulnerable population is viewed as dangerous criminality that must be answered by deportation. Increasingly the solution to the presence of a "dangerous class" of immigrants (Chinese, Mexicans, gang members, sex offenders, criminals) has become banishment, either by locking them up indefinitely or exiling them beyond the boundaries of the nation. After immigrants serve their sentence for an "aggravated felony," they are deported. For immigrants, deportation means separation from homes, communities, and families. It is a de facto life sentence since such people almost never can legally return. For citizens, mandatory minimums and Life without Parole (LWOP) sentences have grown for many categories of crimes.[74] Sex offenders are similarly viewed as part of a "dangerous class" that must be locked away forever, in some cases beyond the time for which they were sentenced to prison for a particular offense. The logic that Mayra Machado must be deported because she is a felon is the same one used to lock up over 2 million citizens. Deporting millions of non-citizens and caging millions of citizens are both strategies of elimination.

Trump's 2016 presidential campaign was peppered with reference to criminal aliens, what he referred to as "rapists and criminals" or simply the "bad hombres." He promised to build a thirty-foot-high border wall visible from space and to deport all of the estimated 11 million undocumented immigrants.[75] It seemed like Americans were going to witness a rapid expansion of apprehensions, detentions, and deportations, but to date this has not come to pass. Apart from hyperbolic rhetoric about a "border invasion" and caravans of gang members trying to sneak into the country, Trump's deportation regime has been less robust than Obama's. In 2017, ICE deported 226,000 and in 2019 this number rose slightly to 267,000. Under Obama, ICE deported an average of 350,000 immigrants each year, with more in the first six years than in the latter two years of his administration.[76]

Even accepting the dubious distinction between criminals and non-criminals, Obama deported a greater proportion of non-criminals than Trump. During Obama's eight years in office, just over half (51 percent) of those removed by ICE were convicted of a crime, whereas under Trump 56 percent of deportees have criminal convictions. Although so far only three years of Trump records are available, the current data indicate that Obama removed more immigrants with no criminal convictions than Trump.[77] The point is not that Trump's immigration policy is better than Obama's, but rather that harsh immigration enforcement has been a bipartisan effort for three decades.

However, the labels of criminality that the state imposes cannot simply be accepted at face value. For example, in 2012, 17 percent of those listed as criminals were guilty of illegal entry, illegal reentry, and minor traffic infractions. In that same year, all of the homicide, rape, sexual assault, and terrorism convictions combined added up to just four-tenths of 1 percent of the total number of deportees.[78] In other words, offenses thought of as depraved crimes of violence were committed by a minuscule part of the population of deportees. Mayra Machado's "aggravated felony" conviction would have put her on the list of the worst-of-the worst criminals, and yet common sense would show that she did not pose a safety or security threat to the nation. The criminal versus non-criminal distinction among immigrants obscures more than it illuminates and reinforces the state logic that criminalizes all forms of unauthorized migration.

BACK TO EL SALVADOR

In late July 2019, Judge Thogersen denied Mayra Machado's asylum claim. The twelve-page opinion, which was delivered six weeks after the second hearing, almost completely ignored all of my expert witness testimony on country conditions in El Salvador that supported Machado's claims. The judge found Machado's testimony not to be credible given what she saw as inconsistencies in her story, and apparent contradictions by some of her own witnesses.[79] According to Judge Thogersen's public Facebook page, she appears to have two sons around the same age as Mayra's two eldest children, but it does not seem as if she identified with Mayra's predicament as a mother separated from her children.[80] In fact, Judge Thogersen brought Mayra to tears in the courtroom when she repeatedly told her that she would not bring her children to such a hearing, implying that Mayra was a bad mother. In reference to this incident, Mayra told me, "I know I'm not a good mother because I am incarcerated. That really got to me."[81]

In November, Machado's petition to the Board of Immigration Appeals was denied; her lawyer appealed to the Fifth Circuit Court. And then all of a sudden, one evening in January 2020, Machado was informed that she was going to be deported that night. Even though she still had a pending appeal, she was shackled, taken to an airport, and put on an ICE Air flight to El Salvador. Her lawyer's last-minute motion for a stay was rejected within an hour. When I spoke with Machado a few days later by Facetime, she was dejected and angry. "I've given immigration four years of my life," she said. She noted that there was little difference between being incarcerated in Louisiana and the constrained life she led in El Salvador. "I went from being in detention to sitting in a room with my phone." Afraid of the gangs in Usulután, Machado remained holed up in her room. "I got dumped in a shithole," she declared.[82]

Machado's arrest in 2018 and deportation in 2020 took place well into Trump's crackdown on immigrants. The Department of Justice had ordered immigration judges not to grant asylum if the threats to the immigrant were based on gangs or criminal organizations. There was also pressure on immigration judges to speed up hearings to address the backlog of nearly a million cases. Immigration advocates have sued Trump at every turn, but the administration has lots of ways to make it hard for immigrants seeking asylum. In 2019, Trump issued a new rule that requires asylum seekers from Central America to remain in Mexico in dangerous border cities while they wait for their asylum hearing in the United States. The Justice Department has also declared a zero-tolerance policy that requires all illegal entrants and asylum seekers to be detained. Although the family separation policy was ended by court order, the new procedure is to lock up entire families. Given the court backlog, immigrants can expect to wait years in prison if they want to claim asylum. And at the end of this detention period, the chances of gaining asylum are low—and almost nonexistent without proper legal representation. Only 29 percent of asylum petitions were granted in 2019.[83] Mayra Machado is just one of millions of immigrants who have been caught in an interlocking criminal justice and immigration system that incarcerates and deports immigrants with no regard for their cultural and familial ties to this country and no sensitivity to the dangers they face in their countries of origin.

Conclusion

A Nation of Immigrant Prisons

Non-citizens have been locked up for a long time in North America. Native Americans were the first to be deprived of their liberty, forced to work for British colonists and enslaved by Spanish settlers and missionaries in what would become the US Southwest. The reservation system and Indian boarding schools were both institutions designed to restrict freedom and mobility. Enslaved Africans were shackled and imprisoned on ships and then forced to work on plantation prisons managed by private individuals but supported by colonial and then state institutions. After a long struggle, Black people gained formal citizenship in 1868 with the Fourteenth Amendment and Native Americans in 1924, but various legal and extralegal means served to disenfranchise both groups. In spite of citizenship, Black citizens are now five times as likely as whites to be imprisoned and much more likely to experience police violence. In the twenty-first century, Native American men are admitted to prison at four times the rate of white men, and Native American women at six times the rate of white women.[1] Incarceration since the 1980s has metastasized and affects everyone, but it disproportionately impacts groups that have historically been considered non-citizens. Non-citizens and their non-white citizen ancestors thus continue to bear the brunt of the carceral cage.

This book, however, focuses on the latest group of non-citizens to be put behind bars since the late nineteenth century. Some of them were charged with immigration-related violations, others with drug and alcohol offenses, and some were labeled "enemy aliens" and kidnapped from their homes in Latin America to be held in camps in the US Southwest. Although these non-citizens were locked up in different kinds of institutions, some in jails and prisons, and others in immigration detention facilities and in insane asylums, it would be a mistake not to see all of these as part of a system designed to deprive foreigners, especially those who are not white, of their liberty. The changes in the bureaucratic labels used for the carceral institutions occludes a fuller picture of immigrant incarceration. Taken together, non-citizens have clearly faced high rates of imprisonment for more than a century and often have been denied constitutional rights of due process to fight for their freedom.

In all the stories in this book, non-citizens faced indefinite detention. They and the lawyers and advocates who represented them fought vigorously for their release and for their claims to be reviewed. Most of the stories end with deportation or death. Only the Higashides ended up gaining US citizenship. Although the Supreme Court limited detention for non-citizens in the first decade of the twenty-first century (Zadvydas [2000] and Martinez [2005]), its most recent decisions indicate that under certain circumstances non-citizens can be held indefinitely behind bars with no possibility of even a bond hearing. In practice, non-citizens deemed excludable from the United States are like the forever prisoners of Guantanamo, exposed to massive state power with few constitutional protections. Even those who are freed from detention and then deported, like Machado, live far from their families in the United States and remain trapped by the violence in their countries of origin. Being a forever prisoner is not just a matter of literally spending the rest of one's life in prison but of being perpetually subject to the deprivation of one's liberty for even the most minor infraction. All non-citizens, and many non-white citizens, live under these conditions of unfreedom.

There is plenty of evidence of immigrants being shackled and beaten by guards in prison, but the most common form of torture is the incarceration itself. The seemingly limitless caging has led to depression and in some cases suicide. One of the nineteen Chinese men locked up at McNeil Island in the late 1880s died while in prison. Nathan Cohen was released from his purgatory on a ship, but he died a year later at thirty-five years of age after being locked up in a private sanitorium in Connecticut. Seiichi Higashide and his family survived their incarceration, but his daughter Elsa was traumatized by seeing her father suddenly snatched from their family home in Peru, and the family still seems to suffer from the racism they experienced in the United States. More than 1,000 of the Mariel Cuban refugees who participated in the uprisings at Atlanta and Oakdale prisons were deported to Cuba, while the rest were paroled into the United States or remained in prison pending deportation. Those paroled have gone on with their lives, but given their tenuous immigration status and fear of deportation, they do not want to share their stories and live in fear of being deported. Although anti-immigrant hysteria and harsh mandatory detention policies under Trump appear novel, they are the latest chapter in a long history of locking up immigrants in the United States. Over the course of more than a century, the numbers of immigrants locked behind bars has waxed and waned, but the infrastructure to detain immigrants has steadily increased.

SITES OF DETENTION

The places where people have been stripped of their liberty stretch from colonial plantations to today's prisons and immigrant detention facilities. McNeil Island prison, where Chinese immigrants were locked up in the late nineteenth century, was officially closed in 2011, but a civil commitment center was built on the island where sex offenders can be locked up after they have completed their prison terms. Crystal City Internment Camp was shuttered in 1948 and a school was built on its site, but today the nation's largest family detention center in the United States sits in Dilley, Texas, less than fifty miles from where Seiichi Higashide and his family were incarcerated during World War II. Hundreds of infants, children, and their families from Guatemala, El Salvador, and Honduras are crammed into the Dilley facility, forced into refrigerated rooms (*hieleras*) and made to sleep on concrete floors under mylar blankets. Overcrowding and lack of medical attention has led to widespread illness in the Dilley Center. "There is a miasma; the often-foul air smells of desperation," one journalist wrote after a visit to Dilley.[2] The Federal Detention Center at Oakdale, Louisiana, where Mariel Cubans staged a prison takeover in 1987, now cages more than 1,000 immigrants, two-thirds of whom are from Mexico.[3]

Immigrant detention today is part of a carceral landscape in the United States that includes more than 2 million citizens behind bars. Some of these prisons are located on former slave plantations like Angola in Louisiana, which became a prison camp that leased convicts to nearby plantations in the late nineteenth century and today holds more than 6,000 men, some of whom are on death row and will be executed at the prison.[4] The name that adorns the largest immigrant family detention facility in the country invokes the name of the man who oversaw convict prison farms in Arkansas and Texas in the 1960s and 1970s. The T. Don Hutto Residential Center near Austin holds more than 500 immigrants including many children, some as young as infants. The immigrant prison is named for the founder of Corrections Corporation of America (now Core Civic), the country's first for-profit private prison, which is worth over $2 billion today. In 1971, a year after the Arkansas prison system was deemed unconstitutional by a judge, T. Don Hutto was named commissioner of the Arkansas Department of Corrections, overseeing the 16,000-acre Cummins plantation prison in Arkansas where Black convicts picked cotton and were forced to stare at the wall while naked for six-hour stretches if they failed to meet their quota, or they were beaten with clubs for refusing to labor in the fields. The Arkansas execution chamber was located on the Cummins plantation, a grim reminder that prisons are often not dissimilar to death camps.[5] The fact that one of the largest immigrant family detention centers in the country is named after Hutto is a reminder that slavery, Black convict prison labor in the twentieth century, and immigrant detention today are part of a long and twisted chain of incarceration.

There is also historical continuity in the high rates of incarceration of people suffering from mental health issues. Whereas in the early twentieth century, Nathan Cohen and others perceived as mentally ill were locked up in insane asylums, today those with mental health issues often find themselves in local jails, and state and federal prisons. A 2006 study by the Bureau of Justice Statistics found that more than half of all people in prison and jail had a mental health problem; nearly two-thirds of people in local jails were diagnosed as mentally ill.[6] There is also a higher proportion of mental illness among detained immigrants than in the general population. One study of immigrant detention and mental illness around the world found that although many immigrants, particularly refugees, had preexisting trauma, the detention process itself was an independent variable that increased the likelihood of mental illness.[7] An estimated 15 to 30 percent of American immigrant detainees have a mental disability, although nobody really knows since accurate data are not recorded.[8] While this number is relatively low compared to the percentage of mentally ill in jails and prisons, immigrant detention by itself seems to cause depression and trauma. Only 21 of 230 ICE facilities have in-person mental health services, and lack of such services is partially responsible for suicides in ICE facilities. Federal inspectors of a California migrant detention center in July 2019 discovered that detainees in three-quarters of the cells they visited had made nooses from bedsheets.[9] Whether some detainees had preexisting suicidal tendencies or not, the desperate conditions in ICE facilities are driving detainees to try to end their lives.

The prisoners held at Guantanamo are not, by any stretch of the imagination, immigrants. They, like the Japanese Peruvians during World War II, were picked up by the US military overseas as part of an ongoing war. And yet the Guantanamo prisoners share with immigrants a lack of protection by the US Constitution and a vulnerability to indefinite detention.

One month before Donald Trump's inauguration, Khalid Qassim, a Yemeni detainee at Guantanamo, waved his artwork in front of a one-way glass as journalists were being given a tour. The artwork depicted a question mark, with a padlock as the dot on the punctuation. News crews captured the image, leading officials at Guantanamo to have to decide whether to censor the image or allow it to be broadcast. Navy Rear Admiral Peter J. Clarke, commander of detention operations, ultimately decided against censorship, commenting, "I would venture to guess that detainee is using his art as a way to express himself."[10] A year later, following an exhibition of Guantanamo detainee art at New York's John Jay College of Criminal Justice, the Pentagon abruptly reversed course, declaring all art produced at Guantanamo to be US government property. Detainees were told that no art would be allowed to leave the prison and that works of art would be burned if and when they were ever released.[11]

Ten months later, in October 2017, Qassim dictated a message to his lawyer Shelby Sullivan-Bennis, "I am in so much pain every minute that I know it can't go on much longer." In the *Guardian* Qassim described a hunger strike that he and other Guantanamo prisoners had undertaken as a peaceful protest against their incarceration for more than fifteen years without being charged with any crime. He had not had any food for twenty-three days, and the doctors had stopped trying to feed him. "They have decided to leave us to waste away and die instead." Torture can take many forms, but the idea of being left to starve is perhaps the cruelest. "These days have been the most terrifying of my 15 years in this place," Qassim stated. "We are used to torture here but this is so slow and so cruel. The people who are supposed to look after us are hurting us. I have been reduced to pleading for my life. I am asking for anyone out there to talk about what's going on here. To ask why Trump is letting us slowly die. I don't have many days left."[12]

This image of the non-violent protestor/artist is at odds with the depiction of Qassim by the US government. What little is known about Khalid Qassim comes from a 2008 Department of Defense secret file on detainees that was released by Wikileaks. Qassim graduated from high school in 1998 with a degree in literature, and then worked as a merchant and fisherman.

He was said to be recruited in 1999 to fight in Afghanistan, where he received military training. After being in combat for a week with the Taliban, he left the front lines, turned in his gun, and attempted to retrieve his passport so he could return to Yemen. On December 18, 2001, as the anti-Taliban Northern Alliance advanced, Qassim was captured in a small village and was turned over to US custody later that month. When he was captured, he had in his possession an identification card, 3,500 Pakistan rupees, and five 100 US dollar bills. The secret file on Qassim alleges that he is a member of al-Qaeda, is "HIGH risk," and is "likely to pose a threat to the US, its interests, and allies." Although it is not clear where the intelligence for these allegations comes from, most evidence appears to be based on interrogations in US custody. The report also claims that Qassim threatened to "kill a US service member by chopping off his head and hands when he gets out" and telling another officer that he "will murder him and drink his blood for lunch." He also allegedly stated that he would "fly planes into houses and prayed that President Bush would die."[13]

If the Chinese on McNeil Island, Nathan Cohen, Seiichi Higashide, the Mariel refugees, and Mayra Machado are generally sympathetic characters, someone like Qassim, accused of being an al-Qaeda agent, is not. This book has focused on non-citizen incarceration in the United States, but even though Guantanamo Bay naval base is officially Cuban territory, it is US-controlled. The Supreme Court has recognized this fact in *Rasul v. Bush* (2004), arguing that federal court "jurisdiction extends to aliens held in a territory over which the United States exercises plenary and exclusive jurisdiction, but not 'ultimate sovereignty.'"[14] The Guantanamo detainees are, like the Japanese Peruvians, clearly not immigrants, but they were forcibly brought under US jurisdiction and now face indefinite detention. While some may object to comparing "innocent" immigrants locked up for no other reason than unauthorized entry to terrorist suspects snatched up in a theater of war, one of the main points of this book is to collapse distinctions reflexively made between alleged criminals and terrorists, on the one hand, and innocent migrants, on the other. If due process is to have any meaning at all, it must also be available to those alleged to have committed the most heinous of crimes, whether that crime be terrorism or a sex offense.

The truth about Khalid Qassim cannot be known with the available evidence. Torturing people is a notoriously unreliable manner for extracting accurate intelligence, so the allegations in the Department of Defense report are highly suspect. Even the CIA admitted in 1989 that "inhumane physical or psychological techniques are counterproductive because they do not produce intelligence and will probably result in false answers."[15] An in-depth Senate investigation led by Senator Dianne Feinstein concluded that there is "overwhelming and incontrovertible" evidence that the CIA tortured Guantanamo detainees both physically and psychologically. Senator Feinstein went on to argue that these interrogation techniques were "cruel, inhuman, and degrading."[16] And because CIA interrogators used torture, it is likely than none of the information obtained would be permissible in a criminal court. This leaves Qassim and others stuck in indefinite detention, the government believing they are high risks, but without the evidence to try them in a criminal legal proceeding because of the way the information was obtained.

Since 2002, almost 800 prisoners have been imprisoned at Guantanamo, most of them, like Qassim, picked up in Afghanistan as part of the War on Terror. Almost all have been released after years in detention with no charges ever being brought against them. Of the eight detainees convicted by the Military Commission, half of them had their convictions overturned by a civilian court or canceled by the Pentagon. As of 2020, forty of them remain at Guantanamo, some having been there for almost two decades. Five of them have been recommended for transfer but have not been allowed to leave, nine have been charged under the Military Commissions System (two of whom have been convicted), and twenty-six are being held in indefinite detention with no possibility of transfer.[17] They are the forever prisoners.

Beyond the prisoners at Guantanamo and at known US military prisons around the globe, the CIA maintains a series of black site prisons in other countries. These are the so-called ghost prisoners. While the 2014 Senate Intelligence committee hearings on CIA interrogation methods and detention centers revealed the existence of some of these ghost prisoners, the full extent of the secret CIA prison system is unknown and remains shrouded in mystery. In 2004, more than 100 such prisoners were being held by the CIA in secret prisons. In that same year, while the Supreme Court was considering a case that may have enabled such prisoners to be eligible for habeas corpus pleas in court, the Department of Justice recommended that four ghost prisoners be transferred out of Guantanamo.[18] Even in Guantanamo, there were secret sites with names like Strawberry Fields and Penny Lane, hidden behind layers of fencing and shrubs. These detainees were not listed among the prisoners on the island and had no access to the Red Cross or lawyers; some of them were even recruited by the CIA and sent back into the field to carry out assassinations.[19] They were there but not there.

Qassim, like dozens of other Guantanamo prisoners, has been held for more than eighteen years to date with no charges and no trial. In response to courts demanding that the detainees' detention be reviewed, the government established Periodic Review Boards, an administrative procedure devoid of the protections or rights that a defendant would have in a criminal trial. There is a long and checkered past of different iterations of review boards at Guantanamo. Complaints about lack of due process and independence led to their demise, with the Periodic Review Boards taking their place in 2011. The new review board, which began hearing cases in 2013, has cleared more Guantanamo detainees than their predecessors, offers detainees more involvement in the process, and has even released one detainee whose identity was mistaken. The requirements of the process include giving advance notice of the hearing date to the detainee with an unclassified summary of the reasons for his continued detention, assigning a military representative, allowing for a private lawyer (not provided by the government), permitting oral and written statements by the detainee and statements of witnesses, and allowing detainees to answer questions posed by the board.[20] Although this is an improvement on previous board procedures, detainees still don't have access to classified information, don't have the ability to cross-examine witnesses, and do not have protections against self-incrimination.

One of the problems with the review board hearings is that they are not designed to hear a plea of innocence. Rather, they are like parole boards where the presumption is that the detainees are guilty, and the boards want to hear contrition and remorse. As Thomas Wilner, one of the Guantanamo detainee lawyers, put it, the review board process "is not based on evidence. You have to be contrite. What do you tell a client who wants to go, 'Fuck you! I'm innocent!'" Haroon Gul, one of the indefinite detainees, went before a review board in 2016 after he was finally able to obtain legal counsel a decade after being locked up there. Gul had been trapped in a catch-22, not being able to send a letter to request a lawyer in the required blue envelopes because not having an active case meant he had no need for the envelopes. Gul's lawyer believes he is innocent, but the review board denied his transfer, explaining that "the Board considered the detainee's . . . failure to acknowledge or accept responsibility for past activities. The Board welcomes seeing the detainee's file in six months with greater candor." If a detainee is innocent and maintains his innocence, the review board will not release him. He must admit his guilt before asking for mercy. Although a secret dossier on Gul, released by WikiLeaks, labels him "high risk" and of "high intelligence value," none of the evidence is available to him. Gul maintains he was just a poor Afghan living in a refugee camp in Pakistan who happened to be caught in the wrong guesthouse in Afghanistan one night because he was on the road selling books and jars of honey to support his family.[21]

Since 2008, scores of Guantanamo detainees, including Qassim, have attempted to pursue habeas corpus claims in the District Court in the District of Columbia, but they keep getting denied access to the courts due to their status as "enemy combatants" in a "non-international armed conflict" being held outside of US territory. Their murky status means that they fall outside the normal rules governing prisoners of war and procedures for criminal suspects in the United States. In this liminal legal space, the US government has been inventing administrative procedures, much as they did for the Mariel refugee review boards, that are neither transparent nor fair. In both cases, the result has been the caging of people who have little hope of ever being able to defend themselves or of leaving behind the prisons in which they are trapped.

In 2018, Qassim sued Donald Trump over his detention, claiming that various circuit court decisions nullified his right to a habeas corpus hearing. Qassim's appeal was based on the Supreme Court ruling in *Boumediene v. Bush* (2008) that clearly stated that Guantanamo detainees "have the habeas corpus privilege." The court rejected the government's arguments that the Constitution did not apply to aliens outside of the country and its claim that the Detainee Treatment Act of 2005 provided sufficient protections.[22] Qassim asserted that the review "panel decisions have created a hollow habeas regime that leaches all substance out of the Supreme Court's governing precedents and effectively shuts down habeas corpus as a remedy for any Guantanamo detainees." While the appeals court judges were sympathetic to this view, they refused to take the case, arguing that the facts of the habeas petitions should first be reviewed by district courts before an appeal could be heard. Judge Tatel argued that Qassim had "attempted to short-circuit the factfinding process."[23] In other words, after sixteen years imprisoned without charge, the courts told Qassim that he needs to follow proper procedure and not rush the process.

The legal fight has thus returned to the district court, with the government arguing that Guantanamo detainees have no due process rights, and even if they did, these rights are satisfied by the review boards. Meanwhile, the Guantanamo detainees maintain that they have been granted no due process rights, including habeas corpus, and that the review boards are not sufficient bodies to insure those rights. In the 2004 *Hamdi v. Rumsfeld* decision the Supreme Court held that it was precisely during times of fear and uncertainty that "our Nation's commitment to due process is most severely tested; and it is in those times that we must preserve our commitment at home to the principles for which we fight abroad."[24] An amicus brief by due process scholars on behalf of the Guantanamo detainees in 2018 reiterated this point, declaring that "perpetual detention without charge is anathema to those very principles and the time has now come for this Court to make clear that this is so and to ensure the foundational principle of freedom from Executive detention without criminal process."[25] Time and again, due process rights for non-citizens have been abridged either based on purported claims of national security, as with the Japanese Peruvians during World War II and the Guantanamo detainees today, or based on spurious claims that some migrants should be considered to be outside of the country and therefore not protected by the Constitution, as was the case with the Mariel Cuban refugees and the Guantanamo detainees. Although the Supreme Court has affirmed the rights to due process and habeas corpus, even for the so-called enemy combatants held in Guantanamo, many of them remain locked up with no formal charges or hearings after sixteen years. De facto, they are forever prisoners without rights.

INCARCERATING THE EXCLUDED

In the summer of 2019, the incessant attacks on immigrants coming from white power activists and the White House led a sixty-eight-year-old anarchist, Willem Von Spronsen, to attack the Northwest Detention Center in Tacoma. In what appears to be a "death-by-cop" suicide mission, Von Spronsen, armed with a rifle, lit a car on fire, threw incendiary devices at the ICE detention center, and attempted to ignite a propane tank. Police shot and killed him within a minute. In a manifesto in which he identified himself as "antifa" and invoked John Brown as his "moral guide" and Emma Goldman as his "political guide," Von Spronsen explained his actions:

> I'm a black and white thinker.
> Detention camps are an abomination.
> I'm not standing by.
> I really shouldn't have to say any more than this.[26]

Von Spronsen's actions were at the extreme edge of a movement that has sought to abolish ICE by blockading detention centers, stopping vans in the process of deporting migrants, and otherwise interrupting the deportation machine through non-violent civil disobedience.

In 2019, President Trump enacted a series of rule changes and executive orders that threaten to massively expand the numbers of immigrants in detention. Trump officials announced the administration would start indefinitely detaining immigrant children and their families in violation of the

1997 Flores agreement that limited detention of children to twenty days. By the end of the fiscal year, immigration authorities had apprehended close to half a million family members and detained almost 38,000 of them.[27] In February 2020, the Justice Department established a section dedicated to denaturalizing "fraudsters" who "unlawfully obtained citizenship," a move that threatens to expand the numbers of people vulnerable to detention and deportation.[28] Zero-tolerance policies, new definitions of deportability based on becoming a public charge, giving political appointees the power to decide appeals rather than immigration judges, and directives requiring mandatory detention of all immigrants applying for asylum for the duration of court proceedings that can stretch out over years is swelling the population of caged immigrants. Not satisfied with only locking up immigrant children, Trump also declared that he was "seriously" considering signing an executive order ending birthright citizenship for the children of unauthorized immigrants.[29] This measure would subject millions of people who were born and raised in the United States to detention and deportation.

The immigrant detention system has been growing in fits and starts from the late nineteenth century to the present, but the rapid growth of incarceration and the raw numbers of immigrants being locked up today is unprecedented. We once imagined ourselves as a nation of immigrants, but we have become a nation of immigrant prisons. Yet the immigrant category does not accurately describe all of the non-citizens and citizens who are incarcerated by the United States at home and abroad. The Mariel Cubans who languished for years in Atlanta and Oakdale prisons were called the excluded, a label apt for the Japanese Peruvians, the Guantanamo prisoners, and so many others who are today behind bars. They are aliens not just in the legal sense of being non-citizens, but as perpetual outsiders.

In March 2020, I spoke with Mayra Machado who had just moved to San Salvador where she had secured a job working with a branch of NDLON. She was excited to be living in a safer neighborhood, helping other deportees, and making money. She was saving to pay several thousand dollars in restitution for her 2005 hot check offense and preparing to petition the governor of Arkansas for a pardon. In the meantime, she has become a paralegal so she can help others with their immigration petitions. In July she helped a friend in prolonged detention win a habeas case in the 5th Circuit, one of the least friendly to immigrants. She still had hope that with the pardon, her asylum claim would be successful and she would be reunited with her three children. Meanwhile, back in the United States, the carceral machine continued to grind on, chewing up millions of immigrants and spitting them out.

NOTES

INTRODUCTION

1. Mayra Machado, telephone communication, 23 August 2019.
2. Details of her arrest are based on my telephone interviews of Mayra Machado while she was at LaSalle Detention center, 23 August 2019.
3. Ruth Ellen Wassem, "U.S. Immigration Policy on Haitian Migrants," Congressional Research Service, 17 May 2011, 4.
4. I capitalize "Black" and "Brown" as a sign of respect to these communities, but "white" will remain lowercase so as not to reinforce the White Power movement's use of capitalization. The inconsistency highlights the socially constructed nature of race and grammar. Michelle Alexander, *The New Jim Crow* (New York: New Press, 2012), 16. One notable exception is Marie Gottschalk, *Caught: The Prison State and the Lockdown of American Politics* (Princeton, NJ: Princeton University Press, 2016).
5. Adam Goodman, *The Deportation Machine: America's Long History of Expelling Immigrants* (Princeton, NJ: Princeton University Press, 2020); Laura Briggs, *Taking Children: A History of American Terror* (Berkeley: University of California Press, 2020); Carl Lindskoog, *Detain and Punish: Haitian Refugees and the Rise of the World's Largest Immigration Detention System* (Gainesville: University of Florida Press, 2018); César Cuauhtémoc García Hernández, *Migrating to Prison: America's Obsession with Locking Up Immigrants* (New York: New Press, 2019); Jenna M. Loyd and Alison Mountz, *Boats, Borders and Bases: Race, the Cold War and the Rise of Migration Detention in the United States* (Berkeley: University of California Press, 2018); Patrisia Macías-Rojas, *From Deportation to Prison: The Politics of Immigration Enforcement in Post-Civil Rights America* (New York: New York University Press, 2016); A. Naomi Paik, *Rightlessness: Testimony and Redress in US Prison Camps Since WWII* (Chapel Hill: University of North Carolina Press, 2016).
6. Vincent J. Cannato, *American Passage: The History of Ellis Island* (New York: Harper, 2009); Erika Lee and Judy Yung, *Angel Island: Immigrant Gateway to America* (New York: Oxford University Press, 2010), 17–20, 57.
7. There is no reference to detention in the index to this comprehensive book about deportation, and the book contains very few explorations of the subject. Daniel Kanstroom, *Deportation Nation: Outsiders in American History* (Cambridge, MA: Harvard University Press, 2007). Kelly Lytle-Hernández's book *City of Inmates*, focusing on the birth and development of the prison in

Los Angeles from the Spanish colonial period to 1965, brings the two fields of migration and prison studies together in a powerful way and shows how immigrants became increasingly criminalized over the course of the twentieth century. Kelly Lytle-Hernández, *City of Inmates: Conquest, Rebellion and Rise of Human Caging in Los Angeles, 1771–1965* (Chapel Hill: University of North Carolina Press, 2017).

8. Kunal M. Parker, *Making Foreigners: Immigration and Citizenship Law in America, 1600–2000* (New York: Cambridge University Press, 2015), 1–16; Evan Taparata, "'Refugees as You Call Them': The Politics of Refugee Recognition in the Nineteenth Century United States," *Journal of American Ethnic History* 38, no. 2 (2019). Briggs, *Taking Children: A History of American Terror*.

9. Briggs, *Taking Children: A History of American Terror*, chs. 1, 2, and 4.

10. Facetime communication with Mayra Machado, 15 January 2020.

11. For an excellent analysis of the making of the idea of the "illegal alien," see Mae Ngai, *Impossible Subjects: Illegal Aliens and the Making of Modern America* (Princeton, NJ: Princeton University Press, 2004).

12. Stephen H. Legomsky, "Immigration Law and the Principle of Plenary Congressional Power," *Supreme Court Review* 1984 (1984).

13. Jennings v. Rodriguez, 583 US (2018). Nielsen v. Preap, 586 US (2019), 12; Nicole Narea, "Justices Leave Room to Challenge Immigrant Detention Law," Law360, https://www.law360.com/articles/1140697/justices-leave-room-to-challenge-immigrant-detention-law.

14. Hernández, *Migrating to Prison*, 9, 47–48; Macías-Rojas, *From Deportation to Prison*, 17.

15. Hidetaka Hirota, *Expelling the Poor: Atlantic Seaboard States and the Nineteenth-Century Origins of American Immigration Policy* (New York: Oxford University Press, 2016), 195–202; Brendan P. O'Malley, "Welcome to New York: Remembering Castle Garden, a Nineteenth-Century Immigrant Welfare State," *Lapham's Quarterly* (2018).

16. Cannato, *American Passage: The History of Ellis Island*, 5; Lee and Yung, *Angel Island: Immigrant Gateway to America*, 8.

17. Bennie Woon Yep, interview with Melody Chin, 24 May 2005. Oral History Project, Angel Island, Pacific Regional Humanities Institute, available at https://escholarship.org/uc/item/7j99z91x.

18. Peter M. Coan, *Ellis Island Interviews: In Their Own Words* (New York: Fall River Press, 1997), xxvii, as cited in Judith Irangika Dingatantrige Perera, "From Exclusion to State Violence: The Transformation of Noncitizen Detention in the United States and Its Implications in Arizona, 1891–present" (PhD dissertation, Arizona State University, 2018), 74.

19. Rachel Buff, *Against the Deportation Terror: Organizing for Immigrant Rights in the Twentieth Century* (Philadelphia: Temple University Press, 2018).

20. US Census Bureau, "Census of Population, 1850 to 2000," 2019, https://www.census.gov/newsroom/pdf/cspan_fb_slides.pdf.

21. Mary L. Dudziak, *Cold War Civil Rights: Race and the Image of American Democracy* (Princeton, NJ: Princeton University Press, 2002).

22. Herbert Brownell Jr., "Address by Honorable Herbert Brownell Jr., Attorney General of the United States at Ebbets Field & Polo Grounds," US Department of Justice, 11 November 1954, https://www.justice.gov/sites/default/files/ag/legacy/2011/09/12/11-11-1954.pdf.

23. Lindskoog, *Detain and Punish*, 2.

24. Although the number of immigrants processed and removed was reaching record-breaking levels, many were repeat offenders who returned after being sent to Mexico, and so these arrests do not represent discrete individuals. Kelly Lytle Hernández, "The Crimes and Consequences of Illegal Immigration: A Cross-Border Examination of Operation Wetback, 1943 to 1954," *Western Historical Quarterly* 37, no. 4 (2006): 429, 440–443.
25. Pearl Buck, "Plight of Immigrants," *New York Times*, 16 November 1954.
26. Perera, "From Exclusion to State Violence," 110–111.
27. The new law was, according to legal historian Daniel Wilsher, "very liberal." Daniel Wilsher, *Immigration Detention: Law, History, Politics* (Cambridge: Cambridge University Press, 2012), 64–65.
28. Hernández, *Migrating to Prison*, 17.
29. Perera, "From Exclusion to State Violence," 111, 115–117.
30. US Department of Justice, *Annual Report of the Immigration and Naturalization Service 1960* (Washington, DC: US Government Printing Office, 1960), 8, Table 23, p. 54.
31. Perera, "From Exclusion to State Violence," p. 124, Table 121, 131.
32. US Department of Justice, *1979 Annual Report of the Immigration and Naturalization Service* (Washington, DC: US Government Printing Office, 1979), 3.
33. Lindskoog, *Detain and Punish*, 16, 33–35.
34. Erika Lee, *America for Americans: A History of Xenophobia in the United States* (New York: Basic Books, 2019).
35. Raymond Lafontant Gerdes, *Fuerte Allen: La diáspora haitiana* (Rio Piedras, Puerto Rico: Plaza Mayor, 1996), 77, 92.
36. Lindskoog, *Detain and Punish*, 52–70, 108–116.
37. Joyce Wadler, "As Others Go Free, 50 Haitians Still Detained Feel Only Despair," *Washington Post*, 25 August 1982.
38. Rudolph Giuliani, as quoted in Hernández, *Migrating to Prison*, 70.
39. Juliet Stumpf, "The Crimmigration Crisis: Immigrants, Crime and Sovereign Power," *American University Law Review* 56, no. 2 (2006): 381–383.
40. US Department of Justice, Office of the Federal Detention Trustee, *Detention Needs Assessment and Baseline Report: A Compendium of Federal Detention Statistics* (Washington, DC: US Government Printing Office, 2002), 14.
41. Immigration and Naturalization Service, US Department of Justice, *1980 Statistical Yearbook of the Immigration and Naturalization Service* (Washington, DC: US Government Printing Office, 1980), Table 63, p. 127; "Immigration Criminal Prosecutions Jump in March 2018," 27 April 2018, https://trac.syr.edu/immigration/reports/510/, Fig. 1.
42. Wilsher, *Immigration Detention*, 70.
43. "US Immigration and Customs Enforcement Fiscal Year 2019 Enforcement and Removal Operation Report," US Immigration and Customs Enforcement, 2019, https://www.ice.gov/sites/default/files/documents/Document/2019/eroReportFY2019.pdf, 5, 10. "FY 2021 Budget in Brief," US Department of Homeland Security, 2020, https://www.dhs.gov/sites/default/files/publications/fy_2021_dhs_bib_0.pdf, 3.
44. Briana Flin, "Growing Up Undocumented When Your Siblings Are Citizens," *The Atlantic*, 22 August 2018.
45. US Department of Justice, *1980 Statistical Yearbook of the Immigration and Naturalization Service*, p. 183, Table 168. Laurence Benenson, "The Math of

Immigration Detention, 2018 Update: Costs Continue to Multiply," National Immigration Forum, 9 May 2018, https://immigrationforum.org/article/math-immigration-detention-2018-update-costs-continue-mulitply/, Figure 2.

46. This list was released by ICE as a part of a Freedom of Information Act request by the Immigrant Legal Resource Center. The list of facilities includes more than 200 whose names and addresses were redacted. "ICE Detention Facilities as of November 2017," National Immigrant Justice Center, 2017, https://immigrantjustice.org/ice-detention-facilities-november-2017. The data can be found at "ICE Facility List Report," 6 November 2017.

47. "New Data on 637 Detention Facilities Used by ICE in FY 2015," Transactional Records Access Clearinghouse, 12 April 2016, http://trac.syr.edu/immigration/reports/422/. In 2016, 352,882 immigrants were put into a civil detention facility. US Department of Homeland Security, "DHS Releases End of Fiscal Year 2016 Statistics," 2016, https://www.dhs.gov/news/2016/12/30/dhs-releases-end-year-fiscal-year-2016-statistics. Michaelangelo Landgrave and Alex Nowrasteh, "Incarcerated Immigrants in 2016: Their Numbers, Demographics, and Countries of Origin," Cato Institute, 2018, https://object.cato.org/sites/cato.org/files/pubs/pdf/irpb7.pdf.

48. The steepest increase has occurred under Trump—in just two years from 38,000 to over 55,000. Emily Ryo and Ian Peacock, *Landscape of Immigrant Detention in the United States* (Washington, DC: American Immigration Council, 2018), Table 1, p. 6. Caitlin Dickerson, "ICE Faces Migrant Detention Crunch as Border Chaos Spills into Interior of the Country," *New York Times*, 22 April 2019 Immigration and Customs Enforcement US Department of Homeland Security, "Currently Detained by Processing Disposition as of 8/17/19," 2019, https://www.ice.gov/detention-management.

49. Bryan Baker, "Immigration Enforcement Actions: 2016," Office of Immigration Statistics, 2017, https://www.dhs.gov/sites/default/files/publications/Enforcement_Actions_2016.pdf, Table 7.

50. Jeffrey S. Passel, "Measuring Illegal Immigration: How Pew Research Center Counts Unauthorized Immigrants in the U.S.," *Pew Research Center: Factank*, 12 July 2019.

51. Figure derived from "Yearbook of Immigration Statistics 2018," Department of Homeland Security, Table 39, https://www.dhs.gov/immigration-statistics/yearbook/2018, and "US Immigration and Customs Enforcement Fiscal Year 2019 Enforcement and Removal Operation Report," US Immigration and Customs Enforcement, 2019, https://www.ice.gov/sites/default/files/documents/Document/2019/eroReportFY2019.pdf, 5. Also, see Goodman, *The Deportation Regime*, 1.

52. Doris Meissner, Donald M. Kerwin, Muzaffar Chishti, and Claire Bergeron, "Immigration Enforcement in the United States: The Rise of a Formidable Machinery," 2013, https://www.migrationpolicy.org/pubs/pillars-reportinbrief.pdf, p. 3, note 7.

53. Although Border Patrol apprehensions have spiked in 2019, they are still far below the previous highs in 1986 and 2000. "Immigration Enforcement Actions: 2017 Data Tables," 2018, https://www.dhs.gov/immigration-statistics/enforcement-actions#, table 35. US Department of Homeland Security, CPB Enforcement Statistics FY 2019.

54. According to an INS study based on 2001 data, migrants who are considered criminals spent an average of 35 days in detention compared to 22 days for

non-criminals. Mexicans spent an average of 15 days in detention compared to others who averaged 63 days. Those from Cuba, Liberia, Sierra Leone, former Yugoslavia, China, Sudan, Bosnia, Algeria, and Haiti all spent an average of 200 to 300 days in detention. The number of migrants spending more than six months in detention increased almost three times from 1994 to 200. US Department of Justice, *Detention Needs Assessment and Baseline Report: A Compendium of Federal Detention Statistics*, 15–16.

55. Deirde M. Maloney, *National Insecurities: Immigrants and US Deportation Policy since 1882* (Chapel Hill: University of North Carolina Press, 2012); "Legal Noncitizens Receive Longest ICE Detention," 3 June 2013, https://trac.syr.edu/immigration/reports/321/.

56. US Department of Homeland Security, Budget in Brief: Fiscal Year 2020, 2019,

57. There has been significant variability in the number of ICE detentions over the last twelve years, going from a low of below 257,000 in 2006 to a high of more than 500,000 in 2019. The average number of ICE detentions from 2006 to 2018 was 371,000 per year. "ICE Initial Book-Ins by Facility Type: FY 2019 through 8/17/2019," 2019, https://www.ice.gov/detention-management.

58. Jack Herrera, "Mexico's Mass Arrests of Central American Migrants Follow Years of US Pressure," *Pacific Standard,* 24 April 2019; Antonio Flores, Luis Noe Bustamante, and Mark Hugo Lopez, "Migrant Apprehensions and Deportations Increase in Mexico, but Remain Below Recent Highs," *Pew Research Center: FacTank*, 12 June 2019; "Mexico: Evolution of the Mérida Initiative, 2007–2020," 28 June 2019, https://fas.org/sgp/crs/row/IF10578.pdf.

59. For a good history of Mexican immigration enforcement on its southern border, see Ana Raquel Minian, "Offshoring Migration Control: Guatemalan Transmigrants and the Construction of Mexico as a Buffer Zone," *American Historical Review* 125, no. 1 (2020).

60. "Global Detention Project: Annual Report 2017," June 2018, 7.

61. Michael Flynn of the Global Detention Project has been trying unsuccessfully to find an accurate dataset for migrant detention around the world. Michael Flynn, personal communication with author, 18 August 2019.

62. Macías-Rojas, *From Deportation to Prison*, 17; Hernández, *Migrating to Prison*, 9.

63. Andrés Reséndez, *The Other Slavery: The Uncovered Story of Indian Enslavement in America* (Boston: Houghton Mifflin Harcourt, 2016); Dan Berger, "Carceral Migrations: Black Power and Slavery in 1970s California Prison Radicalism," in *The Rising Tide of Color: Race, State Violence, and Radical Movements across the Pacific*, ed. Moon-Ho Jung (Seattle: University of Washington Press, 2014).

64. Carolyn Moehling and Anne Morrison Piehl, "Immigration, Crime, and Incarceration in Early Twentieth-Century America" *Demography* 46(2009): 760.

65. Graham C. and Kubrin Ousey, Charis E., "Immigration and Crime: Assessing a Contentious Issue," *Annual Review of Criminology* 1, no. 1 (2018). Tanvi Misra, "For the Last Time, Here's the Real Link Between Immigration and Crime," *City Lab*, 6 Feb. 2019. Michelangelo Landgrave and Alex Nowrasteh, "Criminal Immigrants in 2017: Their Numbers, Demographics and Countries of Origin," 2019, https://object.cato.org/sites/cato.org/files/pubs/pdf/irpb-11.pdf.

66. Daniel Denvir, *All-American Nativism: How the Bipartisan War on Immigrants Explains Politics as We Know It* (New York: Verso, 2020).

67. John F. Kennedy, *A Nation of Immigrants* (New York: Harper Row, 1964).

CHAPTER 1

1. Paul W. Keve, *The McNeil Century: The Life and Times of an Island Prison*, 21–24, 31.
2. Anne Kane Burkly and Steve W. Dunkelberger, *McNeil Island: Images of America* (Charleston: Arcadia, 2019), 7, 41.
3. Burkly and Dunkelberger, *McNeil Island: Images of America*, 9.
4. Keve, *The McNeil Century*, 105–107.
5. W. H. White, US Attorney, Washington Territory, to A. H. Garland, US Attorney General, 8 September 1885, National Archives and Records Administration (NARA) II, Record Group (RG) 60, Department of Justice (DJ) central files, 1884-971-980, box 43.
6. Chinese Exclusion Act (1882).
7. W. H. White, US Attorney, Washington Territory, to A. H. Garland, US Attorney General, 8 September 1885, NARA II, RG 60, DJ central files, 1884-971-980, box 43.
8. "Chinese Immigration Act, 1885," *Statutes of Canada. An Act of Respecting and Regulating Chinese Immigration into Canada, 1885. Ottawa: SC 48-49 Victoria, Chapter 71.*
9. F. F. Maynard, Department of State, to A. M. Garland, US Attorney General, 21 October 1885, NARA II, RG 60, DJ central files, 1884-971-980, box 43.
10. Jean Pfaelzer, *Driven Out: The Forgotten War against Chinese Americans* (Berkeley: University of California Press, 2007), 252–290. Also, see Beth Lew Williams, *The Chinese Must Go: Violence, Exclusion and the Making of the Alien in America* (Cambridge, MA: Harvard University Press, 2018).
11. George Dudley Lawson, "The Tacoma Method," *Overland Monthly and Out West Magazine* March 1886, 235–236.
12. William H. White, as quoted in Pfaelzer, *Driven Out: The Forgotten War against Chinese Americans*, 224.
13. *Tacoma News*, 5 March 1887, as quoted in Pfaelzer, *Driven Out: The Forgotten War against Chinese Americans*, 215–229, 261.
14. Lucy E. Salyer, "'Laws as Harsh as Tigers': Enforcement of the Chinese Exclusion Laws, 1891–1924," in *Entry Denied: Exclusion and the Chinese Community in America, 1882–1943*, ed. Sucheng Chan (Philadelphia: Temple University Press, 1991), 57–93.
15. Lawson, "The Tacoma Method," 237–239. US Attorney White also referred to this incident: W. H. White to Attorney General, 5 December 1885, NARA II, RG 60, DJ central files, 1884-971-980, box 43.
16. W. H. White, US Attorney, Washington Territory, to A. H. Garland, US Attorney General, 5 December 1885, NARA II, RG 60, DJ central files, 1884-971-980, box 43. F. F. Maynard, Department of State, to A. H. Garland, US Attorney General, 17 December 1885, NARA II, RG 60, DJ central files, 1884-971-980, box 43.
17. Lawson, "The Tacoma Method," 237–239.
18. Tel. W. H. White, US Attorney, Washington Territory, to A. H. Garland, US Attorney General, 27 June. 1888, NARA II, RG 60, DJ central files, 1884-980, box 44.
19. T. J. Hamilton, US Marshal, to A. H. Garland, US Attorney General, 17 July 1888, NARA II, RG 60, DJ central files, 1884-980, box 44.
20. Tel. W. H. White, US Attorney, to A. H. Garland, US Attorney General, 2 July 1888, NARA II, RG 60, DJ central files, 1884-980, box 44.
21. Chinese Exclusion Act (1882).

22. W. H. White, US Attorney, Washington Territory, to A. H. Garland, US Attorney General, 16 January 1888, NARA II, RG 60, DJ central files, 1884-980, box 44.
23. Chinese Exclusion Act, May 6, 1882, 47th Congress, Sess. 1, Ch. 126, p. 58–61.
24. 1884 and 1892 Chinese Restriction Acts, US Department of Commerce and Labor, *Treaty, Laws, and Regulations Governing the Admission of Chinese* (Washington, DC: GPO, 1907), 19.
25. Based on database created by archivists at NARA, Seattle. Records of the US Penitentiary, McNeil Island. Washington, NARA, Seattle, 129.8.
26. These sentences are based on 1885–1890 data. Williams, *The Chinese Must Go*, 85.
27. Patrick Winston, district attorney, Spokane, speaking on 2 March 1891 to Select Committee on Immigration and Naturalization, Chinese Immigration, 51st Cong., 2nd sess., 1891, HR Rep 4048 in 51st Cong. 2nd sess., 8–10.
28. These records can be found in the Washington State Archives, Puget Sound Branch, Pierce Frontier Justice collection. The case numbers do not correspond to the archive's document numbering system. One such example is Wong Boy who went before a Grand Jury of the Third Judicial District of Washington Territory court on 23 February 1888.
29. US v. Ah Jim, District Court of Tacoma, Judgment and Sentence, Washington State Archives, Puget Sound Branch, Pierce Frontier Justice Collection, PRC-2248.
30. US v. Ah Sing, 12, July 1888, Washington State Archives, Puget Sound Branch, Pierce Frontier Justice Collection, PRC-6116.
31. C. H. Hanford, Chief Justice Supreme Court, to President Benjamin Harrison, 18 June, 1889, Canada Archives, RG2, Privy Council Office, Series A-1-a. Also cited in Williams, *The Chinese Must Go*, 86.
32. William F. Wharton, Acting Secretary of State, to Attorney General, 3 July 1889, NARA II, RG 60, DJ central files, 1884-980, box 45.
33. Copy of Writ of Deportation, 12 June 1889, District Court, Third Judicial District, Washington Territory, Canada Archives, RG2, Privy Council Office, Series A-1-a.
34. W. H. H. Miller, Secretary of the Treasury, to Department of Justice, 30 June 1891 House US Congress, *Official Opinions of Attorneys General*, vol. 20, Congressional Serial Set (1895) (Washington DC: US Government Printing Office, 1895), 171–172, 178.
35. Blake McKelvey, *American Prisons: A History of Good Intentions* (Montclair, NJ: Patterson Smith, 1977), 229, quoted in Keve, *The McNeil Century*, 51–54.
36. *United States v. On Gee*, Judgment and Sentence, 15 November 1888, Washington State Archives, Puget Sound Branch, Pierce Frontier Justice, File No. PRC-2250.
37. Keve, *The McNeil Century*, 107–109. The McNeil Island Prison Records indicate that On Gee escaped on July 10–11.
38. Charles J. McClain and Laurene Wu McClain, "The Chinese Contribution to the Development of American Law," in *Entry Denied: Exclusion and the Chinese Community in America, 1882–1943*, ed. Sucheng Chan (Philadelphia: Temple University Press, 1991).
39. United States Supreme Court, Fong Yue Ting v. United States, 149 US 698 (1893).
40. Wong Wing v. United States, 163 U.S. (1896).

41. Kelly Lytle Hernández, *City of Inmates: Conquest, Rebellion and Rise of Human Caging in Los Angeles, 1771–1965* (Chapel Hill: University of North Carolina Press, 2017), 89.
42. Wong Wing v. United States, 163 U.S. (1896).
43. Marcus Braun, Immigrant Inspector, New York, to Frank P. Sargent, Commissioner General, Department of Commerce and Labor, Bureau of Immigration and Naturalization, 12 February 1907, NARA, RG 85, entry 9, 52271/74A.
44. Hernández, *City of Inmates*, 137–139.
45. Erika Lee and Judy Yung, *Angel Island: Immigrant Gateway to America* (New York: Oxford University Press, 2010), 57.
46. Case File of the United States v. Edgar Yuen Fong, Scope and Content description in NARA catalog, https://catalog.archives.gov/id/6037243; "Criminal Docket, US v. Edgar Yuen Fong," and "US v. Fong, Transfer 1 Dec. 1936," National Archives Record Administration, Philadelphia, RG 21, Records of District Courts of the United States, 1685–2008, Criminal Case Files, 1791–1988, US District Court for Eastern District of Pennsylvania.
47. Daniel Kanstroom, *Deportation Nation: Outsiders in American History* (Cambridge, MA: Harvard University Press, 2007), 167–186.
48. Levi W. Meyers, US Consul, Victoria, BC, to Edwin F. Uhl, Assistant Secretary of State, 10 April 1894, in NARA II, RG 60, DJ central files, 1884-980-993, box 48. The full court proceedings for Wong Ching, one of the deportees is located in US v. Wong Ching, US Commissioner's Court, Port Townsend, 21 February 1894, NARA II, RG 60, DJ central files, 1884-980-993, box 48.
49. Hidetaka Hirota, *Expelling the Poor: Atlantic Seaboard States and the Nineteenth-Century Origins of American Immigration Policy* (New York: Oxford University Press, 2017).
50. Torie Hester, "Deportability and the Carceral State," *Journal of American History* 102, no. 1 (2015): 142.
51. Bureau of Immigration, *Annual Report of the Commissioner General of Immigration to the Secretary of Labor (1904)* (Washington DC: US Government Printing Office, 1904), Table 1, p. 50, 59, 161.
52. Bureau of Immigration, *Annual Report of the Commissioner General (1904)*, 51, 58, 160.
53. Data from US Department of Commerce (1918: 204, 312, 328–330, 419–21), as cited in Carolyn Moehling and Anne Morrison Piehl, "Immigration, Crime, and Incarceration in Early Twentieth-Century America," *Demography* 46 (2009): Table 1, p. 747.
54. "McNeil Island, Washington, Photos and Records of Prisoners Received, 1887–1939," NARA, Seattle, 1875–1906, image 13 on ancestry.com.
55. "McNeil Island Penitentiary, Photos and Records of Prisoners Received, 1875–1939," Records of the Bureau of Prisons, NARA, Seattle, Record Group 129.
56. Anna Pegler-Gordon, *In Sight of America: Photography and the Development of U.S. Immigration Policy* (Berkeley: University of California Press, 2009). Scholars have studied the development of photographs in these identity documents and passports, but none has analyzed the mug shots of immigrant prisoners. John Torpey, *The Invention of the Passport: Surveillance, Citizenship and the State* (Cambridge: Cambridge University Press, 2000); Craig Robertson, *The Passport in America: The History of a Document* (New York: Oxford University Press, 2010).

57. Elliott Young, *Alien Nation: Chinese Migration in the Americas from the Coolie Era to WWII* (Chapel Hill: University of North Carolina Press, 2014).
58. "District Court Proceedings," *Seattle Post-Intelligencer*, 17 September 1887.
59. US v. Ah Jake, 24 September 1887, Washington State Archives, Puget Sound Branch, Pierce Frontier Justice, File No. KNG-5461.
60. "A Batch of Smuggled Chinese," *Seattle Post-Intelligencer*, 1 May 1894.
61. Pegler-Gordon, *In Sight of Americ*, ch. 2.
62. Fong Sun, inmate 2733, McNeil Island Penitentiary, Photos and Records of Prisoners Received, 1875–1939, NARA, Seattle, 129.8.
63. Photographs of John Doe Shorty and family, Maggie Murray, Florence Farley, and Carrie Sang can be found, in Records of the US Penitentiary, McNeil Island. Washington, NARA, Seattle, 129.8.
64. Allan Sekula, "The Body and the Archive," *October* 39(1986): 30.
65. Case files exist for 2,429 out of 14,379 total inmates during the period 1887–1939; these documents provide information on the precise length of time served as well as a record of letters sent and received and a detailed monthly parole record.
66. Campbell J. and Emily Lennon Gibson, *Historical Census Statistics on the Foreign-Born Population of the United States: 1850–1990* (Washington, DC: US Bureau of the Census, 1999), Table 13.
67. Young, *Alien Nation*.
68. The 1875 Page Act targeting Chinese women, the 1907 Immigration Act and the 1910 Mann Act all served to criminalize the entry of single women. Grace Delgado, "Border Control and Sexual Policing: White Slavery and Prostitution along the U.S.-Mexico Borderlands, 1903–1910," *Western Historical Quarterly* 43(2012).
69. Margaret Werner Cahalan, *Historical Corrections Statistics in the United States, 1850–1984* (Rockville, MD: United States Department of Justice, 1986), 1.
70. US Congress, Chinese Immigration Report 4048, 51st Cong., 2nd sess., 1891.
71. Patrick Winston, district attorney, Spokane, speaking on 2 March 1891 to Select Committee on Immigration and Naturalization, Chinese Immigration, 51st Cong., 2nd sess., 1891, HR Rep 4048 in 51st Cong., 2nd sess., 9.
72. "The Uprising at Seattle," *Washington Standard*, 12 February 1886, 2.
73. US v. Gee Lee, US Ninth Circuit Court of Appeals, October Term 1891, in Patrick H. Winston, US Attorney, to Attorney General, 9 May 1892, NARA II, RG 60, DJ central files, 1884-980, Box 47.
74. Keve, *The McNeil Century*, 109.
75. Thomas R. Brown, US Marshal, to Attorney General, Department of Justice, 26 August 1890, NARA II, RG 60, DJ central files, 1984-980, box 45.
76. Tel. Thomas R. Brown, US Marshal, to Attorney General, Department of Justice, 14 October 1890, NARA II, RG 60, DJ central files, 1984-980, box 45.
77. Leigh Chalmers, Examiner Department of Justice, 5 December 1887, NARA II, RG 60, DJ central files, 1884-980, box 44, p. 1.
78. Geo. W. Schell, Special Assistant US Attorney, to Attorney General, 7 June 1890, NARA II, RG 60, DJ central files, 1984-980, box 45.
79. "Cuban Suspects Arrive," *Semi-Weekly Spokesman Review*, 22 June 1980.
80. "Transfer of McNeil Marks End of Era for Federal Prison," *Semi-Weekly Spokesman Review*, 30 June 1981.
81. Associated Press, "Freedom Still Eludes Some Cubans," *Spokane Chronicle*, 4 August 1980.

82. United Press International, "30 Cubans Stage Strike at McNeil," *Spokane Daily Chronicle*, 26 September 1980.

83. Associated Press, "More Cubans Join Penitentiary Hunger Strike," *Spokesman Review*, 29 March 1980.

84. "18 Cubans from McNeil to Resettle," *Spokane Daily Chronicle*, 17 October 1980.

85. John Craig, "Cuban Refugees' Crimes Mostly Petty, Judge Says," *Spokane Chronicle*, 7 January 1981.

86. "Transfer of McNeil Marks End of Era for Federal Prison."

87. Martha Bellisle, "Man Held at Facility for Sexually Violent Dies," *Seattle Times*, 4 January 2019.

88. Associated Press, "Sole Woman at Washington Facility for Sex Offenders Released," *Seattle Times*, 12 June 2019. Also listen to podcast, Simone Alicea and Paula Wissel, "Not a Prison," *Forgotten Prison* (2019), KNKX, http://www.forgottenprison.org/.

CHAPTER 2

1. James F. Taylor, "The Man without a Country," 18 April 1915, *Pittsburgh Press*; "Grave the Haven of a Homeless Man: Wandering Jew Would Not Be Accepted in Any Country," *Grand Island NE Independent*, 14 March 1916, p. 1, in Find a Grave, https://www.findagrave.com/memorial/177898818.

2. Taylor, "The Man without a Country," https://www.newspapers.com/image/143778865/.

3. "Sea Wanderer Ends 33,740 Mile Journey," *New York Times*, 28 March 1915, https://timesmachine.nytimes.com/timesmachine/1915/03/28/104231692.pdf; "Shipped Back and Forth," *Messenger and Intelligencer* (Wadesboro, NC), 1 April 1915, https://www.newspapers.com/image/93200525/; "Sea Wanderer World Outcast," *Union Springs Herald* (Union Springs, AL), 31 March 1915; "Cohen Back to Brazil Once More," *Bryan Daily Eagle and Pilot.* (Bryan, TX), 24 March 1915; "A Man without a Country," *Outlook with Illustrations* 109 (7 April 1915): 803; "Without a Country and without a Mind," *The Survey*, April–September 34 (1915): 39–40.

4. James F. Taylor, "The Man without a Country," 18 April 1915, *Pittsburgh Press*, https://www.newspapers.com/image/143778865/.

5. Oscar Handlin, *The Uprooted* (Boston: Little, Brown, 1973 [1951]).

6. "New York has Spent Nearly $25,000,000 on Alien Insane," *New York Times*, 7 April 1912; "Too Many Insane Aliens: Lunacy Commission Wants Legislation to Facilitate Their Deportation," *New York Times*, 18 March 1912; "Insane Aliens," *New York Times*, 28 March 1912.

7. Ji-Hye Shin, "Insanity on the Move: The 'Alien Insane' in Modern America, 1882–1930" (PhD dissertation, Rutgers University, 2013), 5.

8. Gerald N. Grob, *Mental Institutions in America: Social Policy to 1875* (New York: Free Press, 1973), 231–238.

9. "Insane and Feeble-Minded in Hospitals and Institutions, 1904" (Washington, DC: US Census Bureau, 1906), Table 12, p. 20. The information from this report was the basis for the 1911 Dillingham Commission report's comments on insane aliens. William Stiles Bennet and William Paul Dillingham, "Abstracts of Reports of the Immigration Commission," in *Reports of the Immigration Commission*, Vols. 1–2 (Washington, 1911), Table 6, p. 234; Table 8, p. 36.

10. The 1910 census indicated that the mental hospital admission rate was 57.9 per 100,000 for native born, compared with 116.3 per 100,000 for foreign born.

Adjusting for the age distribution of each group results in 91.2 for native born and 123.3 for foreign born, still a significant difference but not the 2:1 ratio from the unadjusted numbers. Gerald N. Grob, *Mental Illness and American Society, 1875–1940* (Princeton, NJ: Princeton University Press, 1983), 170.

11. "Too Many Insane Aliens: Lunacy Commission Wants Legislation to Facilitate Their Deportation," *New York Times*, 18 March 1912.

12. Tedd Lutterman, Robert Shaw, William Fisher, and Ronald Manderschied, "Trend in Psychiatric Inpatient Capacity, United States and Each State, 1970–2014" (Alexandria, VA: National Association of State Mental Health Programs, 2014), 16.

13. These data only include commitment to "mental hospitals" and do not include sanitariums, almshouses, and other institutions where immigrants could be found in large numbers. Margaret Werner Cahalan, *Historical Corrections Statistics in the United States, 1850–1984* (Rockville, MD: United States Department of Justice, 1986), 208–210.

14. What is noteworthy about Harcourt's study is that when overall institutionalization was considered, the overall rate of incarceration was actually higher from 1934 through the 1970s than in 2000 near the height of the current moment of "mass incarceration." When people in jails are factored in, the result is that in 2000 the rate of institutionalization is roughly equivalent to what it was from 1934 through the early 1960s. Bernard E. Harcourt, "An Institutionalization Effect: The Impact of Mental Hospitalization and Imprisonment on Homicide in the United States, 1934–2001," *Journal of Legal Studies* 40, no. 1 (2011): 40–43.

15. Grob, *Mental Illness and American Society, 1875–1940*, 180–181.

16. The Russian czar expelled all Jews from Kurland on 28 April 1915, and the area was subsequently occupied by Germany in the same year. In 1919, after briefly being occupied by the Red Army, Kurland became part of the newly independent Latvia. During World War II, the Germans took control of the town of Bausk and murdered the remaining Jews. Only two Jews remained in the town at the end of the war. Dr. S. Lipschitz, "Jewish Communities in Kurland," from *The Jews in Latvia*, ed. Association of Latvian and Esthonian Jews in Israel, 1971, https://www.jewishgen.org/Courland/lipschitz.htm; Museum of Jewish People, "Bauska," https://dbs.bh.org.il/place/bauska.

17. Tara Zahra, *Kidnapped Souls: National Indifference and the Battle for Children in the Bohemian Lands, 1900–1948* (Ithaca, NY: Cornell University Press, 2008), 6–8.

18. "List of Manifest of Alien Passengers for the United States," Ellis Island Foundation, Passenger ID 100896100135, Frame 568, Line 1. There are some references that indicate that Cohen arrived in Baltimore on the *Vasari* on 6 May 1912, but appears at Ellis Island on 4 May. Samuel Littman, HIAS representative at Ellis Island, to Martha Reizenstein, HIAS representative, Baltimore, 23 June 1914, Yidisher Visnshaftlekher Institut (hereafter YIVO), Record Group (hereafter RG) 245.2.

19. Lee W. Formwalt, "The Camilla Massacre of 1868: Racial Violence as Political Propaganda," *Georgia Historical Quarterly* 71, no. 3 (1987).

20. This estimate of Berman's wealth came from a lawsuit brought by Cohen against his uncle. Nathan Cohen v. I. Berman, Jacksonville, Florida, 1 September 1912, YIVO, RG 245.2. Several newspapers contained similar stories. See report in the *Pythian Advocate* published in Minneapolis by Fred E Wheaton, which formed the basis for "A Man without a Country," *Wilmington Dispatch* (Wilmington,

NC), 29 May 1915, 2–3. H. M. Sasnett of the Knights of Pythias in Jacksonville indicated that Cohen spoke very little English when he arrived there. H. M. Sasnett, Jacksonville, to Max Kohn, New York, 23 March 1915, YIVO, RG 245.2.

21. Bureau of Public Health and Marine-Hospital Service, *Book of Instructions for the Medical Inspection of Immigrants* (Washington, DC: US Government Printing Office, 1903), 9–10.

22. John T. E. Richardson, *Howard Andrew Knox: Pioneer of Intelligence Testing at Ellis Island* (New York: Columbia University Press, 2011), 77–78.

23. Howard Markel, "Mental Examination of Immigrants Administration and Line Inspection at Ellis Island," *Public Health Reports (1974–)* 121, no. Supplement 1: Historical Collection, 1878–2005 (2006): 92–98.

24. "Facies" is a medical term for the facial expression linked to a particular condition. Markel, "Mental Examination of Immigrants," 92–97.

25. Markel, "Mental Examination of Immigrants," 97.

26. Markel, "Mental Examination of Immigrants," 99–100.

27. Data culled from *Annual Report of the Commissioner General of Immigration to the Secretary of Labor* (Washington, DC: US Government Printing Office, 1898–1930).

28. Markel, "Mental Examination of Immigrants," 102.

29. Howard A. Knox, "The Moron and the Study of Alien Defectives," *Journal of the American Medical Association* 60 (January 11): 105–106, cited in Richardson, *Howard Andrew Knox*, 79.

30. Richardson, *Howard Andrew Knox*, 259–263.

31. Amy L. Fairchild, *Science at the Borders: Immigrant Medical Inspection and the Shaping of the Modern Industrial Labor Force* (Baltimore: Johns Hopkins University Press, 2003), 169, 99–201; Richardson, *Howard Andrew Knox*, 260–263.

32. "Finds Haven in Grave," *The Sun* (New York), 6 March 1916. "Certificate of Admission of Alien Nathan Cohen," sent from Commissioner of Immigration, Ellis Island, to Commissioner of Immigration, Baltimore, 7 February 1914, National Archives and Records Administration (hereafter NARA), Record Group (hereafter RG) 85, Entry 9, 53751-6.

33. H. M. Sasnett, Jacksonville, to Max Kohn, New York, 23 March 1915, YIVO, RG 245.2; "Without a Country and without a Mind," *The Survey*, 34 (April–September 1915): 39–40.

34. "A Man without a Country," *Wilmington Dispatch* (Wilmington, NC), 29 May 1915, 2–3. "A Man without a Country, Buried," *Rock Island Argus*, 6 March 1916, p. 12; Zeje Jaffe Affidavit taken by William M. Doyas, Immigrant Inspector, Baltimore, 30 December 1913, NARA, RG 85, Entry 9, 53751-6.

35. "Exhibit A: Partnership Agreement between Nathan Cohen and I. Berman," 1 September 1912, YIVO, RG 245.2.

36. "Outcast Finds Home in Death," *Tribune*, 6 March 1916, clipping in YIVO, RG 245.2.

37. Ephraim Bryant, Grand Chancellor, Tallahassee, Florida, http://knightsofpythiasfl.com/leadership/.

38. "Affidavit of A. S. Metzner," Jacksonville, Florida, 19 April 1915, YIVO, RG 245.2.

39. Nathan Cohen v. I. Berman, Duval County, Florida, 26 July 1913, YIVO, RG 245.2.

40. Nathan Cohen v. I. Berman, Duval County, Florida, 26 July 1913, p. 5, Exhibit B, YIVO, RG 245.2.

41. Nathan Cohen v. I. Berman, Duval County, Florida, 26 July 1913, pp. 5–9, YIVO, RG 245.2.
42. Nathan Cohen to F. D. Brennan, Jacksonville, 22 October 1913, YIVO, RG 245.2.
43. Gabriel (Zeje) Jaffe testimony at Nathan Cohen Hearing, 17 February 1914, NARA, RG 85, Entry 9, 53751-6.
44. Jacob Pincus Affidavit, 15 September 1915, YIVO.
45. "Finds Haven in Grave," *The Sun* (New York), 6 March 1916; "A Man without a Country," *Wilmington Dispatch* (Wilmington, NC), 29 May 1915, pp. 2–3.
46. One narrative of Cohen's life indicates that he left Jacksonville in September, but given the date of his last letter to his lawyer sent from Jacksonville at the end of October, it appears he must have left subsequently. Cohen "A Man without a Country," *Wilmington Dispatch* (Wilmington, NC), 29 May 1915, pp. 2–3; "A Man without a Country, Buried," *Rock Island Argus*, 6 March 1916, p. 12.
47. Maryland Federal Naturalization Records, 1795–1931, Gabriel Jaffe, ancestry. com. This also matches his own testimony in Cohen's immigration hearing. Gabriel (Zeje) Jaffe testimony at Nathan Cohen Hearing, 17 February 1914, NARA, RG 85, Entry 9, 53751-6.
48. Information provided by Gabriel Jaffe, Cohen's brother-in-law, to Martha Rezenstein, HIAS representative in Baltimore. Martha Rezenstein, Baltimore, to Irving Lipsitch, Ellis Island, 25 June 1915, YIVO, RG 245.2. Passenger lists from Baltimore show an Itte Cohen arriving in 1905, but that could not have been her because Gabriel only arrived in Baltimore in 1910, and by then they already had six children. Baltimore Passenger Lists, 1820–1964, Itte Cohen, ancestry.com.
49. Cohen gave the same address that Gabriel would later provide during Cohen's deportation hearing. Nathan Cohen, Bay View Hospital Record, 5 December 1913, in NARA, RG 85 Entry 9 53751-6.
50. Martha Rezenstein, Baltimore, to Littman, New York, 3 March 1916, YIVO, RG 245.2.
51. Martha Rezenstein, Baltimore, to Irving Lipsitch, Ellis Island, 25 June 1915, YIVO, RG 245.2.
52. "The Case of Nathan Cohen," YIVO, RG 245.2.
53. Gabriel (Zeje) Jaffe testimony at Nathan Cohen Hearing, 17 February 1914, NARA, RG 85, Entry 9, 53751-6.
54. Gabriel (Zeje) Jaffe testimony at Nathan Cohen Hearing, 17 February 1914, NARA, RG 85, Entry 9, 53751-6.
55. Gabriel (Zeje) Jaffe testimony at Nathan Cohen Hearing, 17 February 1914, NARA, RG 85, Entry 9, 53751-6.
56. H. A. Pratt, C. F. Langworthy, and H. L. Knight, "Dietary Studies in Public Institutions in Baltimore, MD," *Bulletin*, no. 223 (1910): 17.
57. US Census Bureau, *Insane and Feeble-Minded in Institutions* (Washington, DC: US Government Printing Office, 1914), 112.
58. Gabriel (Zeje) Jaffe testimony at Nathan Cohen Hearing, 17 February 1914, NARA, RG 85, Entry 9, 53751-6.
59. Immigration Laws and Regulations of 1907 (Washington, DC: Government Printing Office, 1910), 5, 14.
60. Shin, "Insanity on the Move," 5.
61. Kenneth B. Jones, Physician in Chief, Bay View Hospital, 16 February 1914, NARA, RG 85, Entry 9, 53751-6.
62. Louis Hoffman, Assistant Commissioner of Immigration to Commissioner General of Immigration, 7 March 1914, NARA, RG 85, Entry 9, 53751-6.

63. J. B. Densmore, Acting Secretary of Commerce and Labor, to Busk & Daniels, attorneys for Lamport & Holt Line, 5 February 1915, NARA, RG 85, Entry 9, 53751-6.
64. Busk & Daniels to J. B. Densmore, 8 February 1915, NARA, RG 85, Entry 9, 53751-6.
65. New York Attorney to Attorney General, 24 January 1918, NARA, RG 85, Entry 9, 53751-6.
66. H Snowden Marshall, US Attorney, to Commissioner of Immigration, Ellis Island, 4 February 1915, NARA, RG 85, Entry 9, 53751-6; "The Case of Nathan Cohen," YIVO, RG 245.2.
67. Busk & Daniels, to Commissioner of Immigration, Ellis Island, 15 May 1915, NARA, RG 85, Entry 9, 53751-6.
68. Busk & Daniels to Densmore, 8 February 1915, NARA, RG 85, Entry 9, 53751-6.
69. Busk & Daniels to Senator James A. O'Gorman, 8 February 1915, NARA, RG 85, Entry 9, 53751-6.
70. Densmore to Busk & Daniels, 12 February 1915, NARA, RG 85, Entry 9, 53751-6.
71. Busk & Daniels to Densmore, 15 February 1915, NARA, RG 85, Entry 9, 53751-6.
72. Densmore to Busk & Daniels, 18 February 1915, NARA, RG 85, Entry 9, 53751-6.
73. Busk & Daniels to Densmore, 24 February 1915, NARA, RG 85, Entry 9, 53751-6.
74. Burlingham, Montgomery, and Beecher, to Frederic Howe, 9 March 1915, NARA, RG 85, Entry 9, 53751-6.
75. Bureau of Immigration to Busk & Daniels, 18 March 1915, NARA, RG 85, Entry 9, 53751-6.
76. H. M. Sasnett, Jacksonville, to Max Kohn, New York, 23 March 1915, YIVO, RG 245.2.
77. For more on William Grossman's biography, see Ernest G. Sihler, Henry M. McCraken, and Willis Fletcher Johnson, *Universities and Their Sons: New York University*, ed. Joshua Chamberlain, Vol. 2 (Boston: J. Herndon, 1903), 359.
78. Telegram, H. M. Sasnett, Jacksonville, to William Grossman, New York, 25 March 1915, YIVO, RG 245.2.
79. Telegram, Samuel Littman, New York, to Martha Rezenstein, Baltimore, 20 March 1915; and Telegram, Martha Rezenstein, Baltimore, to Samuel Littman, New York, 26 March 1915, YIVO, RG 245.2.
80. Irving Lipsitch, Representative of HIAS at Ellis Island, to Secretary of Labor through the Commissioner of Immigration at Ellis Island, no date, YIVO.
81. Affidavits for A. S. Metzner, J. M. Stewart, Harry Gerbert, Abe Berman, A. W. Jenks, and A. J. Ducig were all provide to Sasnet on 8–19 April 1915, YIVO.
82. The diagnosis of dementia praecox started declining by the end of the 1920s, and had disappeared by 1939. Richard Noll, *American Madness: The Rise and Fall of Dementia Praecox* (Cambridge, MA: Harvard University Press, 2011), 2–6.
83. J. C., "Experiences of Adults with 'Selective Mutism,' in Their Own Words," *Psychologist* 28, no. 9 (2015): 710.
84. Rezenstein visited Littman in New York but he was in Washington, DC. Martha Rezenstein, Baltimore, to Samuel Littman, New York, 29 March 1915, YIVO, RG 245.2.
85. Samuel Littman to Lamport & Holt, 31 March 1915, YIVO, RG 245.2.
86. Busk & Daniels, representing Lamport & Holt, to Samuel Littman, 1 April 1915, YIVO, RG 245.2.
87. Samuel Littman to Lamport & Holt, 12 April 1915, YIVO, RG 245.2.
88. "The Case of Nathan Cohen," YIVO, RG 245.2.

89. "The Case of Nathan Cohen," YIVO, RG 245.2.
90. "The Case of Nathan Cohen," YIVO, RG 245.2.
91. Newspaper clipping, unknown publication, YIVO, RG 245.2.
92. President of HIAS to Louis S. Barnard, 31 March 1915, YIVO, RG 245.2.
93. Samuel Littman to Physician in Charge, Holbrook Farms, 10 April 1915, YIVO, RG 245.2.
94. General Manager, HIAS, to Alonzo Bell, Knights of Pythias, 13 April 1916, YIVO, RG 245.2.
95. Dr. D. W. McFarland to HIAS, 13 April 1915, YIVO, RG 245.2.
96. Littman to McFarland's Sanitarium, 27 July 1915, YIVO, RG 245.2. Samuel Littman to McFarland, 7 December 1915, YIVO, RG 245.2.
97. McFarland to Littman, 12 May 1915, YIVO, RG 245.2.
98. McFarland to Littman, 4 July 1915, YIVO, RG 245.2.
99. Littman to Grossman, 6 July 1915, YIVO, RG 245.2.
100. McFarland to HIAS, 25 November 1915, YIVO, RG 245.2.
101. Littman to Grossman, 20 April 1915, YIVO, RG 245.2.
102. Littman to Grossman, 7 December 1915, YIVO, RG 245.2.
103. Littman to Henersey, 28 December 1915, YIVO, RG 245.2.
104. Undated fragment of letter from HIAS to unknown recipient, YIVO, RG 245.2.
105. Telegram Littman to Sasnett, 3 March 1915, YIVO, RG 245.2.
106. Telegram Littman to Sasnett, 3 March 1915, YIVO, RG 245.2.
107. Telegram S. M. Mathews to Littman, 3 March 1916, YIVO, RG 245.2.
108. Representative of Lodge of Pythias, to S. M. Mathews, attorney, Jacksonville, 6 March 1916, YIVO, RG 245.2. The primary cause of death is illegible on the certificate. Death Certificate for Nathan Cohen, YIVO RG 245.2.
109. Representative of Lodge of Pythias, to S. M. Mathews, attorney, Jacksonville, 6 March 1916, YIVO, RG 245.2.
110. Martha Rezenstein, Baltimore, to Samuel Littman, New York, 3 March 1916, YIVO, RG 245.2, RG 245.2.
111. "Outcast Finds a Home in Death," *Tribune*, 6 March 1916, YIVO [56]. "Obituary," newspaper clipping, no date, YIVO, RG 245.2.

CHAPTER 3

1. Elsa Kudo, interviewed by Kelli Nakamura, 6 February 2012, Densho Visual History Collection, denshovh-kelsa-01.
2. Seiichi Higashide, *Adiós to Tears: The Memories of a Japanese-Peruvian Internee in US Concentration Camps* (Seattle: University of Washington Press, 2000), 135–137.
3. Higashide, *Adios to Tears*, 136.
4. Kudo, interviewed by Nakamura, 6 February 2012, Densho Visual History Collection, denshovh-kelsa-01.
5. Higashide, *Adios to Tears*, 136.
6. Higashide, *Adios to Tears*, 137–138.
7. Elsa Kudo, interview with author, 4 February 2019.
8. Higashide, *Adios to Tears*, 139–140.
9. Higashide, *Adios to Tears*, 137–140.
10. Higashide, *Adios to Tears*, 140–143.
11. C. Harvey Gardiner, *Pawns in a Triangle of Hate: The Peruvian Japanese and the United States* (Seattle: University of Washington Press, 1981); Thomas Connell, *America's Japanese Hostages* (Westport, CT: Praeger, 2002); Daniel Masterson,

The Japanese in Latin America (Urbana: University of Illinois Press, 2004), ch. 6; Benjamin Jih DuMontier, "Between Menace and Model Citizen: Lima's Japanese-Peruvians, 1936–1963" (PhD dissertation, University of Arizona, 2018); Max Paul Friedman, *Nazis and Good Neighbors: The United States Campaign against the Germans of Latin America in World War II* (Cambridge: Cambridge University Press, 2003); John Christgau, *Enemies: World War II Alien Internment* (San Jose. CA: Authors Choice Press, 1985); Russell W. Estlack, *Shattered Lives, Shattered Dreams: The Disrupted Lives of Families in America's Internment Camps* (Springville, UT: Bonneville Books, 2011); Heidi Gurcke Donald, *We Were Not the Enemy: Remembering the United States Latin American Civilian Internment Program of World War II* (New York: iUniverse, 2006). There are rich collections of oral histories of Japanese Latin Americans compiled by Densho in Seattle (densho. org), and the Japanese Peruvian Oral History project in Berkeley; the German American Internee Coalition (GAIC) has a rich source of digitized documents as well (http://gaic.info/resources/documents/).

12. Higashide, *Adios to Tears*, 12–19.
13. Higashide, *Adios to Tears*, 27–42.
14. Higashide, *Adios to Tears*, 40, 52–56.
15. Higashide, *Adios to Tears*, 62–65.
16. Elsa Kudo, interview with author, 3 February 2019.
17. Seiichi Higashide appears in the first revision of the Proclaimed List along with twenty-eight pages of names from Peru, mostly Japanese. Higashide, *Adios to Tears*, 68–96, 114–115.
18. "The Proclaimed List of Certain Blocked Nationals—Supplement 1–4. Feb. 28-May 1, 1942," 1942, //catalog.hathitrust.org/Record/010592803, http://hdl. handle.net/2027/uc1.b5030504 (Vols.1–3), 98. "The Proclaimed List of Certain Blocked Nationals: Revision II, May 12, 1942," 1942, 116.
19. Friedman, *Nazis and Good Neighbors*, 88–101.
20. Higashide, *Adios to Tears*, 129–132.
21. Higashide, *Adios to Tears*, 78.
22. Elliott Young, *Alien Nation: Chinese Migration in the Americas from the Coolie Era to WWII* (Chapel Hill: University of North Carolina Press, 2014), 77–79.
23. Higashide, *Adios to Tears*, 81–88.
24. Elsa Kudo, interview with author, 3 February 2019.
25. Kudo, interviewed by Nakamura, 6 February 2012, Densho Visual History Collection, denshovh-kelsa-01.
26. This quote is often attributed to Ugarte, but he was citing an unnamed Central American newspaper. Higashide, *Adios to Tears*.
27. Manuel Ugarte, *La Patria Grande* (Buenos Aires: Capital Intelectual, 2010). Connell, *America's Japanese Hostages*, chs. 3–4. Gardiner, *Pawns in a Triangle of Hate*, 12–16.
28. Friedman, *Nazis and Good Neighbors*, 75–78; Carl B. Spaeth and William Sanders, "The Emergency Advisory Committee for Political Defense," *American Journal of International Law* 38, no. 218–241 (1944): 220–221.
29. Gardiner, *Pawns in a Triangle of Hate*, 17–18.
30. *Emergency Advisory Committee for Political Defense, Second Annual Report* (Washington, DC: Pan American Union, 1943), 50–51.
31. Ayumi Takenaka, "The Japanese in Peru: History of Immigration, Settlement, and Racialization," *Latin American Perspectives* 31, no. 3 (2004); José Luis Naupari Robledo, "La presecución a la colectividad japonesa en el Perú

1941–1945" (Master's thesis, Ponticia Universidad Católica del Perú, 2011); Humberto Rodríguez Pastor, *Herederos del dragón: historia de la comunidad china en el Perú* (Lima: Fondo Editorial del Congreso del Perú, 2000).

32. Takenaka, "The Japanese in Peru," 77, 86–87, 90–91.

33. Masterson, *The Japanese in Latin America*, 152.

34. DuMontier, "Between Menace and Model Citizen," 11–13.

35. Masterson, *The Japanese in Latin America*, 154.

36. Manuel Seoane, "The Japanese Are Still in Peru," *Asia and the Americas* 43 (1943), as quoted by Takenaka, "The Japanese in Peru," 92.

37. DuMontier, "Between Menace and Model Citizen," 46–50; James Brown Scott, "Nationality: Jus Soli or Jus Sanguinis," *American Journal of International Law* 24, no. 1 (1930): 59; Takenaka, "The Japanese in Peru," 87; Masterson, *The Japanese in Latin America*, 152.

38. Estimates of people killed range from one to ten, and damage estimates range from $1.6 million to $7 million. Higashide, *Adios to Tears*, 105–110; Masterson, *The Japanese in Latin America*, 156–157; Chikako Yamawaki, *Estrategias de via de los inmigrantes asiáticos en el Perú* (Lima: IEP, JCAS, 2002), 122, as cited in Robledo, "La presecución a la colectividad japonesa en el Perú 1941–1945," 18.

39. Takenaka, "The Japanese in Peru," 93.

40. DuMontier, "Between Menace and Model Citizen," ch. 2.

41. "Resolution Concerning Detention and Expulsion of Dangerous Axis National," Montevideo Resolution, 21 May 1943, US Special War Problems Division, National Archives and Records Administration (hereafter NARA), Record Group (hereafter RG) 59, in http://gaic.info/wp-content/uploads/2016/02/Montevideo-Resol.-21-May-1943.pdf.

42. Elsa Kudo, interview with author, 3 February 2019.

43. Higashide, *Adios to Tears*, 177.

44. White to Lafoon, memorandum in "Statistics," 30 January 1946, NARA, RG 59, Box 70, Special War Problems Division, in http://gaic.info/wp-content/uploads/2016/02/White.Lafoonmemo.lg_.jpg.pdf.

45. H. Glenn Penny, "Latin American Connections: Recent Work on German Interactions with Latin America," *Central European History* 46, no. 2 (2013): 381–385; James Lawrence Tigner, "Shindō Remmei: Japanese Nationalism in Brazil," *Hispanic American Historical Review* 41, no. 4 (1961): 517.

46. Higashide, *Adios to Tears*, 114–115.

47. Gardiner, *Pawns in a Triangle of Hate*, 3–11, 14, 21.

48. White to Lafoon, memorandum in "Statistics," 30 January 1946, NARA, RG 59, Box 70, Special War Problems Division, http://gaic.info/wp-content/uploads/2016/02/White.Lafoonmemo.lg_.jpg.pdf; Connell, *America's Japanese Hostages*, 21–32.

49. Memo from Raymond W. Ickes and James D. Bell, Alien Enemy Control Unit, Department of Justice, to Robert M. Scotten, US Ambassador, San José, Costa Rica, 30 March 1943, NARA, RG 84, US Embassy, San José, Costa Rica, General Records, File 711.5; UD 2353, http://gaic.info/wp-content/uploads/2016/01/Raymond-Ickes-Memorandum-to-the-Minister-30-Mar-1943.pdf .

50. Donald, *We Were Not the Enemy*, xvii–xviiii.

51. *US v. Curtiss-Wright Export Corporation*, 299 US 304 (1936).

52. Christgau, *Enemies*, vii.

53. Jonathan Masters, "Targeted Killings," Council on Foreign Relations, 23 May 2013, https://www.cfr.org/backgrounder/targeted-killings.

54. Lisa C. Miyake, "Forsaken and Forgotten: The US Internment of Japanese Peruvians during WWII," *Asian American Law Journal* 9, no. 5 (2002): 181–182.
55. Byrnes, 64 F. Supp at 234, as quoted in Miyake, "Forsaken and Forgotten," 187.
56. In re Ross, 140 US 453 (1891), as quoted in Miyake, "Forsaken and Forgotten," 188.
57. Miyake, "Forsaken and Forgotten," 189.
58. Miyake, "Forsaken and Forgotten," 190.
59. Gardiner, *Pawns in a Triangle of Hate*, 29.
60. Miyake, "Forsaken and Forgotten," 191; Friedman, *Nazis and Good Neighbors*, 192–209.
61. Cordell Hull to Biddle, 9 November 1942, 74, NARA, RG 59 Central Decimal File, 1940–1944, 0.00115 EW 1939/4570; Box 2835–250/32/19/02, in http://gaic.info/wp-content/uploads/2016/01/Hull-to-Biddle-9-Nov-1942.pdf.
62. George Marshall Memo, 12 December 1942, NARA, Subject Files, 1939–1954, Box 7; Accession Job No. N3-59-87-15, Records of the Special War Problems Division, Department of State, in http://gaic.info/wp-content/uploads/2016/11/Marshall-memo.pdf.
63. "Memorandum regarding the Activities of the United States Government," 3 November 1942, NARA, RG 59, Subject Files, Box 180, location 250/49/23/7, Records of the Special War Problems Division, in http://gaic.info/wp-content/uploads/2016/02/11-42-L.A.memo_.pdf.
64. Connell, *America's Japanese Hostages*, 74–75.
65. Masterson, *The Japanese in Latin America*, 155.
66. Gardiner, *Pawns in a Triangle of Hate*, 10, 22.
67. Gardiner, *Pawns in a Triangle of Hate: The Peruvian Japanese and the United States*, 40.
68. Memorandum from Raymond W. Ickes and James D. Bell to Minister, 30 March 1943, NARA, RG 84; Costa Rica; U.S. Embassy, San Jose; Classified General Records; File 711.5; UD 2353; Box 25 [Old Box 26]—350/53/27/05, p. 2–3, in http://gaic.info/30-mar-1943-raymond-ickes-memo-procedures-to-decide-whom-to-imprison-intern-repatriate/.
69. "Memorandum regarding the Activities of the United States Government, 3 Nov 1942, NARA, RG 59, Subject Files, Box 180, location 250/49/23/7, Records of the Special War Problems Division, http://gaic.info/wp-content/uploads/2016/02/11-42-L.A.memo_.pdf.
70. "Report on traveling conditions of group of German citizens from Costa Rica," 22 February 1943: from folder 383.7, Camp Crystal City, NARA, http://gaic.info/wp-content/uploads/2016/01/22-Feb-1943-ltr_re-Puebla_jpg.pdf.
71. Higashide, *Adios to Tears*, 143–145.
72. Gardiner, *Pawns in a Triangle of Hate*, 76–77.
73. Higashide, *Adios to Tears*, 145–146.
74. Higashide, *Adios to Tears*, 143–146; Robledo, "La presecución a la colectividad japonesa en el Perú 1941-1945," ch. 1.
75. Higashide, *Adios to Tears*, 150.
76. Elsa Kudo, interview with author, 3 February 2019.
77. Higashide, *Adios to Tears*, 155–156.
78. Connell, *America's Japanese Hostages*, 73–74.
79. Higashide, *Adios to Tears*, 156–157; Deborah Cohen, *Braceros: Migrant Citizens and Transnational Subjects* (Chapel Hill: University of North Carolina Press, 2011), 99.

80. Higashide, *Adios to Tears*, 156–157.
81. W. F. Kelly, Chief Supervisor of Border Patrol, Kenedy, Texas, to Commissioner of INS, 2 November 1942, NARA, RG 389, Records of the Office of the Provost Marshal General, Alien Enemy Information Bureau, Records relating to Alien Enemy Civilian Internees, 1941–1946, Box 3, NN3-389-90-1 Kenedy, http://gaic.info/wp-content/uploads/2016/10/31-Oct-1940-Kenedy-census.pdf.
82. Higashide, *Adios to Tears*, 149–150.
83. Connell, *America's Japanese Hostages*, 75–76.
84. Higashide, *Adios to Tears*, 159.
85. Higashide, *Adios to Tears*, 160.
86. Kudo, interviewed by Nakamura, 6 February 2012, Densho Visual History Collection, denshovh-kelsa-01.
87. Higashide, *Adios to Tears*, 161–162.
88. Elsa Kudo, interview with author, 3 February 2019.
89. Kudo, interviewed by Nakamura, 6 February 2012, Densho Visual History Collection, denshovh-kelsa-01.
90. Higashide, *Adios to Tears*, 177.
91. William D. Pawley, as quoted in Gardiner, *Pawns in a Triangle of Hate*, 135.
92. Harry S. Truman, "Proclamation 2662: Removal of Alien Enemies," 1945, https://www.trumanlibrary.org/proclamations/index.php?pid=247&st=immigration&st1=.
93. Miyake, "Forsaken and Forgotten," 191.
94. Higashide, *Adios to Tears*, 178.
95. Elsa Kudo's husband had to postpone his attendance at the University of Illinois as he was not eligible for in-state tuition. Tami Kudo Harnish, Elsa's daughter, email communication, 9 March 2020.
96. Higashide, *Adios to Tears*, 174, 177. A Japanese Brazilian society, Shindo Renmei, had 50,000 members who believed that Japan had won the war. Jeffrey Lesser, *Negotiating National Identity: Immigrants, Minorities and the Struggle for Ethnicity in Brazil* (Durham, NC: Duke University Press, 1999), 138–140.
97. Higashide, *Adios to Tears*, 176–179.
98. "Biggest Vegetable Factory on Earth," *Life*, 3 January 1955, 41.
99. Higashide, *Adios to Tears*, 163; Connell, *America's Japanese Hostages*, 231–232.
100. Higashide, *Adios to Tears*, 180–181.
101. Higashide, *Adios to Tears*, 182.
102. Kudo, interviewed by Nakamura, 6 February 2012, Densho Visual History Collection, denshovh-kelsa-01.
103. *Seabrook at War: A Radio Documentary*. Narrated by Kurt Vonnegut Jr. Written and Produced by Marty Goldensohn and David Steven Cohen. A co-production of WWFM/WWNJ, Trenton and the New Jersey Historical Commission, Department of State, 1995. Clip of interview available at the *Journal for Multimedia History*, Vol. 2, 1999, https://www.albany.edu/jmmh/vol2no1/seabrook.html.
104. Higashide, *Adios to Tears*, 182–183.
105. Higashide, *Adios to Tears*, 185–187; James C. Scott, *Weapons of the Weak: Everyday Forms of Peasant Resistance* (New Haven, CT: Yale University Press, 1985).
106. Higashide, *Adios to Tears*, 193–198.
107. Charles Wollenberg, *Rebel Lawyer: Wayne Collins and the Defense of Japanese American Rights* (Berkeley, CA: Heyday, 2018).

108. Tel. Hajime Kishi to Wayne Collins, 24 April 1946, Wayne Collins Papers, Roll 21, 78/177, Bancroft Library, University of California, Berkeley.

109. Wollenberg, *Rebel Lawyer*.

110. Tel Wayne Collins to Hajime Kishi, 25 April 1946, Wayne Collins Papers, Roll 21, 78/177, Bancroft Library, University of California, Berkeley.

111. Koshiro Mukayama, Crystal City, to Wayne Collins, San Francisco, 29 April 1946, Wayne Collins Papers, Roll 21, 78/177, Bancroft Library, University of California, Berkeley.

112. "Comunicado del Ministerio de Relaciones Exteriores," *El Comercio*, 23 April 1946, as transcribed in Koshiro Mukayama, Crystal City, to Wayne Collins, San Francisco, 29 April 1946, Wayne Collins Papers, Roll 21, 78/177, Bancroft Library, University of California, Berkeley.

113. Connell, *America's Japanese Hostages*, 231.

114. Wayne Collins, San Francisco, to Hajime Kishi, Terminal Island, 25 April 1946, Wayne Collins Papers, Roll 21, 78/177, Bancroft Library, University of California, Berkeley.

115. Higashide's case file does not appear in Collins's voluminous papers. Higashide, *Adios to Tears*.

116. Hajime Kishi, Seabrook Farms, NJ, to Wayne Collins, San Francisco 10 March 1950, Wayne Collins Papers, Roll 21, 78/177, Bancroft Library, University of California, Berkeley.

117. Wayne Collins, San Francisco, to Hajime Kishi, Seabrook Farms, NJ, 13 March 1950, Wayne Collins Papers, Roll 21, 78/177, Bancroft Library, University of California, Berkeley.

118. Kudo, interviewed by Nakamura, 6 February 2012, Densho Visual History Collection, denshovh-kelsa-01.

119. Hajime Kishi, Seabrook Farms, NJ, to Wayne Collins, San Francisco 28 August 1950, Wayne Collins Papers, Roll 21, 78/177, Bancroft Library, University of California, Berkeley; Hajime Kishi, San Diego, to Wayne Collins, San Francisco 2 April 1951, Wayne Collins Papers, Roll 21, 78/177, Bancroft Library, University of California, Berkeley.

120. Wayne Collins, San Francisco, to Hajime Kishi, San Diego, NJ, 8 January 1952, Wayne Collins Papers, Roll 21, 78/177, Bancroft Library, University of California, Berkeley.

121. Wayne Collins, San Francisco, to Yoshihiko Onaga, Los Angeles, 29 April 1953, Wayne Collins Papers, Roll 21, 78/177, Bancroft Library, University of California, Berkeley.

122. Hajime Kishi, San Diego, to Wayne Collins, San Francisco 8 January 1952, Wayne Collins Papers, Roll 21, 78/177, Bancroft Library, University of California, Berkeley.

123. Wayne Collin, "Brief for Masao Kishi Before the Board of Immigration Appeals," Wayne Collins Papers, Roll 21, 78/177.

124. Wayne Collin, "Brief for Masao Kishi Before the Board of Immigration Appeals," Wayne Collins Papers, Roll 21, 78/177, Bancroft Library, University of California, Berkeley.

125. Wayne Collins to Harry S Truman, 16 February 1948, Truman Library, Independence, MO, White House File Record—Collins, as quoted in Connell, *America's Japanese Hostages*, 238.

126. Public Laws, Chapter 783, HR 3566, July 1, 1948, 80th Cong., sess. 2, p. 1206.

127. "Hajimi Kishi Deportation Proceedings," 14 July 1953, Wayne Collins Papers, Roll 21, 78/177, Bancroft Library, University of California, Berkeley.

128. Connell, *America's Japanese Hostages*, 238. Public Law 751, "An Act to Amend the Refugee Relief Act of 1953," 31 August 1954, Chap. 1169, p. 1044.

129. Miyake, "Forsaken and Forgotten," 179.

130. Wayne Collins, San Francisco, to Masao Kishi, San Diego, 19 November 1954, Wayne Collins Papers, Roll 21, 78/177, Bancroft Library, University of California, Berkeley.

131. Higashide, *Adios to Tears*, 223.

132. Higashide, *Adios to Tears*, 224, 237.

133. Higashide, *Adios to Tears*, 242–244.

134. Elsa Kudo, interview with author, 3 February 2019. Event also recounted by Tami Kudo Harnish, Eimi's sister, email communication, 9 March 2020.

135. US Congress, House, Committee on the Judiciary, Treatment of Latin Americans of Japanese Descent, European Americans and Jewish Refugees during World War II, 111th Cong., 1st sess., 2009.

136. Commission on Wartime Relocation and Internment of Civilians, *Personal Justice Denied: Part 2 Recommendations* (Washington, DC: US Government Printing Office, 1983), 9.

137. Commission on Wartime Relocation and Internment of Civilians, *Personal Justice Denied* (Washington, DC: Government Printing Office, 1982), 314.

138. *Civil Liberties Act of 1987*, 100th Congress, HR 442.

139. *Mochizuki v. United States*, (1999).

140. "Litigation," Campaign for Justice, https://jlacampaignforjustice.org/litigation/.

141. "Litigation."

142. Evelyn Iritani, "His Family's Internment Earned Apologies from a Human Rights Commission. Will the U.S. Government Respond?," *Los Angeles Times*, 24 March 2017; Martha Nakagawa, "Obituary: Art Shibayama, Fighter for Japanese Latin American Redress," *Rafu Shimpo* 2018.

143. Karleen C. Chinen, "Former Japanese Peruvian Internees Reunite in Honolulu," *Hawai'i Herald*, 3 October 2014.

144. Kaori Akiyama, personal communication with author, 11 August 2019.

145. Chinen, "Former Japanese Peruvian Internees Reunite in Honolulu."

CHAPTER 4

1. William K. Stevens, "Arkansas Fort Receives First of Thousands of Cubans," *New York Times*, 10 May 1980.

2. Jenna M. Loyd and Alison Mountz, *Boats, Borders and Bases: Race, the Cold War and the Rise of Migration Detention in the United States* (Berkeley: University of California Press, 2018), 59.

3. Stevens, "Arkansas Fort Receives First of Thousands of Cubans."

4. "Two Decades Later, Mariel Boat Lift Refugees Still Feel Effects of Riot," *Los Angeles Times*, 5 May 2001. For more on the KKK protest at Fort Chaffee, see Loyd and Mountz, *Boats, Borders and Bases*, 56–60.

5. US Department of Justice, "Report to Attorney General on the Disturbances at the Federal Detention Center, Oakdale, Louisiana, US Penitentiary, Atlanta, Georgia, 4 February 1988," in US Congress: House, *Mariel Cuban Detainees: Events Preceding and Following the November 1987 Riots: Hearing Before the Subcommittee on Courts, Civil Liberties, and the Administration of Justice*,

February 4 1988, 100th Cong., 2nd Sess. (Washington DC: Government Printing Office, 1989), 272, 292.

6. US Congress, "Supplemental Appropriations Bill, 1986," U.S. Congressional Serial Set (1986), p. 23- 24.

7. Cited by John Lewis, representative of Georgia, in Congressional Record, 27 April 1987, in United States Congress: House, *Mariel Cuban Detainees*, 13.

8. United States Department of Justice, "Report to Attorney General," in US Congress: House, *Mariel Cuban Detainees*, 271-272.

9. Over the years there has been one book-length study of the prison uprising by a criminologist, and several chapters in other books have covered similar ground, mostly relying on government reports and journalistic accounts. Mark S. Hamm, *The Abandoned Ones: The Imprisonment and Uprising of the Mariel Boat People* (Boston: Northeastern University Press, 1995); Mark Dow, *American Gulag inside U.S. Immigration Prisons* (Berkeley: University of California Press, 2004), ch. 14; Gary Leshaw, "Atlanta's Cuban Detainees," *Atlanta Lawyer* (Fourth Quarter 1992): 6–28;Earl Lawson, *The Atlanta Penitentiary Burns: The Cuban Detainees Take Over the Pen with 121 Hostages* (Maitland, FL: Liberty Hill, 2018); Renaldo A. Smith, "The Cuban Detainee Uprising and Riot at the Atlanta Penitentiary November 23, 1987" (Master's thesis, Atlanta University, 1988).

10. Enrique González Sarasa, *Excluibles* (Havana: Ediciones Abril, 1994).

11. Gary Leshaw, interview with author, 21 February 2019; Sally Sandige, interview with author, 19 February 2019.

12. Eoin Higgins, "'Terrible News': US Supreme Court Rules for Indefinite Detention of Immigrants," *Common Dreams*, 19 March 2019.

13. US Department of Justice, "Report to Attorney General," in US Congress: House, *Mariel Cuban Detainees*, 282.

14. US Congress, *Atlanta Federal Penitentiary: Report of the Subcommittee on Courts, Civil Liberties, and the Administration of Justice*, 99th Cong., 2nd sess. (Washington DC: Government Printing Office, 1986), 5-6.

15. Cosme Damian Rodriguez to Deborah Ebel, Atlanta Legal Aid, 2 April 1985, Atlanta History Center (hereafter AHC), Cuba Detainees' Litigation Papers (hereafter CLP), series II, 734, Box 13, Folder 3.

16. Leandro Gandaria, Terre Haute, Indiana, to Mary Donovan, Federal Defender Program, Atlanta, 18 July 1985, AHC, CLP, series II, 734, Box 14, Folder 2.

17. Sarasa, *Excluibles*, 9–10.

18. Roman Jaime to Justice Marvin Shoob, 12 January 1985, AHC, CLP, series II, 734, Box 13, Folder 4.

19. The Reverend Russ Mabry as cited in "Statement of Gary Leshaw," in United States Congress: House, *Mariel Cuban Detainees*, 140–141.

20. US Congress, *Atlanta Federal Penitentiary*, 6, 32.

21. The list of crimes committed by Cuban detainees at the Atlanta Penitentiary was published in "Refugees Languish Amid Prison Violence," *Miami Herald*, 3 April 1986; US Congress, Atlanta Federal Penitentiary, 32.

22. US Congress, *Mariel Cuban Detainees*, 208.

23. Knauff v. Shaughnessy, 338 US 537 *(1950)*. For more on the legal issues related to due process and the entry fiction, see Ethan A. Klingsberg, "Penetrating the Entry Doctrine: Excludable Aliens' Constitutional Rights in Immigration Processes," *Yale Law Journal* 98, no. 3 (1989).

24. US Congress, *Mariel Cuban Detainees*, 122–124.

25. For more on the lack of due process in the INS hearings, see Gary Leshaw's testimony at the congressional hearing. US Congress, *Mariel Cuban Detainees*, 129–132.
26. Kevin Conboy, "Remembrances: Marvin H. Shoob," *Georgia Law Review* 52(2017): v–vi.
27. US Congress, *Mariel Cuban Detainees*, 123.
28. Nishimura Ekiu v. United States, 142 U.S. 651, 660 (1892).
29. United States v. Ju Toy, 198 U.S. 253, 263 (1905).
30. Shaughnessy v. Mezei, 345 U.S. 206 (1953).
31. Leng May Ma v. Barber, 357 U.S. 185, 357 (1958).
32. Carl Lindskoog, *Detain and Punish: Haitian Refugees and the Rise of the World's Largest Immigration Detention System* (Gainesville: University of Florida Press, 2018), 2–3; Loyd and Mountz, *Boats, Borders and Bases*, 42–52.
33. Lindskoog, *Detain and Punish*, 16–18.
34. Hatian Refugee Center v Civiletti, 503 F. Supp. 442, 458 (1980).
35. Lindskoog, *Detain and Punish*, 29–32.
36. Fernandez v. Wilkinson, 505 F. Supp 787, 795, 800 (1980).
37. Rodriguez-Fernandez v. Wilkinson, 654 F 2d 1382(1981).
38. Fernandez-Roque v. Smith, 567 F. Supp. 1115, 1129 (1983).
39. Fernandez-Roque v. Smith, 734 F.2d 576 584 (1984). At the same time, in the Haitian case Jean v. Nelson (1984) the 11th Circuit decided that excludable aliens had no constitutional protections. Jean v. Nelson, 727 F.2d 957 (1984).
40. In a 1987 case involving Jamaican stowaways, the 5th Circuit Court held that excludable aliens had due process rights as articulated in the Fifth and Fourteenth Amendments. Nonetheless, the Circuit Courts were divided on the issue. The 10th Circuit in Rodriguez-Fernandez v. Wilkinson (1981) and the 5th Circuit both argued that excludable aliens have Fifth Amendment protections if they are held indefinitely. However, the 11th and the 4th Circuit Courts held that no such rights existed for excludable aliens. Lynch v. Cannatella, 810 F 2d 1363 (5th Cir. 1987). For a legal analysis of this decision, see Klingsberg, "Penetrating the Entry Doctrine: Excludable Aliens' Constitutional Rights in Immigration Processes," 644–645; Rodriguez-Fernandez v. Wilkinson, 654 F 2d (10th Cir. 1981).
41. Jean v. Nelson, 472 U.S. 846(1985); Mary Jane Lapointe, "Discrimination in Asylum Law: The Implications of Jean v. Nelson," *Indiana Law Journal* 62, no. 1 (1986): 128–129.
42. US Congress, *Atlanta Federal Penitentiary*, 9-10, 20.
43. US Congress, *Mariel Cuban Detainees*, 75.
44. US Congress, *Mariel Cuban Detainees*, 123.
45. Roberto Salabarria Gomez to Senator Paula Hawkins, 9 August 1984, AHC, CLP, series II, 734, Box 13, Folder 3. Roberto Salabarria Gomez to Senator Mack Mattingly, 9 August 1984, AHC, CLP, series II, 734, Box 13, Folder 3.
46. Sally Sandige, Coalition to Support Cuban Detainees, testimony before Congress, 4 February 1988, in US Congress, *Mariel Cuban Detainees*, 239–241.
47. US Congress, An Amendment to the Various Acts Relative to Immigration and the Importation of Alien under Contract or Agreement to Perform Labor, Fifty-First, II, 1891, Ch. 551, 1084.
48. Colorado v. Jose Borcello Pozo, Colorado Court of Appeals, 6 June 1985, in AHC, CLP, series II, 734, Box 14, Folder 1.

49. William C. Thompson, Atlanta Legal Aid, to Jane S. Hazen, Denver, 21 October 1985, AHC, CLP, series II, 734, Box 14, Folder 1.
50. Sarasa, *Excluibles*, 51.
51. US Congress, *Mariel Cuban Detainees*, 99.
52. Hamm, *The Abandoned Ones*, 27.
53. John M. Crewdson, "Refugees Straining Center in Key West," *New York Times*, 6 May 1980.
54. Alexander Stephens, "'I Hope They Don't Come to Plains': Race and the Detention of Mariel Cubans 1980–1981" (Master's thesis, University of Georgia, 2016), 110.
55. Carol Whitlock, "A Refugee Sponsor's Diary of Love," *Miami Herald*, December 21, 1980, as cited in Stephens, "'I Hope They Don't Come to Plains'," 98–102.
56. Hamm, *The Abandoned Ones*, 55–58.
57. C.L.S., "Los Impacientes," *La Vida Nueva*, May 28, 1980, p. 1, as quoted in Jana Lipman, "A Refugee Camp in America: Fort Chaffee and Vietnamese and Cuban Refugees, 1975–1982," *Journal of American Ethnic History* 33, no. 2 (2014): 77. For more on earlier resistance at Fort Chaffee see, Kristina Karin Shull, "'Nobody Wants These People': Reagan's Immigration Crisis and America's First Private Prisons" (PhD dissertation, University of California, 2014), ch. 2.
58. Jo Thomas, "Refugees at Ft. Chaffee Wait in Boredom and Un- certainty," *New York Times*, June 6, 1980, as cited in Lipman, "A Refugee Camp in America," 75.
59. Rosendo Tabio as cited in Thomas, "A Refugee Camp in America," 75.
60. George Volsky, "55 Cubans Riot in Bus Traveling to Atlanta Prison," *New York Times*, 30 May 1986.
61. Leshaw, "Atlanta's Cuban Detainees," 12.
62. "Guards Quell Cuban Inmates," *New York Times*, 2 November 1984.
63. William E. Schmidt, "Atlanta Prison Lockup of Cubans Continues," *New York Times*, 25 October 1984.
64. Telephone interview with Patrick O'Neil, 28 December 2018.
65. US Department of Justice, "Report to Attorney General," in US Congress, *Mariel Cuban Detainees,* 391–392. The $5 million cost from the 1984 rebellion was cited in US Congress, *Atlanta Federal Penitentiary*, 4.
66. US Congress, *Mariel Cuban Detainees*, 125.
67. US Department of Justice, "Report to Attorney General," in US Congress, *Mariel Cuban Detainees* , 393–394.
68. US Department of Justice, "Report to Attorney General," in US Congress, *Mariel Cuban Detainees*, 394; US Congress, *Atlanta Federal Penitentiary*, 5.
69. "50 Cuban Prisoners Force Fed in Atlanta," *New York Times*, 2 September 1985.
70. Although this letter is dated October 13, it likely was written September 13 given the timing of Ann Woolner's article two days later: 33 Detainees to Editor, 13 October 1985, AHC, CLP, series II, 734, Box 14, Folder 2.
71. Ann Woolner, "Hope Wanes for Cubans at the Pen," *Atlanta Constitution*, 15 September 1985.xxxxx
72. 33 Detainees to Editor, 13 October 1985, AHC, CLP, series II, 734, Box 14, Folder 2.
73. Tracy Thompson, "Cubans, Guards Trapped in Cycle of Violence at Atlanta Pen," *Atlanta Journal Constitution*, 19 April 1987. Leshaw, "Atlanta's Cuban Detainees," 12. Hamm, *The Abandoned Ones*, 97–100.
74. "FBI Investigates Death of Cuban Removed from Cell at Atlanta Pen," *Atlanta Journal Constitution*, 20 February 1987; Thompson, "Cubans, Guards Trapped in

Cycle of Violence at Atlanta Pen"; "Prison Officials Get 2nd Autopsy on Cuban Inmate," *Atlanta Journal Constitution*, 22 April 1987.

75. Leshaw, "Atlanta's Cuban Detainees," 12; Hamm, *The Abandoned Ones*, 97–100.

76. Estela Bravo, *The Cuban Excludables* (Bravo Films, 1997).

77. Larry Copeland and Adam Gelb, "Leader in '84 Atlanta Disturbance Identified," *Miami News*, 1 December 1987.

78. Thompson, "Cubans, Guards Trapped in Cycle of Violence at Atlanta Pen."

79. US Department of Justice, "Report to Attorney General," in US Congress, *Mariel Cuban Detainees*, 306–309.

80. Michael Kozak testimony in US Congress, *Mariel Cuban Detainees*, 46–47.

81. This account of the disturbances at Oakdale is based on the after-action report to the attorney general by Oakdale FDC, which itself was derived from interviews with hundreds of participants. US Department of Justice, "Report to Attorney General," in US Congress, *Mariel Cuban Detainees*, 310–311.

82. US Department of Justice, "Report to Attorney General," in US Congress, *Mariel Cuban Detainees*, 396–399.

83. US Department of Justice, "Report to Attorney General," in US Congress, *Mariel Cuban Detainees*, 312.

84. US Department of Justice, "Report to Attorney General," in US Congress, *Mariel Cuban Detainees*, 314–317.

85. US Department of Justice, "Report to Attorney General," in US Congress, *Mariel Cuban Detainees*, 317–321.

86. US Department of Justice, "Report to Attorney General," in US Congress, *Mariel Cuban Detainees*, 396–399.

87. US Department of Justice, "Report to Attorney General," in US Congress, *Mariel Cuban Detainees*, 400–406.

88. Mark S. Hamm, "Santeria in Federal Prisons: Understanding a Little-Known Religion," *Federal Prisons Journal*, no. 4 (1992).

89. Hamm, "Santeria in Federal Prisons," 42.

90. Associated Press, "Many Offered But Few Got Call to Help in Prison Crisis with PM-Cubans-Atlanta, Bjt," 4 December 1987.

91. US Department of Justice, "Report to Attorney General," in US Congress, *Mariel Cuban Detainees*, 408–411.

92. Sally Sandige, interview with author, 19 February 2019.

93. US Department of Justice, "Report to Attorney General," in US Congress, *Mariel Cuban Detainees*, 408–411.

94. Heather Ann Thompson, *Blood in the Water: The Attica Prison Uprising of 1971 and Its Legacy* (New York: Pantheon Books, 2016).

95. Hamm, *The Abandoned Ones*, 30.

96. US Department of Justice, "Report to Attorney General," in US Congress, *Mariel Cuban Detainees*, 327–330.

97. Hamm, *The Abandoned Ones*, 9.

98. Hamm, *The Abandoned Ones*, 23–24.

99. Jerry Schwartz, "A Deal to Release Prison Hostages in Atlanta Collapses at Deadline," *New York Times*, 27 November 1987 1987. US Department of Justice, "Report to Attorney General," in US Congress, *Mariel Cuban Detainees*, 417.

100. Sarasa, *Excluibles*, 10.

101. US Department of Justice, "Report to Attorney General," in US Congress, *Mariel Cuban Detainees* , 422–424

102. Leshaw, "Atlanta's Cuban Detainees," 14.

103. US Department of Justice, "Report to Attorney General," in US Congress, *Mariel Cuban Detainees*, 418.
104. Agustín Román, "Importancia de la misericordia," as quoted in Daniel Shoer Roth, *Pastor profeta patriarca* (Miami: Ermita de la Caridad, 2015), 254.
105. Hamm, *The Abandoned Ones*, 173–175.
106. US Department of Justice, "Report to Attorney General," in US Congress, *Mariel Cuban Detainees*, 334–338.
107. Wood, Katie, and Brenda L. Mooney, "What Really Happened at the Atlanta Pen," *Fulton County Daily Report*, 14 December 1987, 10.
108. Wood and Mooney, "What Really Happened at the Atlanta Pen," 3; José Peña Perez's name also appears in Hamm, *The Abandoned Ones*, 10–11.
109. Wood and Mooney, "What Really Happened at the Atlanta Pen," 11.
110. Wood and Mooney, "What Really Happened at the Atlanta Pen," 12.
111. Sarasa, *Excluibles*, 10.
112. Wood and Mooney, "What Really Happened at the Atlanta Pen," 12.
113. Wood and Mooney, "What Really Happened at the Atlanta Pen," 3.
114. Sally Squires, "Held Hostage," *Washington Post*, 12 January 1988.
115. Robert Pear, "Behind the Prison Riots: Precautions Not Taken," *New York Times*, 6 December 1987.
116. US Department of Justice, "Report to Attorney General," in US Congress, *Mariel Cuban Detainees*, 426–430.
117. William Robbins, "US Schedules Interviews on Fate of Cuban Inmates," *New York Times*, 8 February 1988.
118. Juan Sarria Miranda to Gary Leshaw, 18 December 1987, Sally Sandige Papers, Atlanta Legal Aid Society.
119. Jose Narbona Sanchez to Gary Leshaw, 14 December 1987, Sally Sandige Papers, Atlanta Legal Aid Society.
120. Gustavo Pique Perez to Gary Leshaw, 15 September 1989, Sally Sandige Papers, Atlanta Legal Aid Society.
121. Manuel Diaz Bandera to Carla Dudeck, 17 April 1990, Sally Sandige Papers, Atlanta Legal Aid Society.
122. Ronald Smothers, "Release of Cubans Stepped Up in 5 Months Since US Riots," *New York Times*, 30 April 1988.
123. Ronald Smothers, "US Plans First Deportations after Reviews of Cuban Cases," *New York Times*, 18 November 1988.
124. Ronald Smothers, "Court Orders Five Deported to Cuba," *New York Times*, 1 December 1988.
125. Ronald Smothers, "At End of a Long Road, Cuban Inmates Revolt," *New York Times*, 23 Aug. 1991 1991.
126. Linda Calhoun, interview with author, 10 March 2019.
127. Ronald Smothers, "No Progress Seen in Siege at Prison," *New York Times*, 25 Aug. 1991.
128. Steven Lee Meyers, "31 Inmates in Prison Siege Are Returned to Cuba," *New York Times*, 1 September 1991 1991.
129. Bravo, *The Cuban Excludables*.
130. Bravo, *The Cuban Excludables*.
131. Frances Robles, "'Marielitos' Face Long-Delayed Reckoning: Expulsion to Cuba," *New York Times*, 14 January 2017.
132. "Man Freed from Prison Faces Possible Deportation," *CBS Miami*, 18 May 2017.

133. Jay Weaver and Mimi Whitfield, "Some Cuban Felons, including 2,000 Murderers, Could Face Deportation under New Policy," *Miami Herald*, 16 January 2017.

134. David Goodhue, "A Judge Has Canceled an Immigrant's Drug Conviction. It Saved Him from Deportation," *Miami Herald*, 31 Aug. 2017.

135. Nora Gámez-Torres, "More Than 1,300 Cuban Migrants Are Being Held in Detention Centers across the US," *Miami Herald*, 28 July 2017.

136. Jenny Jarvie, "After Living in the U.S. for More Than Half a Century, This Cuban Activist May Be Deported," *Los Angeles Times*, 20 February 2020.

CHAPTER 5

1. Judgment and Disposition Order, Mayra Jackeline Machado, Circuit Court, Washington County, Arkansas, 1 September 2004, CR 2004-1707-4.

2. "Arrest Warrant in the Circuit Court, Washington County, Arkansas, Mayra Jackeline Machado," 14 January 2005, CR 2004-1402-1, 2004-2414-2, 20004, 1707-4; "Arkansas Parole Board Report No. PCAR 552E, Re Mayra Jackline Machado," 7 Nov. 2018.

3. "The 287(g) Program," August 2019, 3.

4. Cindy Carcamo, "Immigrants Fear that Definition of 'Criminal' will Be Stretched Under Trump," *Los Angeles Times*, 26 November 2016.

5. Kate Linthicum, "A Mother Risked Her Life to Reunite with Her Kids in the US. Now She Faces Prison Time," *Los Angeles Times*, 15 September 2018.

6. *Arkansas Sentencing Standards Grid & Seriousness Reference Table*, 14 June 2017, http://www.arkansas.gov/asc/pdfs/Proposed-Seriousness-Reference-Table-and-Grid-MARK-UP-COPY.pdf.

7. Immigration and Nationality Act, 8 USC, Ch. 12, Section 1101 (43).

8. César Cuauhtémoc García Hernández, "Creating Crimmigration," *Bringham Young University Law Review* (2013): 1457–1515.

9. Anti-Drug Abuse Act of 1988, Pub. L. 100-690, §§ 7342, 7344, 102 Stat. 4469, 4470.

10. "Aggravated Felonies," December 2016, https://www.americanimmigrationcouncil.org/sites/default/files/research/aggravated_felonies.pdf, 1.

11. Marie Gottschalk, *Caught: The Prison State and the Lockdown of American Politics* (Princeton, NJ: Princeton University Press, 2016), 220–221; Juliet Stumpf, "The Crimmigration Crisis: Immigrants, Crime and Sovereign Power," *American University Law Review* 56, no. 2 (2006): 383; Hernández, "Creating Crimmigration," 1468–1469.

12. Susan Stellin, "How Many *Legal*; Immigrants Are We Deporting?," *Los Angeles Times*, 21 August 2016.

13. "Budget Trend Data 1975 through the President's 2003 Request to the Congress," US Department of Justice, https://www.justice.gov/archive/jmd/1975_2002/2002/html/page104-108.htm; Immigration and Naturalization Service; Executive Office of the President, "Stronger Border Security," 2019, https://www.whitehouse.gov/wp-content/uploads/2018/02/FY19-Budget-Fact-Sheet_Border-Security.pdf; Doris Meissner, Donald M. Kerwin, Muzaffar Chishti, and Claire Bergeron, "Immigration Enforcement in the United States: The Rise of a Formidable Machinery," Migration Policy Institute, 2013, https://www.migrationpolicy.org/pubs/pillars-reportinbrief.pdf, Figure 1, p. 4;

César Cuauhtémoc García Hernández, *Migrating to Prison: America's Obsession with Locking Up Immigrants* (New York: New Press, 2019), 67–69.

14. Meissner et al., "Immigration Enforcement in the United States," Figure 2, p. 12.
15. Jessica Boltner and Doris Meissner, "Crisis at the Border? Not by the Numbers," Migration Policy Institute, 2018, https://www.migrationpolicy.org/news/crisis-border-not-numbers, Figure 3; Miriam Valverde, "Has the Number of Border Patrol Quadrupled since 2005," *Politifact*, 1 February 2019.
16. US Department of Homeland Security, "Yearbook of Immigration Statistics: 2017," 2017, https://www.dhs.gov/immigration-statistics/yearbook/2017/, Table 39, "Aliens Removed or Returned: Fiscal Years 1892 to 2017."
17. Gottschalk, *Caught*, 223.
18. Chris Cillizza, "The Remarkable History of the Family Separation Crisis," *CNN*, 18 June 2018.
19. Department of Justice, "Alien Incarceration Report Fiscal Year 2018, Quarter 2," 16 April 2019, https://www.justice.gov/opa/page/file/1154711/download, 14. Michaelangelo Landgrave and Alex Nowrasteh, "Incarcerated Immigrants in 2016: Their Numbers, Demographics, and Countries of Origin," Cato Institute, 2018, https://object.cato.org/sites/cato.org/files/pubs/pdf/irpb7.pdf, 1.
20. Stephen A. Camarota, "Non-Citizens Committed a Disproportionate Share of Federal Crimes, 2011–16," Center for Immigration Studies, https://cis.org/Camarota/NonCitizens-Committed-Disproportionate-Share-Federal-Crimes-201116; Steven A. Camarota and Jessica Vaughan, "Immigration and Crime: Assessing a Conflicted Issue," 2009, http://cis.org/ImmigrantCrime.
21. Landgrave and Nowrasteh, "Incarcerated Immigrants in 2016," https://object.cato.org/sites/cato.org/files/pubs/pdf/irpb7.pdf, 2–4. The 2017 data are consistent with those of 2016. Michelangelo Landgrave and Alex Nowrasteh, "Criminal Immigrants in 2017: Their Numbers, Demographics and Countries of Origin," Cato Institute, 2019, https://object.cato.org/sites/cato.org/files/pubs/pdf/irpb-11.pdf, 2–3.
22. Anna Flag, "Is There a Connection between Undocumented Immigrants and Crime?," *New York Times*, 13 May 2019.
23. Wendy Sawyer and Peter Wagner, "Mass Incarceration: The Whole Pie 2019," Prison Policy Inititiave, https://www.prisonpolicy.org/reports/pie2019.html.
24. Federal Bureau of Prisons, "Population Statistics," 7 May 2019, https://www.bop.gov/about/statistics/population_statistics.jsp.
25. "Alien Incarceration Report Fiscal Year 2018, Quarter 2," https://www.justice.gov/opa/page/file/1154711/download, 3–5, 11–12.
26. General Accountability Office, "Criminal Alien Statistics: Information on Incarcerations, Arrests, Convictions, Costs, and Removals," 2018, https://www.gao.gov/assets/700/693162.pdf, 44.
27. Transactional Records Access Clearinghouse. "Immigration Criminal Prosecutions Jump in March 2018," 27 April 2018, https://trac.syr.edu/immigration/reports/510/.
28. Transactional Records Access Clearinghouse. "Immigration Prosecutions for January 2020," 19 February 2020, https://trac.syr.edu/tracreports/bulletins/immigration/monthlyjan20/fil/.
29. Transactional Records Access Clearinghouse, "Federal Prosecution Levels Remain at Historic Highs," 12 December 2018, https://trac.syr.edu/tracreports/crim/540/.

30. Transactional Records Action Clearinghouse, "Despite Rise in Felony Charges, Most Immigration Convictions Remain Misdemeanors," 26 June 2014, https://trac.syr.edu/immigration/reports/356/.

31. Linthicum, "A Mother Risked Her Life to Reunite with Her Kids."

32. Kristen McCabe, Randy Capps, Michael Fix, and Ying Huang, *A Profile of Immigrants in Arkansas: Changing Workforce and Family Demographics*, Vol. 1, Migration Policy Institute, January 2013, https://www.immigrationresearch.org/system/files/MPI_-_Changing_Workforce_and_Family_Demographics_0.pdf, 11, 27.

33. Transactional Records Access Clearinghouse, "ICE Apprehensions Half Levels of Five Years Ago," 12 June 2018, https://trac.syr.edu/immigration/reports/517/.

34. Karla Mari McKanders, "Immigration Enforcement and the Fugitive Slave Acts: Exploring Their Similarities," *Catholic University Law Review* 61, no. 4 (2014).

35. American Civil Liberties Union, "ICE Detainers and the Fourth Amendment: What do Recent Federal Court Decisions Mean?," 13 November 2014, https://www.aclu.org/other/backgrounder-ice-detainers-and-fourth-amendment-what-do-recent-federal-court-decisions-mean.

36. Marc R. Rosenblum, "Understanding the Potential Impact of Executive Action on Immigration Enforcement," Migration Policy Institute, 2015, https://www.americanimmigrationcouncil.org/research/secure-communities-fact-sheet, 17–19.

37. Mayra Machado, interview with author, 23 August 2019.

38. Shannon Dooling, director, "What's Waiting for Deported Salvadorans Inside 'La Chacra,'" *WBUR*, aired 30 August 2018; Bridget Hickley and Eileen Grench, "Donald Trump: For People Deported to El Salvador in US Immigration Crackdown, Life Is About to Get Much Harder," *ABC News*, 9 January 2018.

39. Cindy Carcamo, "Immigrants Fear that Definition of 'Criminal Will Be Stretched under Trump," *Los Angeles Times*, 26 November 2016; Vikki Vargas, "'We Have No Time': Woman on Brink of Deportation," NBC News, Los Angeles, 30 November 2016; Teresa Wiltz, "What Crimes Make Immigrants Eligible for Deportation?" PBS NewsHour, 28 December 2016; Araceli Martínez Ortega, "Joven madre lucha contra reloj para no ser deportada a El Salvador," *La Opinion*, 1 December 2016; Ana Milena Varón, "Llevaba una vida ejemplar, pero ahora pudiera ser deportada por un error en su juventud," *Hoy Los Angeles*, 15 December 2016; "Salvadoreña sería deportada y seperada de sus tres hijos," *Elsalvador.com*, 2 December 2016.

40. Mayra Machado, "Declaration of Mayra Machado in Support of Application for Withholding of Removal and Convention Against Torture," 7 April 2019, in the author's possession.

41. Jill H. Wilson, "Recent Migration to the United States from Central America: Frequently Asked Questions," Congressional Research Service, 2019, https://crsreports.congress.gov, 2–5.

42. United States Border Patrol, "Southwest Border Sectors: Total Ilegal Alien Apprehensions by Fiscal Year, 1960–2018," 2019, https://www.cbp.gov/sites/default/files/assets/documents/2019-Mar/bp-southwest-border-sector-apps-fy1960-fy2018.pdf. For a history of Mexican-Guatemalan border control, see Ana Raquel Minian, "Offshoring Migration Control: Guatemalan Transmigrants and the Construction of Mexico as a Buffer Zone," *American Historical Review* 125, no. 1 (2020).

43. Donald Trump, "Remarks by President Trump on the National Security and Humanitarian Crisis on our Southern Border," 15 February 2019, https://www.whitehouse.gov/briefings-statements/remarks-president-trump-national-security-humanitarian-crisis-southern-border/; United States Border Patrol, "Southwest Border Sectors: Total Ilegal Alien Apprehensions by Fiscal Year, 1960–2018," https://www.cbp.gov/sites/default/files/assets/documents/2019-Mar/bp-southwest-border-sector-apps-fy1960-fy2018.pdf.
44. This account of Machado's time at La Hacienda is from Mayra Machado, "Declaration of Mayra Machado in Support of Application for Withholding of Removal and Convention Against Torture," 7 April 2019, in the author's possession. The names of people in El Salvador havebeen changed to preserve their anonymity and safety.
45. Mayra Machado, interview with author, 23 August 2019.
46. Linthicum, "A Mother Risked Her Life to Reunite with Her Kids."
47. Jo Tuckman, "Survivor Tells of Escape from Mexican Massacre in which 72 Were Left Dead," *Guardian*, 25 August 2010.
48. Linthicum, "A Mother Risked Her Life to Reunite with Her Kids."
49. Linthicum, "A Mother Risked Her Life to Reunite with Her Kids."
50. Transactional Records Access Clearinghouse, "Deportations under ICE's Secure Communities Program," 25 April 2018, https://trac.syr.edu/immigration/reports/509/.
51. Linthicum, "A Mother Risked Her Life to Reunite with Her Kids."
52. Lex Talamo, "'My Story as a Jena 6': Racism and Justice in a Small Louisiana Town," *Shreveport Times*, 5 July 2017.
53. Fox Butterfield, "Privately Run Juvenile Prison in Louisiana Is Attacked for Abuse of 6 Inmates," *New York Times*, 16 March 2000.
54. *Southern Poverty Law Center v. Department of Homeland Security* (District Court, District of Columbia, 4 April 2018).
55. Maria Clark, "In Tiny Jena, Immigration Debate Plays Out at Largest Detention Center in the Gulf South," *NOLA.com*, 24 October 2018.
56. Monsy Alvarado, "'These People Are Profitable': Under Trump, Private Prisons Are Cashing In on ICE Detainees," *USA Today*, 20 December 2019; Lauren-Brooke "L.B." Eisen, "Trump's First Year Has Been the Private Prison Industry's Best," Brennan Center for Justice, 15 January 2018, https://www.brennancenter.org/blog/trump%E2%80%99s-first-year-has-been-private-prison-industry-best.
57. Geo Group, "Annual Report," 2018, http://investors.geogroup.com/Cache/397601808.PDF?O=PDF&T=&Y=&D=&FID=397601808&iid=4144107, 3, 14, 122.
58. Yuki Noguchi, "Unequal Outcomes: Most ICE Detainees Held in Rural Areas Where Deportation Risks Soar," NPR: *Morning Edition*, 15 August 2019.
59. Transactional Records Access Clearinghouse, "Judge-by-Judge Asylum Decisions in Immigration Courts FY 2013–2018," 2018, https://trac.syr.edu/immigration/reports/judge2018/denialrates.html.
60. US Department of Homeland Security. Immigration and Customs Enforcement, "Over 72-hour ICE Detention Facilities," 2019, https://www.ice.gov/detention-management.
61. Noguchi, "Unequal Outcomes."
62. US Department of Justice, "Executive Office for Immigration Review Swears in 46 Immigration Judges," 28 September 2018, https://www.justice.gov/eoir/page/file/1097241/download.

63. Alex Nowrasteh, "Deportation Rates in Historical Perspective," Cato Institute, 2019, https://www.cato.org/blog/deportation-rates-historical-perspective. In his first three years in office (2017–19), Trump removed 749,462 people, far below Obama's deportation rate. US Department of Homeland Security, Immigration and Customs Enforcement, "U.S. Immigration and Customs Enforcement Fiscal Year 2019 Enforcement and Removal Operations Report," 2019, Figure 14, p. 19.

64. President Barack Obama, "Remarks by the President in Address to the Nation on Immigration," Office of the Press Secretary, White House, 20 November 2014, https://obamawhitehouse.archives.gov/the-press-office/2014/11/20/remarks-president-address-nation-immigration.

65. Elliott Young, "The Hard Truths about Obama's Deportation Priorities," *HuffPost*, 1 March 2017.

66. Ginger Thompson and Sarah Cohen, "More Deportations Follow Minor Crimes, Records Show," *New York Times*, 6 April 2014.

67. Transactional Records Access Clearinghouse, "Secure Communities and ICE Deportation: A Failed Program?," 8 April 2014, https://trac.syr.edu/immigration/reports/349/.

68. Young, "The Hard Truths about Obama's Deportation Priorities."

69. Nicholas Kulish, Caitlin Dickerson, and Ron Nixon, "Immigration Agents Discover New Freedom to Deport under Trump," *New York Times*, 25 February 2017.

70. Christie Thompson and Anna Flag, "Who Is ICE Deporting?," Marshall Project, 26 September 2016, https://www.themarshallproject.org/2016/09/26/who-is-ice-deporting.

71. US Department of Homeland Security, "DHS Immigration Enforcement: 2016," December 2016, https://www.dhs.gov/sites/default/files/publications/DHS%20Immigration%20Enforcement%202016.pdf.

72. John F. Pfaff, *Locked In: The True Cause of Mass Incarceration and How to Achieve Real Reform* (New York: Basic Books, 2017), 32–33.

73. Gottschalk, *Caught*, 195.

74. Pfaff argues that although some sentences have been lengthened and LWOP is significant in some states, the actual time served by the average inmate has not dramatically grown in the last three decades. Pfaff, *Locked In*, 56–59.

75. Team Fix, "The CNN-Telemundo Republican Debate Transcript, Annotated," *Washington Post*, 25 February 2016.

76. US Department of Homeland Security, Immigration and Customs Enforcement, "ICE Enforcement and Removal Operations Report: Fiscal Year 2015," 2015, Figure 1, p. 2; US Department of Homeland Security, Immigration and Customs Enforcement, "U.S. Immigration and Customs Enforcement Fiscal Year 2019 Enforcement and Removal Operations Report," 2019, Figure 13, p. 19.

77. Immigration and Customs Enforcement, "ICE Enforcement and Removal Operations Report: Fiscal Year 2015," Figure 1, p. 2; US Department of Homeland Security, Immigration and Customs Enforcement, "U.S. Immigration and Customs Enforcement Fiscal Year 2019 Enforcement and Removal Operations Report," 2019, Figure 16, p. 22.

78. Transactional Records Access Clearinghouse. "Historical Data: Immigration and Customs Enforcement Removals," 2016, https://trac.syr.edu/phptools/immigration/removehistory/.

79. Mayra Machado, interview with author, 23 August 2019; "Mayra Jacqueline Machado, Decision and Order of the Immigration Judge," 23 July 2019, in the author's possession.
80. Cassie Thogersen, Facebook page, accessed 15 August 2019.
81. Mayra Machado, interview with author, 23 August 2019.
82. Mayra Machado, personal communication with author, 15 January 2020.
83. Transactional Records Access Clearinghouse, "Asylum Decisions: 2019," 2019, https://trac.syr.edu/phptools/immigration/asylum/.

CONCLUSION

1. Leak Sakala, "Breaking Down Mass Incarceration in the 2010 Census: State-by-State Incarceration Rates by Race/Ethnicity," Prison Policy Initiative, 28 May 2019, https://www.prisonpolicy.org/reports/rates.html; Prison Policy Initiative, *American Indians Are Overrepresented in United States Prisons and Jails*, 2014, https://www.prisonpolicy.org/graphs/2010percent/US_American_Indian_2010.html; Lakota People's Law Project, "Native Lives Matter," 2015, https://s3-us-west-1.amazonaws.com/lakota-peoples-law/uploads/Native-Lives-Matter-PDF.pdf, p. 6.
2. Martin Garbus, "What I Saw at the Dilley, Texas, Immigrant Detention Center," *The Nation*, 26 March 2019.
3. Federal Bureau of Prisons, "FCI Oakdale II," 2019, https://www.bop.gov/locations/institutions/oad/index.jsp; Transactional Resource Action Clearinghouse, "Detainees Leaving ICE Detention from the Oakdale Federal Detention Center," 2008, https://trac.syr.edu/immigration/detention/200803/BOPOAD/exit/.
4. Angola Prison Museum, "History of Angola," https://www.angolamuseum.org/history-of-angola.
5. I want to thank Christen Smith for making me aware of the connection between Hutto and the prison-plantation system. Arkansas Department of Corrections, *2006 Facts Brochure*, 2006, https://web.archive.org/web/20090806120702/http://www.adc.arkansas.gov/pdf/facts_brochure2006.pdf, 25; "Shockingly Candid Photos of Life on an Arkansas Prison Farm," *Mother Jones*, 9 August 2017.
6. Doris J. James and Lauren E. Glaze, *Mental Health Problems of Prison and Jail Inmates*, Bureau of Justice Statistics, September 2006, 1.
7. M. von Werthern et al., "The Impact of Immigration Detention on Mental Health: A Systematic Review," *BMC Psychiatry* 18, no. 1 (2018): 14–15.
8. Human Rights Watch and ACLU, *Deportation by Default: Mental Disability, Unfair Hearings, and Indefinite Detention in the U.S. Immigration System*, July 2010, 3; Renuka Rayasam, "Migrant Mental Health Crisis Spirals in ICE Detention Facilities," *Politico*, 21 July 2019.
9. Rayasam, "Migrant Mental Health Crisis Spirals in ICE Detention Facilities."
10. Carol Rosenberg, "Wondering and Waiting at Guantánamo Bay," *Miami Herald*, 16 December 2016.
11. Carol Rosenberg, "After Years of Letting Captives Own Their Artwork, Pentagon Calls it U.S. Property. And May Burn It," *Miami Herald*, 16 December 2017.
12. Khalid Ahmed Qassim v. Donald Trump et al. (United States District Court, District of Columbia 2017); Khalid Qasim, "I Am in Guantánamo Bay. The US Government Is Starving Me to Death," *Guardian*, 13 October 2017.

13. S E C R E T / / NOFORN / / 20330407, "JTF-GTMO Detainee Assessment for Khalid Ahmed Qasim," 7 April 2008, http://media.miamiherald.com/static/images/escenic-images/gitmopdfs/us9ym-000242dp.pdf, 3–11.

14. Rasul v. Bush, 542 US 466 (2004).

15. John L. Helgerson, Director of Congressional Affairs, to Vice Chairman William S. Cohen, Senate Select Committee on Intelligence, re: SSCI Questions on XXXXXX, at 7–8 (DTS #1989-0131), as quoted in US Congress, Committee Study of the Central Intelligence Agency's Detention and Interrogation Program, 113th Cong., 2nd sess., 2014.

16. Dianne Feinstein, "Foreword," in US Senate, Select Committee on Intelligence, "Intelligence Committee Study of the Central Intelligence Agency's Detention and Interrogation Program," 2014, https://fas.org/irp/congress/2014_rpt/ssci-rdi.pdf, 4.

17. Carol Rosenberg, "Guantánamo by the Numbers," *Miami Herald*, 25 October 2018; Andrei Schneikman, Alan McLean, Jeremy Ashkenas, Archie Tse, and Jacob Harris, "Guantanamo Docket," in *New York Times* (2018).

18. Helgerson, "Committee Study of the Central Intelligence Agency's Detention and Interrogation Program," 141–143.

19. Adam Goldman and Matt Apuzzo, "Penny Lane: Gitmo's Other Secret CIA facility," Associated Press, 26 November 2013.

20. Andrea Harrison, "Periodic Review Boards for Law-of-War Detention in Guantanamo: What's Next?," *Journal of International and Comparative Law* 24, no. 3 (2018): 568–572.

21. Amos Barshad, "Guantanamo, Forever," *Marshal Project and Longreads*, 28 February 2018.

22. Boumediene v. Bush, 553 US 723 (2008).

23. Khalid Ahmed Qassim v. Donald J. Trump (US Court of Appeals, District of Columbia 14 August 2018).

24. Hamdi v. Rumsfeld, 542 US 507 (2004).

25. Eric M. Freedman, "Brief of Proposed Amici Curiae Due Process Scholars in Support of Petitioners," 2018, https://assets.documentcloud.org/documents/4432504/Due-Process-Scholars-Amicus.pdf, 11.

26. Willem Von Spronsen, "Final Statement," 13 July 2019, in Crimethinc, "On Willem Van Spronsen & His Final Statement," *It's Going Down*, 14 July 2019, https://itsgoingdown.org/on-william-van-spronsen/.

27. Department of Homeland Security, US Immigration and Customs Enforcement, "US Immigration and Customs Enforcement Fiscal Year 2019 Enforcement and Removal Operation Report," 2019, https://www.ice.gov/sites/default/files/documents/Document/2019/eroReportFY2019.pdf, 9.

28. US Department of Justice, "The Department of Justice Creates Section Dedicated to Denaturalization Cases," 26 February 2020, https://www.justice.gov/opa/pr/department-justice-creates-section-dedicated-denaturalization-cases.

29. Jack Crowe, "Trump Claims He Is 'Seriously' Considering Ending Birthright Citizenship for Children of Illegal Immigrants," *National Review*, 21 August 2019.

BIBLIOGRAPHY

ARCHIVES
AHC Atlanta History Center. Atlanta, Georgia.
Canada Archives. Ottawa, Canada.
NARA National Archives and Records Administration. College Park, MD and Seattle.
Sally Sandige Papers, Atlanta Legal Aid Society. Atlanta, Georgia.
Washington State Archives, Puget Sound Regional Archives. Bellevue, Washington.
Wayne Collins Papers. Bancroft Library, University of California, Berkeley.
YIVO, Yidisher Visnshaftlekher Institut (Institute for Jewish Research).
    New York City.

BIBLIOGRAPHY
Alexander, Michelle. *The New Jim Crow*. New York: New Press, 2012.
Alvarado, Monsy. "'These People are Profitable': Under Trump, Private Prisons Are
    Cashing In on ICE Detainees." *USA Today*, 20 December 2019.
American Civil Liberties Union. "ICE Detainers and the Fourth Amendment: What
    Do Recent Federal Court Decisions Mean?" 13 November 2014. https://www.
    aclu.org/other/backgrounder-ice-detainers-and-fourth-amendment-what-do-
    recent-federal-court-decisions-mean.
American Immigration Council. *Aggravated Felonies*. December 2016. https://www.
    americanimmigrationcouncil.org/sites/default/files/research/aggravated_
    felonies.pdf.
American Immigration Council. "The 287(g) Program: An Overview." August
    23, 2019. https://www.americanimmigrationcouncil.org/research/
    287g-program-immigration.
Angola Prison Museum. "History of Angola." 2019. https://www.angolamuseum.org/
    history-of-angola.
Anti-Drug Abuse Act of 1988, Pub. L. 100-690, §§ 7342, 7344, 102 Stat. 4469, 4470.
Arkansas Sentencing Standards Grid & Seriousness Reference Table. 14 June. 2017.
    http://www.arkansas.gov/asc/pdfs/Proposed-Seriousness-Reference-Table-
    and-Grid-MARK-UP-COPY.pdf.
"Arrest Warrant in the Circuit Court, Washington County, Arkansas, Mayra Jackeline
    Machado," 14 January 2005, CR 2004-1402-1, 2004-2414-2, 20004, 1707-4;
    "Arkansas Parole Board Report No. PCAR 552E, Re Mayra Jackline Machado,"
    7 Nov. 2018.
Associated Press. "Freedom Still Eludes Some Cubans." *Spokane Chronicle*,
    4 August 1980.

Associated Press. "Many Offered but Few Got Call to Help in Prison Crisis with PM-Cubans-Atlanta, Bjt." 4 December 1987.

Associated Press. "More Cubans Join Penitentiary Hunger Strike." *Spokesman Review*, 29 March 1980.

Associated Press. "Sole Woman at Washington Facility for Sex Offenders Released." *Seattle Times*, 12 June 2019.

Barshad, Amos. "Guantanamo, Forever." *Marshal Project and Longreads*, 28 February 2018.

Bellisle, Martha. "Man Held at Facility for Sexually Violent Dies." *Seattle Times*, 4 January 2019.

Benenson, Laurence. *The Math of Immigration Detention, 2018 Update: Costs Continue to Multiply*. 9 May 2018. https://immigrationforum.org/article/math-immigration-detention-2018-update-costs-continue-mulitply/.

Berger, Dan. "Carceral Migrations: Black Power and Slavery in 1970s California Prison Radicalism." In *The Rising Tide of Color: Race, State Violence, and Radical Movements across the Pacific*, edited by Moon-Ho Jung. Seattle: University of Washington Press, 2014.

Bolter, Jessica, and Doris Meissner. *Crisis at the Border? Not by the Numbers*. Migration Policy Institute. 2018. https://www.migrationpolicy.org/news/crisis-border-not-numbers.

Boumediene v. Bush, 553 723 (2008).

Bravo, Estela. *Cuban Excludables*. Bravo Films, 1997.

Briggs, Laura. *Taking Children: A History of American Terror*. Berkeley: University of California Press, 2020.

Brownell, Herbert. "Address by Honorable Herbert Brownell Jr., Attorney General of the United States at Ebbets Field & Polo Grounds. Jr." 11 November 1954, https://www.justice.gov/sites/default/files/ag/legacy/2011/09/12/11-11-1954.pdf.

Buck, Pearl. "Plight of Immigrants." *New York Times*, 16 November 1954.

"Budget Trend Data 1975 through the President's 2003 Request to the Congress," US Department of Justice, https://www.justice.gov/archive/jmd/1975_2002/2002/html/page104-108.htm;

Buff, Rachel. *Against the Deportation Terror: Organizing for Immigrant Rights in the Twentieth Century*. Philadelphia: Temple University Press, 2018.

Bureau of Immigration. *Annual Report of the Commissioner General of Immigration to the Secretary of Labor*. Washington, DC: US Government Printing Office, 1898–1930.

Burkly, Anne Kane, and Steve W. Dunkelberger. *McNeil Island: Images of America*. Charleston: Arcadia, 2019.

Butterfield, Fox. "Privately Run Juvenile Prison in Louisiana Is Attacked for Abuse of 6 Inmates." *New York Times*, 16 March 2000.

Cahalan, Margaret Werner. *Historical Corrections Statistics in the United States, 1850–1984*. Rockville, MD: United States Department of Justice, 1986.

Camarota, Steven A. "Non-Citizens Committed a Disproportionate Share of Federal Crimes, 2011–16." Center for Immigration Studies. 2018. https://cis.org/Camarota/NonCitizens-Committed-Disproportionate-Share-Federal-Crimes-201116.

Camarota, Steven A., and Jessica Vaughan. *Immigration and Crime: Assessing a Conflicted Issue*. Center for Immigration Studies. 2009. http://cis.org/ImmigrantCrime.

Campaign for Justice. "Litigation." 2019. https://jlacampaignforjustice.org/litigation/.

Cannato, Vincent J. *American Passage: The History of Ellis Island*. New York: Harper, 2009.

Capps, Randy, Kristen McCabe, Michael Fix, and Ying Huang. *A Profile of Immigrants in Arkansas: Changing Workforce and Family Demographics*, Vol. 1. Migration Policy Institute. January 2013. https://www.immigrationresearch.org/system/files/MPI_-_Changing_Workforce_and_Family_Demographics_0.pdf.

Carcamo, Cindy. "Immigrants Fear that Definition of 'Criminal' Will Be Stretched under Trump." *Los Angeles Times*, 26 November 2016.

Chinen, Karleen C. "Former Japanese Peruvian Internees Reunite in Honolulu." *Hawai'i Herald*, 3 October 2014.

Christgau, John. *Enemies: World War II Alien Internment*. San Jose: Authors Choice Press, 1985.

Cillizza, Chris. "The Remarkable History of the Family Separation Crisis." *CNN*, 18 June 2018.

C. J. "Experiences of Adults with 'Selective Mutism,' in Their Own Words." *Psychologist* 28, no. 9 (2015): 710–711.

Clark, Maria. "In Tiny Jena, Immigration Debate Plays Out at Largest Detention Center in the Gulf South." *NOLA.com*, 24 October 2018.

C.L.S. "Los Impacientes." *La Vida Nueva*, May 28, 1980.

Cohen, Deborah. *Braceros: Migrant Citizens and Transnational Subjects*. Chapel Hill: University of North Carolina Press, 2011.

Commission on Wartime Relocation and Internment of Civilians. *Personal Justice Denied*. Washington, DC: US Government Printing Office, 1982.

Commission on Wartime Relocation and Internment of Civilians. *Personal Justice Denied: Part 2 Recommendations*. Washington, DC: US Government Printing Office, 1983.

Conboy, Kevin. "Remembrances: Marvin H. Shoob." *Georgia Law Review* 52 (2017): i–vii.

Congressional Research Service. "Mexico: Evolution of the Mérida Initiative, 2007–2020." 28 June 2019. https://fas.org/sgp/crs/row/IF10578.pdf.

Connell, Thomas. *America's Japanese Hostages*. Westport, CT: Praeger, 2002.

Copeland, Larry, and Adam Gelb. "Leader in '84 Atlanta Disturbance Identified.'" *Miami News*, 1 December1987.

Craig, John. "Cuban Refugees' Crimes Mostly Petty, Judge Says." *Spokane Chronicle*, 7 January 1981.

Crewdson, John M. "Refugees Straining Center in Key West." *New York Times*, 6 May 1980.

Crimethinc. "On Willem Van Spronsen & His Final Statement." *It's Going Down*, 14 July 2019. https://itsgoingdown.org/on-william-van-spronsen/.

Crowe, Jack. "Trump Claims He Is 'Seriously' Considering Ending Birthright Citizenship for Children of Illegal Immigrants." *National Review*, 21 August 2019.

"Cuban Suspects Arrive." *Semi-Weekly Spokesman Review*, 22 June 1980.

Delgado, Grace. "Border Control and Sexual Policing: White Slavery and Prostitution along the U.S.-Mexico Borderlands, 1903–1910." *Western Historical Quarterly* 43 (2012): 157–178.

Denvir, Daniel. *All-American Nativism: How the Bipartisan War on Immigrants Explains Politics as We Know It*. New York: Verso, 2020.

Dickerson, Caitlin. "ICE Faces Migrant Detention Crunch as Border Chaos Spills into Interior of the Country." *New York Times*, 22 April 2019.

Donald, Heidi Gurcke. *We Were Not the Enemy: Remembering the United States Latin American Civilian Internment Program of World War II*. New York: iUniverse, 2006.

Dooling, Shannon, director. "What's Waiting for Deported Salvadorans inside 'La Chacra.'" WBUR, 2018.

Dow, Mark. *American Gulag inside U.S. Immigration Prisons*. Berkeley: University of California Press, 2004.

Dudziak, Mary L. *Cold War Civil Rights: Race and the Image of American Democracy*. Princeton, NJ: Princeton University Press, 2002.

DuMontier, Benjamin Jih. "Between Menace and Model Citizen: Lima's Japanese-Peruvians, 1936–1963." PhD dissertation, University of Arizona, 2018.

"18 Cubans from McNeil to Resettle." *Spokane Daily Chronicle*, 17 October 1980.

Eisen, Lauren-Brooke. "Trump's First Year Has Been the Private Prison Industry's Best." *Brennan Center for Justice*. 15 January 2018. https://www.brennancenter.org/blog/trump%E2%80%99s-first-year-has-been-private-prison-industry-best.

Elsa Kudo, interviewed by Kelli Nakamura, 6 February 2012, Densho Visual History Collection, denshovh-kelsa-01.

Estlack, Russell W. *Shattered Lives, Shattered Dreams: The Disrupted Lives of Families in America's Internment Camps*. Springville, UT: Bonneville Books, 2011.

Executive Office of the President. "Stronger Border Security." 2019. https://www.whitehouse.gov/wp-content/uploads/2018/02/FY19-Budget-Fact-Sheet_Border-Security.pdf.

Fairchild, Amy L. *Science at the Borders: Immigrant Medical Inspection and the Shaping of the Modern Industrial Labor Force*. Baltimore: Johns Hopkins University Press, 2003.

"FBI Investigates Death of Cuban Removed from Cell at Atlanta Pen." *Atlanta Journal Constitution*, 20 February 1987.

Federal Bureau of Prisons. "FCI Oakdale II." 2019. https://www.bop.gov/locations/institutions/oad/index.jsp.

Federal Bureau of Prisons. "Population Statistics." 2019. https://www.bop.gov/about/statistics/population_statistics.jsp.

Feinstein, Dianne. "Foreword." In US Senate, Select Committee on Intelligence, "Intelligence Committee Study of the Central Intelligence Agency's Detention and Interrogation Program." 2014. https://fas.org/irp/congress/2014_rpt/ssci-rdi.pdf.

Fernandez v. Wilkinson, 505 F. Supp 787 (1980).

Fernandez-Roque v. Smith, 567 F. Supp. 1115 (1983).

Fernandez-Roque v. Smith, 734 F.2d 576 584 (1984).

"50 Cuban Prisoners Force Fed in Atlanta," *New York Times*, 2 September 1985.

Flag, Anna. "Is There a Connection between Undocumented Immigrants and Crime?" *New York Times*, 13 May 2019.

Flin, Briana. "Growing Up Undocumented When Your Siblings Are Citizens." *The Atlantic*, 22 August 2018.

Flores, Antonio, Luis Noe Bustamante, and Mark Hugo Lopez. "Migrant Apprehensions and Deportations Increase in Mexico, but Remain below Recent Highs." *Pew Research Center: FacTank*, 12 June 2019.

Formwalt, Lee W. "The Camilla Massacre of 1868: Racial Violence as Political Propaganda." *Georgia Historical Quarterly* 71, no. 3 (1987): 399–426.

Freedman, Eric M. *Brief of Proposed Amici Curiae Due Process Scholars in Support of Petitioners*. 2018. https://assets.documentcloud.org/documents/4432504/Due-Process-Scholars-Amicus.pdf.

Friedman, Max Paul. *Nazis and Good Neighbors: The United States Campaign against the Germans of Latin America in World War II*. Cambridge: Cambridge University Press, 2003.

Gámez-Torres, Nora. "More than 1,300 Cuban Migrants Are Being Held in Detention Centers across the US." *Miami Herald*, 28 July 2017.

Garbus, Martin. "What I Saw at the Dilley, Texas, Immigrant Detention Center." *The Nation*, 26 March 2019.

Gardiner, C. Harvey. *Pawns in a Triangle of Hate: The Peruvian Japanese and the United States*. Seattle: University of Washington Press, 1981.

General Accountability Office. "Criminal Alien Statistics: Information on Incarcerations, Arrests, Convictions, Costs, and Removals." 2018. https://www.gao.gov/assets/700/693162.pdf.

Geo Group. *Annual Report*. 2018. https://issuu.com/epatton/docs/2018_annual_report__the_geo_group_large.

Gerdes, Raymond Lafontant. *Fuerte Allen: La diáspora haitiana*. Rio Piedras, Puerto Rico: Plaza Mayor, 1996.

Gibson, Campbell J. and Emily Lennon. *Historical Census Statistics on the Foreign-Born Population of the United States: 1850–1990*. US Census Bureau, 1999. https://www.census.gov/population/www/documentation/twps0029/twps0029.html.

Global Detention Project. *Global Detention Project: Annual Report 2017*. June. https://www.globaldetentionproject.org/global-detention-project-annual-report-2017.

Goldman, Adam, and Matt Apuzzo. "Penny Lane: Gitmo's Other Secret CIA facility." Associated Press, 26 November 2013.

Goodhue, David. "A Judge Has Canceled an Immigrant's Drug Conviction. It Saved Him from Deportation." *Miami Herald*, 31 August 2017.

Goodman, Adam. *The Deportation Machine: America's Long History of Expelling Immigrants*. Princeton, NJ: Princeton University Press, 2020.

Gottschalk, Marie. *Caught: The Prison State and the Lockdown of American Politics*. Princeton, NJ: Princeton University Press, 2016.

Grob, Gerald N. *Mental Illness and American Society, 1875–1940*. Princeton, NJ: Princeton University Press, 1983.

Grob, Gerald N. *Mental Institutions in America: Social Policy to 1875*. New York: Free Press, 1973.

"Guards Quell Cuban Inmates." *New York Times*, 2 November 1984.

Hamdi v. Rumsfeld, 542 507 (2004).

Hamm, Mark S. *The Abandoned Ones: The Imprisonment and Uprising of the Mariel Boat People*. Boston: Northeastern University Press, 1995.

Hamm, Mark S. "Santeria in Federal Prisons: Understanding a Little-Known Religion." *Federal Prisons Journal* 4 (1992): 37–42.

Handlin, Oscar. *The Uprooted*. Boston: Little, Brown, 1973 [1951].

Harcourt, Bernard E. "An Institutionalization Effect: The Impact of Mental Hospitalization and Imprisonment on Homicide in the United States, 1934–2001." *Journal of Legal Studies* 40, no. 1 (2011): 39–83.

Harrison, Andrea. "Periodic Review Boards for Law-of-War Detention in Guantanamo: What's Next?" *Journal of International and Comparative Law* 24, no. 3 (2018): 541–578.

Haitian Refugee Center v. Civiletti, 503 F. Supp. 442 (1980).

Helgerson, John L., Director of Congressional Affairs, to Vice Chairman William S. Cohen, Senate Select Committee on Intelligence, re: SSCI Questions on XXXXXX, at 7–8 (DTS #1989-0131), as quoted in US Congress, Committee Study of the Central Intelligence Agency's Detention and Interrogation Program, 113th Cong., 2nd sess., 2014.

Hernández, César Cuauhtémoc García. "Creating Crimmigration." *Brigham Young University Law Review* (2013): 1457–1516.

Hernández, César Cuauhtémoc García. *Migrating to Prison: America's Obsession with Locking Up Immigrants*. New York: New Press, 2019.

Hernández, Kelly Lytle. *City of Inmates: Conquest, Rebellion and Rise of Human Caging in Los Angeles, 1771–1965*. Chapel Hill: University of North Carolina Press, 2017.

Hernández, Kelly Lytle. "The Crimes and Consequences of Illegal Immigration: A Cross-Border Examination of Operation Wetback, 1943 to 1954." *Western Historical Quarterly* 37, no. 4 (2006): 421–444.

Herrera, Jack. "Mexico's Mass Arrests of Central American Migrants Follow Years of US Pressure." *Pacific Standard*, 24 April 2019.

Hester, Torie. "Deportability and the Carceral State." *Journal of American History* 102, no. 1 (2015): 141–151.

Hickley, Bridget, and Eileen Grench. "Donald Trump: For People Deported to El Salvador in US Immigration Crackdown, Life Is About to Get Much Harder." *ABC News*, 9 January 2018.

Higashide, Seiichi. *Adiós to Tears: The Memories of a Japanese-Peruvian Internee in US Concentration Camps*. Seattle: University of Washington Press, 2000.

Higgins, Eoin. "'Terrible News': US Supreme Court Rules for Indefinite Detention of Immigrants." *Common Dreams*, 19 March 2019.

Hirota, Hidetaka. *Expelling the Poor: Atlantic Seaboard States and the Nineteenth-Century Origins of American Immigration Policy*. New York: Oxford University Press, 2017.

Human Rights Watch and ACLU. *Deportation by Default: Mental Disability, Unfair Hearings, and Indefinite Detention in the U.S. Immigration System*. July 2010.

Immigration and Nationality Act. 8 USC, Ch. 12, Section 1101 (43).

Immigration and Naturalization Service; Executive Office of the President, "Stronger Border Security," 2019, https://www.whitehouse.gov/wp-content/uploads/2018/02/FY19-Budget-Fact-Sheet_Border-Security.pdf.

Iritani, Evelyn. "His Family's Internment Earned Apologies from a Human Rights Commission. Will the U.S. Government Respond?" *Los Angeles Times*, 24 March 2017.

James, Doris J., and Lauren E. Glaze. *Mental Health Problems of Prison and Jail Inmates*. Washington, DC: US Department of Justice, Office of Justice Programs, Bureau of Justice Statistics, September 2006.

Jarvie, Jenny. "After Living in the U.S. for More Than Half a Century, This Cuban Activist May Be Deported." *Los Angeles Times*, 20 February 2020.

Jean v. Nelson, 727 F.2d 957 (1984).

Jean v. Nelson, 472 U.S. 846 (1985).

Kanstroom, Daniel. *Deportation Nation: Outsiders in American History*. Cambridge, MA: Harvard University Press, 2007.

Kennedy, John F. *A Nation of Immigrants*. New York: Harper Row, 1964.

Keve, Paul W. *The McNeil Century: The Life and Times of an Island Prison*. Chicago: Nelson-Hall, 1984.

Khalid Ahmed Qassim v Donald Trump et al., (2017).

Khalid Ahmed Qassim v. Donald J. Trump, (2018).

Khalid Ahmed Qassim v. Donald J. Trump (US Court of Appeals, District of Columbia 14 August 2018).

Klingsberg, Ethan A. "Penetrating the Entry Doctrine: Excludable Aliens' Constitutional Rights in Immigration Processes." *Yale Law Journal* 98, no. 3 (1989): 639–658.

Knauff v. Shaughnessy. 338 US 537 (1950).

Knight, H. L., H. A. Pratt, and C. F. Langworthy. "Dietary Studies in Public Institutions in Baltimore, MD." *Bulletin*, no. 223 (1910): 15–87.

Kulish, Nicholas, Caitlin Dickerson, and Ron Nixon. "Immigration Agents Discover New Freedom to Deport under Trump." *New York Times*, 25 February 2017.

Lakota People's Law Project. "Native Lives Matter." 2015. https://s3-us-west-1.amazonaws.com/lakota-peoples-law/uploads/Native-Lives-Matter-PDF.pdf.

Landgrave, Michelangelo, and Alex Nowrasteh. *Criminal Immigrants in 2017: Their Numbers, Demographics and Countries of Origin*. Cato Institute, March 4, 2019. https://object.cato.org/sites/cato.org/files/pubs/pdf/irpb-11.pdf.

Lapointe, Mary Jane. "Discrimination in Asylum Law: The Implications of Jean v. Nelson." *Indiana Law Journal* 62, no. 1 (1986): 127–149.

Lawson, Earl. *The Atlanta Penitentiary Burns: The Cuban Detainees Take Over the Pen with 121 Hostages*. Maitland, FL: Liberty Hill, 2018.

Lawson, George Dudley. "The Tacoma Method." *Overland Monthly and Out West Magazine*, 1886, 234–239.

Lee, Erika. *America for Americans: A History of Xenophobia in the United States*. New York: Basic Books, 2019.

Lee, Erika, and Judy Yung. *Angel Island: Immigrant Gateway to America*. New York: Oxford University Press, 2010.

Legomsky, Stephen H. "Immigration Law and the Principle of Plenary Congressional Power." *Supreme Court Review* 1984 (1984): 255–307.

Leng May Ma v. Barber, 357 U.S. 185 (1958).

Leshaw, Gary. "Atlanta's Cuban Detainees." *Atlanta Lawyer* (Fourth Quarter 1992): 6–15, 28.

Lesser, Jeffrey. *Negotiating National Identity: Immigrants, Minorities and the Struggle for Ethnicity in Brazil*. Durham, NC: Duke University Press, 1999.

Lewis, John, representative of Georgia, in Congressional Record, 27 April 1987. In United States Congress: House. *Mariel Cuban Detainees: Events Preceding and Following the November 1987 Riots: Hearing Before the Subcommittee on Courts, Civil Liberties, and the Administration of Justice*. February 4 1988, 100th Congress, 2nd Session, 1989.

Lindskoog, Carl. *Detain and Punish: Haitian Refugees and the Rise of the World's Largest Immigration Detention System*. Gainesville: University of Florida Press, 2018.

Linthicum, Kate. "A Mother Risked Her Life to Reunite with Her Kids in the US. Now She Faces Prison Time." *Los Angeles Times*, 15 September 2018.

Lipman, Jana. "A Refugee Camp in America: Fort Chaffee and Vietnamese and Cuban Refugees, 1975–1982." *Journal of American Ethnic History* 33, no. 2 (2014): 57–87.

Loyd, Jenna M., and Alison Mountz. *Boats, Borders and Bases: Race, the Cold War and the Rise of Migration Detention in the United States*. Berkeley: University of California Press, 2018.

Lutterman, Tedd, Robert Shaw, William Fisher, and Ronald Manderschied. *Trend in Psychiatric Inpatient Capacity, United States and Each State, 1970–2014*. Alexandria, VA: National Association of State Mental Health Programs, 2014.

Lynch v. Cannatella, 810 F 2d 1363 (1987).

Machado, Mayra Jackeline. Judgment and Disposition Order, Circuit Court, Washington County, Arkansas, 1 September 2004, CR 2004-1707-4.

Macías-Rojas, Patrisia. *From Deportation to Prison: The Politics of Immigration Enforcement in Post–Civil Rights America*. New York: New York University Press, 2016.

Maloney, Deirde M. *National Insecurities: Immigrants and US Deportation Policy since 1882*. Chapel Hill: University of North Carolina Press, 2012.

"Man Freed from Prison Faces Possible Deportation." *CBS Miami*, 18 May 2017.

Markel, Howard. "Mental Examination of Immigrants Administration and Line Inspection at Ellis Island." *Public Health Reports (1974–)* 121, no. Supplement 1: Historical Collection, 1878–2005 (2006): 92–103.

Masters, Jonathan. "Targeted Killings." Council on Foreign Relations. 2013. https://www.cfr.org/backgrounder/targeted-killings.

Masterson, Daniel. *The Japanese in Latin America*. Urbana: University of Illinois Press, 2004.

McClain, Charles J., and Laurene Wu McClain. "The Chinese Contribution to the Development of American Law." In *Entry Denied: Exclusion and the Chinese Community in America, 1882–1943*. Edited by Sucheng Chan, 3–24. Philadelphia: Temple University Press, 1991.

McCraken, Henry M., Ernest G. Sihler, and Willis Fletcher Johnson. *Universities and Their Sons: New York University*. Edited by Joshua Chamberlain. Vol. 2, Boston: J. Herndon, 1903.

McKanders, Karla Mari. "Immigration Enforcement and the Fugitive Slave Acts: Exploring Their Similarities." *Catholic University Law Review* 61, no. 4 (2014): 925–954.

Meissner, Doris, Donald M. Kerwin, Muzaffar Chishti, and Claire Bergeron. "Immigration Enforcement in the United States: The Rise of a Formidable Machinery." Migration Policy Institute. 2013. https://www.migrationpolicy.org/pubs/pillars-reportinbrief.pdf.

Meyers, Steven Lee. "31 Inmates in Prison Siege are Returned to Cuba." *New York Times*, 1 September 1991.

Misra, Tanvi. "For the Last Time, Here's the Real Link between Immigration and Crime." *City Lab*, 6 February 2019.

Miyake, Lisa C. "Forsaken and Forgotten: The US Internment of Japanese Peruvians during WWII." *Asian American Law Journal* 9, no. 5 (2002): 163–193.

Mochizuki v. United States. 41 Fed. Cl. 54 (1998).

Moehling, Carolyn, and Anne Morrison Piehl. "Immigration, Crime, and Incarceration in Early Twentieth-Century America." *Demography* 46 (2009): 739–763.

Nakagawa, Martha. "Obituary: Art Shibayama, Fighter for Japanese Latin American Redress." *Rafu Shimpo* (Los Angeles Japanese Daily News), August 8, 2018.

Narea, Nicole. "Justices Leave Room to Challenge Immigrant Detention Law." Law360. 2019. https://www.law360.com/articles/1140697/ justices-leave-room-to-challenge-immigrant-detention-law.

National Immigrant Justice Center. "ICE Detention Facilities as of November 2017." https://immigrantjustice.org/ice-detention-facilities-november-2017.

Ngai, Mae. *Impossible Subjects: Illegal Aliens and the Making of Modern America.* Princeton, NJ: Princeton University Press, 2004.

Nishimura Ekiu v. United States, 142 U.S. 651 (1892).

Noguchi, Yuki. "Unequal Outcomes: Most ICE Detainees Held in Rural Areas Where Deportation Risks Soar." NPR, *Morning Edition,* 15 August 2019.

Noll, Richard. *American Madness: The Rise and Fall of Dementia Praecox.* Cambridge, MA: Harvard University Press, 2011.

Nowrasteh, Alex. "Deportation Rates in Historical Perspective." Cato Institute, 2019. https://www.cato.org/blog/deportation-rates-historical-perspective.

Nowrasteh, Alex, and Michaelangelo Landgrave. "Incarcerated Immigrants in 2016: Their Numbers, Demographics, and Countries of Origin." Cato Institute, 2018. https://object.cato.org/sites/cato.org/files/pubs/pdf/irpb7.pdf.

Obama, Barack. "Remarks by the President in Address to the Nation on Immigration." Washington, DC: White House. Office of the Press Secretary, 2014.

O'Malley, Brendan P. "Welcome to New York: Remembering Castle Garden, a Nineteenth-Century Immigrant Welfare State." *Lapham's Quarterly* (12 September 2018).

Ortega. Areceli Martínez. "Joven madre lucha contra reloj oara no ser deportada a El Salvador." *La Opinion,* 1 December 2016.

Ousey, Graham C., and Charis E. Kubrin. "Immigration and Crime: Assessing a Contentious Issue." *Annual Review of Criminology* 1, no. 1 (2018): 63–84.

Paik, A. Naomi. *Rightlessness: Testimony and Redress in US Prison Camps since WWII.* Chapel Hill: University of North Carolina Press, 2016.

Pan American Union. *Emergency Advisory Committee for Political Defense, Second Annual Report.* Washington, DC: 1943.

Parker, Kunal M. *Making Foreigners: Immigration and Citizenship Law in America, 1600–2000.* New York: Cambridge University Press, 2015.

Passel, Jeffrey S. "Measuring Illegal Immigration: How Pew Research Center Counts Unauthorized Immigrants in the U.S." *Pew Research Center: Factank,* 12 July 2019.

Pastor, Humberto Rodríguez. *Herederos del dragón: historia de la comunidad china en el Perú.* Lima: Fondo Editorial del Congreso del Perú, 2000.

Pear, Robert. "Behind the Prison Riots: Precautions Not Taken." *New York Times,* 6 December 1987.

Pegler-Gordon, Anna. *In Sight of America: Photography and the Development of U.S. Immigration Policy.* Berkeley: University of California Press, 2009.

Penny, H. Glenn. "Latin American Connections: Recent Work on German Interactions with Latin America." *Central European History* 46, no. 2 (2013): 362–394.

Pentagon Calls It U.S. Property. And May Burn It." *Miami Herald,* 16 December 2017.

Perera, Judith Irangika Dingatantrige. "From Exclusion to State Violence: The Transformation of Noncitizen Detention in the United States and Its Implications in Arizona, 1891-present." PhD dissertation, Arizona State University, 2018.

Pfaelzer, Jean. *Driven Out: The Forgotten War against Chinese Americans.* Berkeley: University of California Press, 2007.

Pfaff, John F. *Locked In: The True Cause of Mass Incarceration and How to Achieve Real Reform*. New York: Basic Books, 2017.

Presidential Proclamation. *Proclamation 2662: Removal of Alien Enemies*.1945. https://www.trumanlibrary.org/proclamations/index.php?pid=247&st=immigration&st1=.

"Prison Officials Get 2nd Autopsy on Cuban Inmate." *Atlanta Journal Constitution*, 22 April 1987.

Prison Policy Initiative. *American Indians Are Overrepresented in United States Prisons and Jails*. 2014. https://www.prisonpolicy.org/graphs/2010percent/US_American_Indian_2010.html.

Qassim, Khalid. "I Am in Guantánamo Bay. The US Government Is Starving Me to Death." *The Guardian*, 13 October 2017.

Raquel Minian, Ana. "Offshoring Migration Control: Guatemalan Transmigrants and the Construction of Mexico as a Buffer Zone." *American Historical Review* 125, no. 1 (2020): 89–111.

Rasul v Bush, 466 (2004).

Rayasam, Renuka. "Migrant Mental Health Crisis Spirals in ICE Detention Facilities." *Politico*, 21 July 2019.

"Refugees Languish Amid Prison Violence," *Miami Herald*, 3 April 1986.

Reséndez, Andrés. *The Other Slavery: The Uncovered Story of Indian Enslavement in America*. Boston: Houghton Mifflin Harcourt, 2016.

Richardson, John T. E. *Howard Andrew Knox: Pioneer of Intelligence Testing at Ellis Island*. New York: Columbia University Press, 2011.

Robbins, William. "US Schedules Interviews on Fate of Cuban Inmates." *New York Times*, 8 February 1988.

Robertson, Craig. *The Passport in America: The History of a Document*. New York: Oxford University Press, 2010.

Robledo, José Luis Naupari. "La presecución a la colectividad japonesa en el Perú 1941–1945." Master's thesis, Ponticia Universidad Católica del Perú, 2011.

Robles, Frances. "'Marielitos' Face Long-Delayed Reckoning: Expulsion to Cuba." *New York Times*, 14 January 2017.

Rodriguez-Fernandez v. Wilkinson, 654 F 2d 1382 (1981).

Rosenberg, Carol. "After Years of Letting Captives Own Their Artwork, Pentagon Calls It U.S. Property. And May Burn It," *Miami Herald*, 16 December 2017.

Rosenberg, Carol. "Guantánamo by the Numbers." *Miami Herald*, 25 October 2018.

Rosenberg, Carol. "Wondering and Waiting at Guantánamo Bay." *Miami Herald*, 16 December 2016.

Rosenblum, Marc R. "Understanding the Potential Impact of Executive Action on Immigration Enforcement." American Immigration Council. 2015. https://www.americanimmigrationcouncil.org/research/secure-communities-fact-sheet.

Roth, Daniel Shoer. *Pastor, profeta, patriarca*. Miami: Ermita de la Caridad, 2015.

Ryo, Emily, and Ian Peacock. *Landscape of Immigrant Detention in the United States*. Washington, DC: American Immigration Council, 2018.

Sakala, Leak. "Breaking Down Mass Incarceration in the 2010 Census: State-by-State Incarceration Rates by Race/Ethnicity." Prison Policy Initiative, 28 May 2019. https://www.prisonpolicy.org/reports/rates.html.

"Salvadoreña sería deportada y seperada de sus tres hijos." *Elsalvador.com*, 2 December 2016.

Salyer, Lucy E. "'Laws as Harsh as Tigers': Enforcement of the Chinese Exclusion Laws, 1891–1924." In *Entry Denied: Exclusion and the Chinese Community in America, 1882-1943*. Edited by Sucheng Chan, 57–93. Philadelphia: Temple University Press, 1991.

Sarasa, Enrique González. *Excluibles*. Havana: Ediciones Abril, 1994.

Sawyer, Wendy, and Peter Wagner. "Mass Incarceration: The Whole Pie 2019." Prison Policy Initiative. 2019. https://www.prisonpolicy.org/reports/pie2019.html.

Schmidt, William E. "Atlanta Prison Lockup of Cubans Continues." *New York Times*, 25 October 1984.

Schneikman, Andrei, Alan McLean, Jeremy Ashkenas, Archie Tse, and Jacob Harris. "Guantanamo Docket." *New York Times*, 2 May 2018.

Schwartz, Jerry. "A Deal to Release Prison Hostages in Atlanta Collapses at Deadline." *New York Times*, 27 November 1987.

Scott, James Brown. "Nationality: Jus Soli or Jus Sanguinis." *American Journal of International Law* 24, no. 1 (1930): 58–64.

Scott, James C. *Weapons of the Weak: Everyday Forms of Peasant Resistance*. New Haven, CT: Yale University Press, 1985.

Seabrook at War: A Radio Documentary. Narrated by Kurt Vonnegut Jr. Written and Produced by Marty Goldensohn and David Steven Cohen. A co-production of WWFM/WWNJ, Trenton and the New Jersey Historical Commission, Department of State, 1995. Clip of interview available at the *Journal for Multimedia History*, Vol. 2, 1999, https://www.albany.edu/jmmh/vol2no1/seabrook.html.

S E C R E T / / NOFORN / / 20330407. *JTF-GTMO Detainee Assessment for Khalid Ahmed Qasim*. 7 April 2008. http://media.miamiherald.com/static/images/escenic-images/gitmopdfs/us9ym-000242dp.pdf.

Sekula, Allan. "The Body and the Archive." *October* 39 (1986): 3–64.

Seoane, Manuel. "The Japanese Are Still in Peru." *Asia and the Americas* 43 (1943).

Shaughnessy v. Mezei, 345 U.S. 206 (1953).

Shin, Ji-Hye. "Insanity on the Move: The 'Alien Insane' in Modern America, 1882–1930." PhD dissertation, Rutgers University, 2013.

"Shockingly Candid Photos of Life on an Arkansas Prison Farm." *Mother Jones*, 9 August 2017.

Shull, Kristina Karin. " 'Nobody Wants These People': Reagan's Immigration Crisis and America's First Private Prisons." PhD dissertation, University of California, 2014.

Smith, Renaldo A. "The Cuban Detainee Uprising and Riot at the Atlanta Penitentiary November 23, 1987." Master's, thesis, Atlanta University, 1988.

Smothers, Ronald. "At End of a Long Road, Cuban Inmates Revolt." *New York Times*, 23 August 1991.

Smothers, Ronald. "Court Orders Five Deported to Cuba." *New York Times*, 1 December 1988.

Smothers, Ronald. "No Progress Seen in Siege at Prison." *New York Times*, 25 August 1991.

Smothers, Ronald. "Release of Cubans Stepped Up In 5 Months Since US Riots." *New York Times*, 30 April 1988.

Smothers, Ronald. "US Plans First Deportations after Reviews of Cuban Cases." *New York Times*, 18 November 1988.

Southern Poverty Law Center v. Department of Homeland Security. US District Court, District of Columbia. 4 April 2018.

Spaeth, Carl B., and William Sanders. "The Emergency Advisory Committee for Political Defense." *American Journal of International Law* 38, no. 2 (1944): 218–241.

Squires, Sally. "Held Hostage." *Washington Post*, 12 January 1988.

Stellin, Susan. "How Many *Legal*; Immigrants Are We Deporting?" *Los Angeles Times*, 21 August 2016.

Stephens, Alexander. "'I Hope They Don't Come to Plains': Race and the Detention of Mariel Cubans 1980–1981." Master's thesis, University of Georgia, 2016.

Stevens, William K. "Arkansas Fort Receives First of Thousands of Cubans." *New York Times*, 10 May 1980.

Stumpf, Juliet. "The Crimmigration Crisis: Immigrants, Crime and Sovereign Power." *American University Law Review* 56, no. 2 (2006): 367–419.

Takenaka, Ayumi. "The Japanese in Peru: History of Immigration, Settlement, and Racialization." *Latin American Perspectives* 31, no. 3 (2004): 77–98.

Talamo, Lex. "'My Story as a Jena 6': Racism and Justice in a Small Louisiana Town." *Shreveport Times*, 5 July 2017.

Taparata, Evan. "'Refugees as You Call Them': The Politics of Refugee Recognition in the Nineteenth Century United States." *Journal of American Ethnic History* 38, no. 2 (Winter 2019): 9–35.

Team Fix. "The CNN-Telemundo Republican Debate Transcript, Annotated." *Washington Post*, 25 February 2016.

Thomas, Jo. "Refugees at Ft. Chaffee Wait in Boredom and Uncertainty," *New York Times*, 6 June 1980.

Thompson, Christie, and Anna Flag. "Who Is ICE Deporting?" Marshal Project. 26 September 2016. https://www.themarshallproject.org/2016/09/26/who-is-ice-deporting.

Thompson, Ginger, and Sarah Cohen. "More Deportations Follow Minor Crimes, Records Show." *New York Times*, 6 April 2014.

Thompson, Heather Ann. *Blood in the Water: The Attica Prison Uprising of 1971 and Its Legacy*. New York: Pantheon Books, 2016.

Thompson, Tracy. "Cubans, Guards Trapped in Cycle of Violence at Atlanta Pen." *Atlanta Journal Constitution*, 19 April 1987.

Tigner, James Lawrence. "Shindō Remmei: Japanese Nationalism in Brazil." *Hispanic American Historical Review* 41, no. 4 (1961): 515–532.

Torpey, John. *The Invention of the Passport: Surveillance, Citizenship and the State*. Cambridge: Cambridge University Press, 2000.

Transactional Records Access Clearinghouse. "Asylum Decisions: 2019." 2019. https://trac.syr.edu/phptools/immigration/asylum/.

Transactional Records Access Clearinghouse. "Deportations under ICE's Secure Communities Program." 25 April 2018. https://trac.syr.edu/immigration/reports/509/.

Transactional Records Access Clearinghouse. "Despite Rise in Felony Charges, Most Immigration Convictions Remain Misdemeanors." 26 June 2014. https://trac.syr.edu/immigration/reports/356/.

Transactional Records Access Clearinghouse. "Detainees Leaving ICE Detention from the Oakdale Federal Detention Center." 2008. https://trac.syr.edu/immigration/detention/200803/BOPOAD/exit/.

Transactional Records Access Clearinghouse. "Federal Prosecution Levels Remain at Historic Highs." 12 December 2018. https://trac.syr.edu/tracreports/crim/540/.

Transactional Records Access Clearinghouse. "Historical Data: Immigration and Customs Enforcement Removals." 2016. https://trac.syr.edu/phptools/immigration/removehistory/.

Transactional Records Access Clearinghouse. "ICE Apprehensions Half Levels of Five Years Ago." 12 June 2018. https://trac.syr.edu/immigration/reports/517/.

Transactional Records Access Clearinghouse. "Immigration Criminal Prosecutions Jump in March 2018." 27 April 2018. https://trac.syr.edu/immigration/reports/510/.

Transactional Records Access Clearinghouse. "Immigration Prosecutions for February 2019." 27 March 2019. https://trac.syr.edu/tracreports/bulletins/immigration/monthlyfeb19/fil/.

Transactional Records Access Clearinghouse. "Immigration Prosecutions for January 2020." 19 February 2020. https://trac.syr.edu/tracreports/bulletins/immigration/monthlyjan20/fil/.

Transactional Records Access Clearinghouse. "Judge-by-Judge Asylum Decisions in Immigration Courts FY 2013-2018." 2018. https://trac.syr.edu/immigration/reports/judge2018/denialrates.html.

Transactional Records Access Clearinghouse. "Legal Noncitizens Receive Longest ICE Detention." 3 June 2013. https://trac.syr.edu/immigration/reports/321/.

Transactional Records Access Clearinghouse. "New Data on 637 Detention Facilities Used by ICE in FY 2015." 12 April 2016. http://trac.syr.edu/immigration/reports/422/. https://trac.syr.edu/immigration/detention/200803/BOPOAD/exit/.

Transactional Records Access Clearinghouse. "Secure Communities and ICE Deportation: A Failed Program?" 8 April 2014. https://trac.syr.edu/immigration/reports/349/.

"Transfer of McNeil Marks End of Era for Federal Prison." *Semi-Weekly Spokesman Review*, 30 June 1981.

Truman, Harry S. "Proclamation 2662: Removal of Alien Enemies," 1945, https://www.trumanlibrary.org/proclamations/index.php?pid=247&st=immigration&st1=.

Tuckman, Jo. "Survivor Tells of Escape from Mexican Massacre in which 72 Were Left Dead." *Guardian*, 25 August 2010.

"Two Decades Later, Mariel Boat Lift Refugees Still Feel Effects of Riot." *Los Angeles Times*, 5 May 2001.

Trump, Donald. 2019. "Remarks by President Trump on the National Security and Humanitarian Crisis on Our Southern Border." https://www.whitehouse.gov/briefings-statements/remarks-president-trump-national-security-humanitarian-crisis-southern-border/.

2006 Facts Brochure. 2006. https://web.archive.org/web/20090806120702/http://www.adc.arkansas.gov/pdf/facts_brochure2006.pdf.

Ugarte, Manuel. *La Patria Grande*. Buenos Aires: Capital Intelectual, 2010.

United Press International. "30 Cubans Stage Strike at McNeil." *Spokane Daily Chronicle*, 26 September 1980.

United States Congress: House. *Mariel Cuban Detainees: Events Preceding and Following the November 1987 Riots: Hearing Before the Subcommittee on Courts, Civil Liberties, and the Administration of Justice, 100th Congress, 2nd Session, February 4, 1988*. Washington DC: US Government Printing Office, 1989.

United States v. Ju Toy, 198 U.S. 253 (1905).

"The Uprising at Seattle." *Washington Standard*, 12 February 1886.

US Census Bureau. *Census of Population, 1850 to 2000.* 2019. https://www.census.gov/newsroom/pdf/cspan_fb_slides.pdf.

US Census Bureau. *Insane and Feeble-Minded in Hospitals and Institutions, 1904.* Washington DC: US Government Printing Office, 1906. https://archive.org/details/cu31924032599650.

US Census Bureau. *Insane and Feeble-Minded in Institutions.* Washington, DC: US Government Printing Office, 1914.

US Congress. An Amendment to the Various Acts Relative to Immigration and the Importation of Aliens under Contract or Agreement to Perform Labor. Fifty-First Congress, Session 2, 1891.

US Congress. Committee on the Judiciary. *Atlanta Federal Penitentiary: Report of the Subcommittee on Courts, Civil Liberties, and the Administration of Justice.* 99th Congress, 2nd Session. Washington DC: Government Printing Office, 1986.

US Congress. Urgent Supplemental Appropriations Bill, 1986. U.S. Congressional Serial Set (1986).

US Congress. House. Chinese Immigration Report 4048. 51st Congress. 2nd Session, 1891.

US Congress. House. Committee on the Judiciary. Atlanta Federal Penitentiary: Report of the Subcommittee on Courts, Civil Liberties, and the Administration of Justice. 99th Congress, 2nd Session, 1986.

US Congress. House. Committee on the Judiciary. *Treatment of Latin Americans of Japanese Descent, European Americans and Jewish Refugees during World War II.* Washington, DC: US Government Printing Office, 2009.

US Congress. House. *Official Opinions of Attorneys General.* Congressional Serial Set (1895). Vol. 20, Washington, DC: US Government Printing Office, 1895.

US Congress. *Senate Select Committee on Intelligence. Committee Study of the Central Intelligence Agency's Detention and Interrogation Program.* 113th Congress, 2nd Session, 2014.

US Congress. Senate. Abstracts of Reports of the Immigration Commission. 61st Congress. 3rd Session, 1911.

US Department of Commerce and Labor. Bureau of Immigration and Naturalization. Immigration Laws and Regulations of 1907. 1910.

US Department of Commerce and Labor. *Treaty, Laws, and Regulations Governing the Admission of Chinese.* Washington, DC: US Government Printing Office, 1907.

US Department of Homeland Security. "DHS Immigration Enforcement: 2016." December 2016. https://www.dhs.gov/sites/default/files/publications/DHS%20Immigration%20Enforcement%202016.pdf.

US Department of Homeland Security. "FY 2021 Budget in Brief." 2020. https://www.dhs.gov/sites/default/files/publications/fy_2021_dhs_bib_0.pdf.

US Department of Homeland Security. "Immigration Enforcement Actions: 2017 Data Tables." 2018. https://www.dhs.gov/immigration-statistics/enforcement-actions#.

US Department of Homeland Security. "Yearbook of Immigration Statistics: 2017." 2017. https://www.dhs.gov/immigration-statistics/yearbook/2017/.

US Department of Homeland Security. *Budget in Brief: Fiscal Year 2020.* 2019. https://www.dhs.gov/sites/default/files/publications/DHS%20BIB%202019.pdf.

US Department of Homeland Security. Customs and Border Protection. "CPB Enforcement Statistics FY 2019." 2019. https://www.cbp.gov/newsroom/stats/cbp-enforcement-statistics.

US Department of Homeland Security. Customs and Border Protection. "Southwest Border Sectors: Total Illegal Alien Apprehensions by Fiscal Year, 1960–2018. Patrol, United States Border." 2019. https://www.cbp.gov/sites/default/files/assets/documents/2019-Mar/bp-southwest-border-sector-apps-fy1960-fy2018.pdf.

US Department of Homeland Security. Immigration and Customs Enforcement. *Currently Detained by Processing Disposition as of 8/17/19.* 2019. https://www.ice.gov/detention-management.

US Department of Homeland Security. Immigration and Customs Enforcement. "Fiscal Year 2018 ICE Enforcement and Removal Operations Report." 2018. https://www.ice.gov/doclib/about/offices/ero/pdf/eroFY2018Report.pdf.

US Department of Homeland Security. Immigration and Customs Enforcement. "ICE Enforcement and Removal Operations Report: Fiscal Year 2015." 2015. https://www.ice.gov/sites/default/files/documents/Report/2016/fy2015removalStats.pdf.

US Department of Homeland Security. Immigration and Customs Enforcement. "ICE Facility List Report." 6 November 2017. National Immigrant Justice Center https://immigrantjustice.org/ice-detention-facilities-november-2017.

US Department of Homeland Security. Immigration and Customs Enforcement. "ICE Initial Book-Ins by Facility Type: FY 2019 through 8/17/2019." 2019. https://www.ice.gov/detention-management.

US Department of Homeland Security. Immigration and Customs Enforcement. "Over 72-hour ICE Detention Facilities." 2019. https://www.ice.gov/detention-management.

US Department of Homeland Security. Immigration and Customs Enforcement. "US Immigration and Customs Enforcement Fiscal Year 2019 Enforcement and Removal Operation Report." 2019. https://www.ice.gov/sites/default/files/documents/Document/2019/eroReportFY2019.pdf.

US Department of Homeland Security. Office of Immigration Statistics. "Immigration Enforcement Actions: 2016." 2017. https://www.dhs.gov/sites/default/files/publications/Enforcement_Actions_2016.pdf.

US Department of Homeland Security, "Yearbook of Immigration Statistics: 2017," 2017, https://www.dhs.gov/immigration-statistics/yearbook/2017/, Table 39, "Aliens Removed or Returned: Fiscal Years 1892 to 2017."

US Department of Justice. "Budget Trend Data 1975 Through the President's 2003 Request to the Congress." 2002. https://www.justice.gov/archive/jmd/1975_2002/2002/html/page104-108.htm.

US Department of Justice. "Executive Office for Immigration Review Swears in 46 Immigration Judges." 2018. https://www.justice.gov/eoir/page/file/1097241/download.

US Department of Justice. "Alien Incarceration Report Fiscal Year 2018, Quarter 2." 16 April 2019. https://www.justice.gov/opa/page/file/1154711/download.

US Department of Justice. "The Department of Justice Create Section Dedicated to Denaturalization Cases." 26 February 2020. https://www.justice.gov/opa/pr/department-justice-creates-section-dedicated-denaturalization-cases.

US Department of Justice. *1979 Annual Report of the Immigration and Naturalization Service.* Washington, DC: US Government Printing Office, 1979.

US Department of Justice. *1980 Statistical Yearbook of the Immigration and Naturalization Service.* Washington, DC: US Government Printing Office, 1980.

US Department of Justice. *Annual Report of the Immigration and Naturalization Service 1960*. Washington DC: US Government Printing Office, 1960.

US Department of Justice. Executive Office for Immigration Review. "Mayra Jacqueline Machado, Decision and Order of the Immigration Judge," 23 July 2019.

US Department of Justice. Federal Bureau of Prisons. *Report to Attorney General on the Disturbances at the Federal Detention Center, Oakdale, Louisiana, US Penitentiary, Atlanta, Georgia*. Washington, DC: US Government Printing Office, 1988.

US Department of Homeland Security. Immigration and Customs Enforcement. "Fiscal Year 2018 ICE Enforcement and Removal Operations Report." 2018. https://www.ice.gov/doclib/about/offices/ero/pdf/eroFY2018Report.pdf.

US Department of Justice. Office of the Federal Detention Trustee. *Detention Needs Assessment and Baseline Report: A Compendium of Federal Detention Statistics*. Washington, DC: US Government Printing Office, 2002.

US Department of State. *The Proclaimed List of Certain Blocked Nationals—Supplement 1-4. Feb. 28-May 1, 1942*. Washington, DC: US Government Printing Office, 1942.

US Department of State. *The Proclaimed List of Certain Blocked Nationals: Revision II, May 12, 1942*. Washington, DC: US Government Printing Office, 1942.

US Department of Treasury. Bureau of Public Health and Marine-Hospital Service. *Book of Instructions for the Medical Inspection of Immigrants*. Washington, DC: US Government Printing Office, 1903.

US House of Representatives. *Civil Liberties Act of 1987*. HR 442. 100th Congress. 10 August 1988.

Valverde, Miriam. "Has the Number of Border Patrol Quadrupled since 2005?" *Politifact*, 1 February 2019.

Vargas, Vikki. "'We Have No Time': Woman on Brink of Deportation," NBC News, Los Angeles, 30 November 2016. Varón, Ana Milena. "Llevaba una vida ejemplar, pero ahora pudiera ser deportada por un error en su juventud." *Hoy Los Angeles*, 15 December 2016.

Volsky, George. "55 Cubans Riot in Bus Traveling to Atlanta Prison." *New York Times*, 30 May 1986.

Von Spronsen, Willem. "Final Statement," 13 July 2019. In Crimethinc, "On Willem Van Spronsen & His Final Statement," *It's Going Down*, 14 July 2019. https://itsgoingdown.org/on-william-van-spronsen/.

von Werthern, M., K. Robjant, Z. Chui, R. Schon, L. Ottisova, C. Mason, and C. Katona. "The Impact of Immigration Detention on Mental Health: A Systematic Review." *BMC Psychiatry* 18, no. 1 (2018): 382.

Wadler, Joyce. "As Others Go Free, 50 Haitians Still Detained Feel Only Despair." *Washington Post*, 25 August 1982.

Wassem, Ruth Ellen. "U.S. Immigration Policy on Haitian Migrants." Washington, DC: Congressional Research Service, 17 May 2011.

Weaver, Jay, and Mimi Whitfield. "Some Cuban Felons, including 2,000 Murderers, Could Face Deportation under New Policy." *Miami Herald*, 16 January 2017.

Whitlock, Carol. "A Refugee Sponsor's Diary of Love," *Miami Herald*, December 21, 1980.

Williams, Beth Lew. *The Chinese Must Go: Violence, Exclusion and the Making of the Alien in America*. Cambridge, MA: Harvard University Press, 2018.

Wilsher, Daniel. *Immigration Detention: Law, History, Politics*. Cambridge: Cambridge University Press, 2012.

Wilson, Jill H. "Recent Migration to the United States from Central America: Frequently Asked Questions." Washington, DC: Congressional Research Service, 2019. https://crsreports.congress.gov.

Wissel, Paula, and Simone Alicea. "Not a Prison." In *Forgotten Prison*: KNKX, 2019.

Wiltz, Teresa. "What Crimes Make Immigrants Eligible for Deportation?" PBS NewsHour, 28 December 2016.

Wollenberg, Charles. *Rebel Lawyer: Wayne Collins and the Defense of Japanese American Rights*. Berkeley, CA: Heyday, 2018.

Wong Wing v. United States 163 U.S. 228 (1896).

Wood, Katie, and Brenda L. Mooney. "What Really Happened at the Atlanta Pen." *Fulton County Daily Report*, 14 December 1987.

Woolner, Ann. "Hope Wanes for Cubans at the Pen," *Atlanta Constitution*, 15 September 1985.

Yamawaki, Chikako. *Estrategias de via de los inmigrantes asiáticos en el Perú*. Lima: IEP, JCAS, 2002.

Young, Elliott. *Alien Nation: Chinese Migration in the Americas from the Coolie Era to WWII*. Chapel Hill: University of North Carolina Press, 2014.

Young, Elliott. "The Hard Truths about Obama's Deportation Priorities." *HuffPost*, 1 March 2017.

Zahra, Tara. *Kidnapped Souls: National Indifference and the Battle for Children in the Bohemian Lands, 1900–1948*. Ithaca, NY: Cornell University Press, 2008.

INDEX

For the benefit of digital users, indexed terms that span two pages (e.g., 52–53) may, on occasion, appear on only one of those pages.

deportation to El Salvador (2020) of,
  5–6, 18–19, 183–84
detention at La Salle Detention Center
  of, 1–2, 5–6, 158, 166–68, 173–74
early childhood in El Salvador of, 2
felony conviction for fraudulent
  checks (2004) of, 2–3, 159, 160–62,
  166–67, 172–73, 181–83, 195
felony conviction for receipt of stolen
  property (2005) by, 162–63
Fifth Circuit Court of Appeals case
  of, 18–19
immigration to United States (1990)
  by, 159
immigration to United States (2017)
  by, 171–72
life in El Salvador after 2017 of, 168–
  72, 177, 183, 186, 195
photos of, 161f, 173f
probation following felony plea
  (2004–14) for, 159–60, 162
probation violation arrest (2005)
  of, 159–60
traffic accident arrest (2018) of, 173–
  74, 177, 183–84
traffic stop arrest (2015) of, 1–2, 159,
  160, 161, 166–67
Macias, Humberto, 156–57
Madison, James, 98–99
Malaysia, 17–18
Marcello, Carlos, 34–35
Mariel Boatlift (Cuba, 1980),
  11–12, 119–20
Marrero González, Carlos, 151–52
Marshall, George, 100
Martineau, Bolivar, 136, 156
Martinez Leon, Julia, 131–32
Martinez Perez Rodriguez, Robert, 146
Mas Canosa, Jorge, 146
Maynard, F. F., 25, 26–27
McCarren-Walter Act of 1952, 8–9
McCarty, Mac, 119
McCune, Gary, 149–51
McNeil Island Federal Prison
  (Washington State)
  Canadian immigrants detained at, 45,
  46f, 48f, 48–49
  Chinese immigrants detained at, 19,
  23–25, 26–32, 37–44, 45–51, 46f,
  48f, 186–87

conditions of detention at, 32, 51–52
  Cuban refugees detained during 1980s
  at, 11–12, 51–53, 120
  drug crimes and, 46–49
  establishment (1875) of, 23–24
  location of, 23–24
  Mexican immigrants detained at, 37,
  45, 46f, 48f, 48–49
  Native Americans imprisoned at, 24,
  43–44f, 43–44
  photographs of prisoners from,
  37–44, 38–44f
  Special Commitment Center for sex
  offenders at, 52–53, 187
  statistical breakdown of charges for all
  foreign-born inmates at, 47f
  statistical breakdown of foreign-born
  inmates by nationality in, 46f
  Three Prisons Act (1891) and, 23–24
Medina, Isabel, 174, 176
Meese, Edwin, 146, 147, 151
mental illness. See also insane asylums
  and mental hospitals
  Cohen case and, 54, 56f, 57, 58–60,
  67–68, 71, 72–76, 78–81, 82–84,
  90, 188
  dementia praecox diagnoses
  and, 79–80
  deportation and, 63f, 68–69
  Ellis Island screenings for, 65–70
  eugenics and, 69–70
Mérida Initiative, 16–17
Mesa-Rodriguez, Geraldo, 137–38
Metzner, A. S., 70–71
Mexican immigrants
  Bracero program (1940s) and, 103–4
  criminalization of immigration and, 34
  deportations during 2010s
  of, 13, 169
  drug crimes and, 48–49
  McNeil Island Federal Prison
  detentions of, 37, 45, 46f,
  48f, 48–49
  "Operation Wetback" (1954)
  deportations of, 9, 115–16
Mexico
  Axis nationals in Mexico during World
  War II and, 100
  Central American immigrants
  deported from, 16–17, 18f